THE INFORMATION ECOLOGY OF E-GOVERNMENT

Informatization Developments and the Public Sector

A series based on

I.Th.M. Snellen, W.B.H.J. van de Donk and J.P. Baquiast (Eds.), Expert Systems in Public Administration. Evolving Practices and Norms

Volume 9

Previously published in this series

ISSN 0928-9038

The Information Ecology of E-Government

E-Government as Institutional and Technological Innovation
in Public Administration

Edited by

Victor Bekkers

*Erasmus University Rotterdam, Faculty of Social Sciences, Public
Administration, The Netherlands*

and

Vincent Homburg

*Erasmus University Rotterdam, Faculty of Social Sciences, Public
Administration, The Netherlands*

IOS
Press

Amsterdam • Berlin • Oxford • Tokyo • Washington, DC

ISBN 1 58603 483 9
Library of Congress Control Number: 2004116328

Publisher
IOS Press
Nieuwe Hemweg 6B
1013 BG Amsterdam
The Netherlands
fax: +31 20 620 3419
e-mail: order@iospress.nl

Distributor in the UK and Ireland
IOS Press/Lavis Marketing
73 Lime Walk
Headington
Oxford OX3 7AD
England
fax: +44 1865 750079

Distributor in the USA and Canada
IOS Press, Inc.
4502 Rachael Manor Drive
Fairfax, VA 22032
USA
fax: +1 703 323 3668
e-mail: iosbooks@iospress.com

This book is dedicated to
Gerard G. Homburg (1927-2004)

Preface

With this book, we have tried to increase our knowledge about how to understand the technological and institutional innovations in public administration that usually go by the name of electronic government. It is founded on the premise that, in order to understand electronic government, one has to scrutinize the various environments and contexts in which e-government is developed and implemented. As such, it builds upon the biological and environmental lines of reasoning that have been suggested by authors like Bonnie Nardi and Vicky O'Day, and Thomas Davenport and Laurence Prusak.

The first ideas for a book on the information ecology or e-government emerged while preparing a panel session at the IRSPM VII conference, to be held in Hong Kong in the spring of 2003. Many – but not all - of the contributors to this book planned to attend this conference. It is rather ironic for a book in which a biological perspective is propagated, that the conference in fact had to be cancelled because of the vigorous spread of the SARS virus in South-East Asia at that time. But in retrospect, it might have been for the better: maybe the urge to publish the book was fuelled by the cancellation of the conference and the missed opportunity for the envisaged participants to discuss and reflect on the antecedents, consequences and contexts of e-government.

So, in this book, yet another perspective on e-government is presented. Is that not pretty presumptuous? Maybe. But, on the other hand, it seems that only a short time ago, numerous academics and practitioners in the field were somewhat blinded by the successes of the dot-com developments in the private sector, and some of them enthusiastically claimed that public administration was to be revolutionized. But that did not happen, and also the dot-com soap bubble burst. This suggests that there is much yet to be learned about innovation in public administration, especially about innovations at the cornerstones of technological and institutional transformations. New and more fully developed formulations of theory into practice are needed. We hope that with this book, we have at least contributed to some aspects of the understanding of e-government. It is most likely too early to tell whether a solid base, on which to advance, has been constructed. But if this volume could stimulate further thinking, experimenting and reflection, maybe it is possible to innovate.

Unsurprisingly, for a book like this, it is very hard to acknowledge each and every one that has made this book possible. However, we feel that we should at least acknowledge the sheltering institutions of the authors of the various chapters, for supporting, encouraging and facilitating the research efforts that are the bases for the chapters. Furthermore, we would like to thank the Netherlands Institute of Government (NIG) for their financial support, and Julie Raadschelders for her help in editing and correcting the original manuscripts.

Rotterdam, September 2004

Victor Bekkers & Vincent Homburg

List of Tables

List of Figures

Contents

The Information Ecology of E-Government
V.J.J.M. Bekkers and V.M.F. Homburg (Eds.)
IOS Press, 2005

E-Government as an Information Ecology: Backgrounds and Concepts

Victor BEKKERS and Vincent HOMBURG
Erasmus University Rotterdam, Faculty of Social Sciences,
Public Administration Group, PO Box 1738, 3000 DR Rotterdam, The Netherlands

Abstract. This chapter introduces e-government, defined as the redesign of information relations between governments and their stakeholders. It is argued that e-government can be analysed in terms of evolving interactions and relations between a diversity of actors, their practices, values and technology within a specific and local (thus unique) environment. This view on e-government is analysed further in the remainder of this book.

1. E-Government as a Policy Window

E-government - or electronic government – is one of the innovations proposed in discussions about modernising public administration. The concept of e-government is often associated with the more or less strategic use of modern information and communication technologies (ICTs) within the public sector [1]. In practice, the concept is defined and implemented in a variety of forms and shapes [2, 3]. Before we present our working definition and our conceptualisation of e-government, we give our attention to a number of socio-political and administrative developments in the environment of public administration. To some extent, a number of developments that have occurred since the 1990s have influenced the content of e-government programmes in many countries. The following developments can be noted.

1.1 The Crisis of Representative Democracy

Since the 1990s, representative democracy has been put under a lot of pressure. The traditional institutions of the liberal and constitutional democracy, its main actors and its practices are in a frail condition. Some scholars talk about a cleavage between the citizen and politics. Elected representatives often do not represent the 'will of the people' and are prone to elitism [4].

Two strategies are put forward to overcome this crisis of representative democracy [4, 5]. The first strategy aims at increasing the (permanent) participation of citizens in the political and public debate. A lively democracy is not only built on the number of people who actually vote in general, local and regional elections. A really 'strong' democracy should also embrace the idea of political debate and political action and should stimulate and facilitate citizens to raise their voice and to be politically active [6]. Strong democracy and 'active citizenship' are seen as the two sides of the same coin. Interactive decision-making and participatory planning processes are examples of this strategy. The second strategy addresses the citizen primarily as a consumer or client of government services and products. Much of the criticism directed at government and politics refers to the bureaucratic structures and culture of government in which demand-orientation and customer-friendliness is lacking. The assumption is that improved service delivery restores citizens' trust in politics. That is why it has become an important issue in the political programme of politicians who want to bridge the gap between citizens and government [5].

1.2   Responsive Public Service Delivery

The attention that was paid to the responsiveness of public service delivery in the early 1990s was also inspired by two other developments. First, in the private sector a strong focus on customer needs in relation to the quality of goods and services to be produced became a major source of competitive advantage. It has led to the introduction of all kinds of elaborated quality and marketing systems. For a long time, these quality systems were absent in public organisations. Another development, which stimulated the call for better public services, was the emergence of the 'empowered citizen'. He not only demanded better and faster services, but he was also able to enforce his arguments and claims and rights. To some extent, the process of individualisation and the collapse of the great ideologies of the 19th century have eroded the legitimacy of the claims and arguments that were put forward by government and politics on behalf of the citizen. The citizen himself, his individual interests, needs and beliefs have moved into the centre of the political and administrative system [5, 7]. The result was a call for easier, more rapid and more integrated and responsive ways of public service delivery.

1.3   Business Process Redesign and the Re-Invention of Government

The growing awareness that the lack of quality of public services has become a serious threat to the legitimacy of the public sector has forced public organisations to look critically at their own internal business processes, especially the process of service delivery. The challenge was to redesign these processes in a more customer-friendly and efficient way. At the same time, we can observe another trend, even a 'hype', which in the late 1980s and early 1990s became very popular in the private sector. This trend was called business process redesign (BPR), and it was presented as a paradigm-shift: the main criterion for the productivity of organisations was no longer the reformulation and reorganisations of tasks, but the outcomes of business processes [8]. Information technology was seen as an important tool that enables organisations to reorganise around processes. For instance, the structure of former Dutch Tax Administration reflected the major tax laws in the Netherlands, but the growing abuse of taxes, tax evasion and the fact that tax payers (as empowered citizens) increasingly appealed their assessments, has put the structure and functioning of the agency under a lot of pressure. The former organisation was based on task-oriented departments that executed specific tax laws and regulations, which led to all kinds of coordination problems. The increased workload urged the agency to alter their organisation and to scrutinise their working processes. Using the ideas of BPR, reorganisation took place. The new agency was organised around client-groups of taxpayers, which led to the integration of formerly separate tax handling processes and procedures [9].

1.4 From Government towards Governance

In the 1990s we also observe a shift in the dominant 'steering' paradigm. Traditionally, the government was put in the centre of all kinds of societal developments and problems. The idea that government could effectively influence and intervene in societal developments and try to solve societal problems from a centralised and hierarchical position, detached from society, and according to the goals laid down in a policy programme, met with a lot of criticism. Ineffective government interventions were primarily seen as flaws in the 'machinery of government', as the result of imperfect knowledge about the nature and effects of the problem, and as the product of a mismatch between the policy instruments that were used and the policy goals that were formulated. In the 1990s we can observe the emergence of a new steering paradigm which is called the 'governance paradigm' in contrast to the classical 'government paradigm'. This shift from government towards governance implies that:
- Government is not entity but a conglomerate of actors;
- Government is not the only actor who tries to influence societal developments, and
- Government interventions are interventions in a policy network, in which power, resource dependency, and strategic behaviour are vital elements.

Successful government interventions depend on the complex interplay between public, private and semi-public actors which is aimed at the creation of a shared understanding about the nature of the policy problems and the way these should be handled [10]. The idea of governance reflects the attention that should be paid to the processes themselves in which actors with different interests, resources and beliefs co-produce policy practices that they share. The paradigm shift from 'government to governance' gives government organisations a position in a complex network of the exchange, (inter)dependency and communication relations which it actually maintains or wants to maintain with relevant stakeholders in its environments (other governments, citizens, companies and societal organisations).

1.5 Responsibility and Accountability

Attention should also be paid to another trend. During the 1990s, there was a growing concern about waste, delays and mismanagement in the public sector, all of which contributed to inefficiency and inefficacy in the conversion of public expenditures (and tax money) into policy outcomes and public services. Two causes were suggested [7, 11]. First, due to centralisation and bureaucratisation, policymakers and decision makers were too remote from the locus of decision information and action; second, the existing accountability arrangements and procedures were in poor shape or were even absent. Not only did the call for better hierarchical accountability measures become louder, but a plea was made for new, more horizontally-oriented accountability arrangements that would reflect the need for customer-oriented accountability information; information that can be made accessible through the use of modern ICT.

1.6 The Connectivity of Network Technology

It is tempting to regard e-government as the public sector equivalent of – what is nowadays called the bubble of – the Internet and dot-com developments in the private sector that rose to high at the start of the new millennium. And it may be assumed that policymakers were not immune to the attractions of the often-proclaimed successes of innovative commercial applications on the World Wide Web [12]. However, looking at the policy developments of e-government in various countries, there is reason to believe that the concept of e-government is more than the result of technological mimicry. Even before the emergence of the World Wide Web (WWW) in 1993, policymakers at different levels of government discussed the need to establish new information infrastructures and networks in the public sector in order to reform government. However, the rise of the Internet and the WWW in the beginning of the 1990s opened their eyes to the possibilities that network technology, especially the open nature of the Internet network, could generate. Before the emergence of the Internet, network technology was primarily seen as EDI technology, in which well-defined data could be processed according to heavily formalised and standardised exchange procedures and formats.

One of the most important features of network technology, and especially the Internet, is the potential to connect, which enables individuals, groups of individuals and organisations to overcome numerous organisational, functional, temporal and geographical boundaries and barriers. Connectivity enables people and organisations to exchange and share information and knowledge and to become engaged in various kinds of communication and other interactions. Modern network technology makes it rather easy 'to reach out and touch', which opens new horizons to redesign government in order to improve the quality of its service and the political participation of citizens, companies and societal organisations.

In sum, the popularity of e-government at the turn of the millennium can be understood from the idea that at that moment, a number of developments and reforms, which already appeared during the 1990s, have come together. A policy window existed that gave politicians, public managers, citizens, companies and societal organisations a glimmer of a new and better government. In this policy window, ICT was seen as an important solution that would enable government organisations to improve the quality and efficiency of public services to meet the rising demands of the citizens who saw themselves as clients; enable government organisations to redesign their internal and external information exchange and communication processes and with relevant stakeholders; offer new ways to improve internal and external accountability, and open a new perspective on political and public participation and debate.

In order to explore the concept of e-government, we first look at how e-government has been used in practice (i.e., to what ends, and in what contexts it is applied) and second, what view of technology can be adhered to.

2. Manifestations of E-Government

In many respects, e-government developments have been pioneered by the United States, with parallel developments in the United Kingdom, Australia, Canada, New Zealand and Singapore. In these countries, there was an initial focus on electronic service delivery, and in particular on re-engineering public sector bureaucracies to enable electronic service channels. In the beginning of the 1990s, especially in the United States [13] and the United Kingdom [14, 15], various e-government initiatives emerged that focused on one-stop shopping (either in real life, by means of call centres or on the Internet) for citizens and corporations. In the American policy programmes National Performance Review and Access America, unequivocal information provision to citizens and corporations, and the possibility of electronic transactions between government executive institutions and citizens were announced and implemented in the government portal Firstgov.gov (http://www.firstgov.gov). The Firstgov.gov line of thinking with respect to e-government (a central portal linking various information and transaction services provided by various executive institutions at various levels of government) has by now been implemented in various countries. Characteristic for many of the initiatives is that they seem to focus on electronic service delivery enabled by ICTs and organisation-wide re-engineering [8, 11]. The emphasis is on *re-engineering the relationship between administration and citizens* (especially in their roles as consumers of products offered by the public sector). Dunleavy and Margetts claim that e-government actually is a specific implementation of the re-engineering thought embodied in New Public Management [16-19]. It at least shows that many e-government initiatives are embedded within re-engineering operations inspired by New Public Management style of thinking.

Developments in the United Kingdom pioneered a different perspective on e-government. The first Blair government announced a strategic response to both the weaknesses of 'conventional' public administration [20, 21], and, especially, the fragmenting effects of the decentralisation and privatisation operations of the preceding governments. This strategic response was labelled 'joined-up government' and it focused on improving intra-state relationships and managing relationships between state agencies, civil society and private companies. Although similar joining-up initiatives were undertaken in Australia, Canada, the Netherlands, New Zealand, Sweden and the United States, the term 'joined-up government' was most vigorously used in the UK. The 'joined-up government' (JUG) approach consists of various ways of aligning formally distinct organisations in pursuit of the objectives of the government of the day [20]. The report *Wiring it up* [22] summarises the various dimensions of JUG as new types of organisations, new accountabilities and incentives, new ways of working across organisations and new ways of delivering services.

Fostering partnerships is not an easy task. Instruments of joined-up government include the use of pooled budgets, joint teams and shared leadership which sound neutral, but may have a profound effect on the participating organisations' internal life (such as its culture and values, training, and way of dealing with and structuring information). Therefore, truly cooperative relationships go beyond the use of hyperlinks to various governmental organisations in national or federal government portal sites. As Ling states, "[n]ew service models are said to be about partnerships, networks, 'flat' relationships, and trust" [20: 624].

What is interesting here is that it is acknowledged that service delivery and one-stop shopping require cooperative relationships within and surrounding the public sector and, more importantly, that this implies new ways of working within public organisations [see also 23, 24, 25]. The focus of the re-engineering is not so much the executive organisation, but more on the network of public, voluntary and private sector organisations that are in one way or the other involved in service delivery. Borrowing from the private sector, this can be referred to as *network re-engineering* or *network redesign* [26].

Another development in the context of e-government is concerned with participation of citizens. Nowadays, communication technologies are used throughout the world, not only to communicate with citizens but also to enable citizens to speak up and to enable true interaction between governments and citizens. In a way, the coming of Internet technology has enabled a direct form of democracy (which doesn't say technology created this form of democracy) in which interaction is regarded as constitutive of democracy itself [27]. In this view on e-government, technology is not primarily used as a medium for delivering services, but as a basis for a 'cyber civil society' in which the knowledge to be used as a basis for democratic decision making is discussed, disputed and contested in open forums. The interaction and knowledge gathered in these discussions is also referred to in the research on social capital.

2.1   The Concept of E-Government

Looking at the concept of e-government as it has been used in many government documents [for an overview, see 12], we may state that e-government is a phenomenon with many faces [3]. It is a policy and managerial concept that has very little theoretical foundation. The theoretical concept of e-government is not well elaborated, although there is a large amount of empirical research available focused on the effects of ICT on the functioning of public administration [23, 28-30]. The intellectual roots of e-government can be found in policy documents and consulting reports, in the practice of Internet and web applications in public administrations and in other related managerial concepts and practices such as e-commerce, e-business etc. Due to this fuzzy variety of concepts and practices, the concept of e-government is not well defined and is based on pragmatic experiences and visions [13, 15, 31].

We describe e-government as the use of modern information and communication technologies, especially Internet and web technology, by a public organisation to support or redefine the existing and/or future (information, communication and transaction) relations with 'stakeholders' in the internal and external environment in order to create added value [3, 32, 33]. Relevant stakeholders are citizens, companies, societal organisations, other government organisations and civil servants [2]. Added value can be found in the following goals: increasing the access to government, facilitating the quality of service delivery, stimulating internal efficiency, supporting public and political accountability, increasing the political participation of citizens, and improving interorganisational cooperation and relations.

E-government is often described in relation to the kind of services to be provided [2, 32]. The following services can be distinguished:
- Information services. They are focused on the disclosure of government information, for instance the possibility of downloading brochures, policy reports, regulations and other official documents. Other examples include the possibility of searching in relevant databases or looking at benchmark information about the results of an agency.
- Contact services, which refer to the possibility of contacting the public administration. For instance, to ask questions of civil servants and politicians about the application of certain rules and programmes, or to make a complaint.
- Transaction services refer to the electronic intake and further handling of certain requests and applications of personal rights, benefits and obligations, like digital tax assessments, the render of permits, licenses and subsidies;
- Participation services address more than just the possibility of electronic voting. Electronic forums and virtual communities can provide citizens, interest groups and other parties a channel for getting involved in the formulation and evaluation of policy programmes, like the reconstruction of a neighbourhood, a shopping mall or the planning of a rail road;
- Data transfer services, which refer to the exchange and sharing of (basic and standard) information between government agencies and between government and private organisations.

In many writing on e-government, the development of e-government is viewed as a linear process in which certain phases of a sequence of 'qualitative jumps' can be distinguished [3, 12, 32].

The first jump is the transition from passive, supply-oriented information services to more interactive services, like contact and transaction services. Due to the increased interaction with, for instance, citizens that make a digital request for a license, the effects on the internal working processes increase. Existing procedures, routines and operation procedures need to be described, scrutinised, (re-) formalised, standardised and to some extent integrated.

The second jump is the development of transaction services. Transaction services presupposes the integration of working routines, as well as the vertical and horizontal integration of information domains in which the development of interorganisational data bases and data transfer services play an important role. In essence, the exchange and sharing of information and knowledge between specific back offices and between front office and back office in order to execute transaction services implies the integration of information domains, each with their own legal framework, their own systems, data definitions, routines, procedures, knowledge and frames of reference [29, 34].

The development of data transfer services can be seen as the third jump. The next jump is the transition from service delivery innovation toward democratic innovation. Participatory services like online opinion polling, online surveys and participation in online forums and digital platforms can conflict with the dominant model of representative democracy. Moreover, in a service delivery orientation of e-government, the citizen is viewed as a consumer, while in a participatory orientation of e- government the citizen is viewed as a voter and co-creator of public policy. E-government is also about the ability to generate competing ideas, innovative views and reframing problem definitions that could be considered in the policy process [5].

The last jump to be made is broadening the scope of e-government beyond service delivery toward citizens and companies. A major challenge is how to relate a vision on the use of ICT in public administration to major policy problems like, for instance, the social cohesion and security in neighbourhoods and to broader policy programmes, like the restructuring of the public health sector [12].

Although the sequence of these jumps suggests a linear and progressive trajectory, it is important to note that the practice of e-government is less evolutionary and more chaotic than this sequence of jumps suggests [3]. Moreover, we argue later that the idea of e-government as an information-ecology will fundamentally question this evolutionary perspective on the development of e-government.

2.2   The Language of E-Government: The Promise of a New and Better Government?

In the OECD definition of e-government, it has been described as the use of information and communication technologies, and particularly the Internet, as a tool to achieve better government [12: 23]. This definition can be seen as the expression of an e-government ideology which is present in many countries, certainly if we compare it with the definition we have introduced in this chapter. This ideology is based on two pillars.

First, the promise that ICT will bring a better government, which is more open, more accessible, more responsive, more collaborative and more demand-oriented than government in the pre-Internet era. ICT has the potential to break down all kinds of barriers which clients face. If it is used properly, a seamless and integrated government that operates as a whole become reality. For instance, in the documents of the United Kingdom, which are called 'Modernising Government' [14] and 'E-Government: A Strategic Framework for Public Services in the Information Age' [35], e-government (defined as information age government) is an aspect of modernising government which has only one purpose: to make life better for citizens and business.

The second pillar consists of the idea that technology should be seen as a neutral and willing instrument that can be applied according to the preferences of the user. For instance, in the UK vision on technology, the various promises of ICT are written in the imperative: *ICT will,* for instance, make our life easier [14]. Moreover, ICT is a revolutionising force. It changes our lives: the way we work, they way we do business, the way we communicate with each other, the way we spend our time. The British government intends to be at the head of the developments, using them to give effect to the goals established in the policy document. In Dutch programmes like *'Digital Delta'* and *'Action Programme for Electronic Government'*, there is a strong belief and trust in the possibilities of modern ICT. Optimism prevails about the progress ICT will bring. Things that were previously unthinkable will now happen, especially in the field of electronic service delivery. And, according to the Dutch government, this is just the beginning. The blessings that ICT will bring cannot be denied. Public administration has a moral duty to use ICT and to adjust to these promised blessings by using the most advanced 'tools'.

Moreover, the tool-oriented nature of many e-government programmes leads to a fixation on ICT applications. For example, the OECD states that characteristic to many, if not all, e-government initiatives is that they seem to focus on Internet-based applications. They are the concrete tools to achieve better government [12]. Additionally, in this orientation on the use of ICT as tools, the realisation of e-government is primarily seen as an issue of information management and project management. It is seen as a matter of setting goals, formulating action plans, allocating budgets, formulating clear roles and responsibilities which very often implies a plea for more centralisation.

To some extent we can state that these two pillars reflect two myths that can be questioned by using the idea of the 'information ecology'. The first myth relates to e-government as a new and better government and the second myth deals with idea of technological progress and instrumentality. The fostering of these two myths can be seen as a possible reason for the cleavage between the rhetoric and practice of e-government, why the goals that are formulated in may policy documents are not yet being accomplished. For instance, Teicher and Dow [36] conclude, while looking at the e-government experience in Australia - which by many experts is viewed as a frontrunner in e-government - that although the e-government promises major changes, the actual achievements are quite modest. Joined-up government especially is still far away.

Before we go into the concept of the information ecology as it has been formulated by Davenport [37] and Nardi and O'Day [38], we first want to look at some literature on the effects of ICT in public administration in order to assess, if the claim of a new and better government is a realistic one. This exercise will show us that the outcomes of ICT interventions are more ambiguous and diffuse. The idea of the information ecology helps us to understand these effects by questioning the omnipotent power of technology, as we later argue.

The dominant view on technology that lays behind many policy documents on e-government is a combination of a determinism and voluntarism. These two positions reflect two old positions in the so-called 'technology debate'. The deterministic position reflects the idea that ICT is an autonomous, exogenous power. The effects that will occur are a given with the characteristics of the technology, and they will occur. Technology is defining technology [39]. References to the emergence of an omnipotent information society should underline this position. The voluntarists presuppose that ICT is a neutral set of tools that enables individuals to realise their goals. Technology is viewed as an enabling technology, as a set of instruments that are willing instruments in the hands of their masters and the goals they want to accomplish. The effects that ICT will realise are primarily goal-driven and depend on the effective and efficient use of ICT. ICT is seen as a set of instruments that can be controlled by the people who use them. The challenge is to apply the right tools in the right way. Both positions can be combined by the following assumption that is dominant in many policy documents on e-government. The emergence of the information society produces new technologies that cannot be denied, and because they are available they should be applied in the most proper way so that they can produce effects that support the reinvention of government.

However, research into the effects of ICT in public, but also private, organisations [25, 29, 30, 40, 41] show that the effects that are generated by the use of ICT in public administration are not general, but specific and context-driven. In many policy documents, the existing political, socio-organisational and institutional setting in which ICT and e-government is introduced is neglected. So we can question the claim of a more open, client-oriented and more responsive government that can be realised by the proper use of ICT. There are hardly any general effects. Effects are limited to the specific setting in which ICT is introduced.

The main reason that these effects are limited and context-driven is that the introduction of ICT in public administration is a social intervention in a policy network, which influences the position, interests, values and (information) domains of the actors involved. Thus, the introduction and use of ICT is not a neutral intervention, but a political one. Choices with respect to ICT influences the access, use and distribution of information and communication and information relations and patterns between the actors in the policy network, and thus the effects that will occur [25, 42]. Dutton and Guthrie [43] analyse the development of the Santa Monica Public Electronic Network as an 'ecology of games', in which an interrelated system of actors within a certain territory develop a number of games with changing players that influence the use of ICT. McLoughlin [44] draws attention to the dynamic interaction between organisational and individual power in order to understand the effects of technology interventions in organisation. Referring to Brigham and Corbett's work on the effects of e-mail - which is an important communication device in e-government, he concludes that there is little point in talking about the impacts of e-mail by focusing on the inherent technical features of e-mail, but rather on the emergent properties of e-mail which result from the micro-political interaction between the technical features of e- mail, but rather on the emergent properties of e-mail which result from the micro-political interaction between the technical features of e-mail and the organisational context in which email is introduced and used. The effects of email that have occurred have not been as general as previously claimed. They are limited and contradictory.

Evaluating the success and failures of business process redesign by ICT, Davenport [37] also questions the general claim of business process redesign. He concludes that the effects that occur can only be understood sensibly by looking at the evolving interactions and relations between a diversity of actors, their practices, values and technology within a specific and local (thus unique) environment. It is important to stress that social and technological aspects of an environment co-evolve [37, 38]. This is an important conclusion because e-government (especially related to transaction services) is, to a large extent, a matter of business process redesign of working, information and communication processes between front and back offices and between back offices which lay behind many sophisticated websites.

The general effects that are being claimed in many e-government documents cannot be found in the research about the use of ICT in public and private organisations. This is one of the possible explanations as to why there is a cleavage between the rhetoric of e-government, the lagging implementation of e-government and the local effects that occur when a number of measures and actions have been undertaken. Who benefits from these limited effects? Research shows that ICT in the public sector very often strengthens the existing frames of reference, power relations and positions within a policy sector [41, 45].

However, this so-called reinforcement hypothesis stems from the period before the massive introduction of network technology like the Internet. Does this hypothesis survive the age of the Internet? Up until now research findings are scarce, and if they are present they are ambiguous and based on a single or a few case studies. For instance, Taylor and Hurt [46] have looked at e-government initiatives of parliaments by examining their websites. They conclude that a parliament-centric view prevails. The information they provide is information about the parliament, its history, its functioning, its agenda, its members. Access is also given to relevant documents that are discussed in the parliament. However, Internet and web technology is hardly used for debate and for citizen participation, in terms of participation services. The explanation that Taylor and Hurt [46] give refers to the dominance of the institutionalised paradigm of representative democracy, in which strong citizenship and active participation of citizens is seen as a threat for the institutions of the representative democracy. However, only 'young democracies' which an emerging new parliamentary tradition like the Scottish and Slovenian parliament, used the Internet for discussion and citizen participation; this emphases the importance of looking at the institutional context in which also the new technologies like the Internet is being introduced and used. Taylor and Hurt [46], Coleman, Taylor and Van de Donk [47], Bellamy and Raab [48], Hague and Loader [4] draw the conclusion that the potential of innovation (in terms of contributing towards strong, participatory democracy and enhancing the responsiveness of democracy) up until now has been used fully to address the crisis in the established representative democracies. Looking at the Australian practice, Teicher and Dow [36] conclude that a fundamental reshaping of bureaucratic structures does not take place.

Hence, we must conclude that the progress that ICT government can bring is not supported by research. The effects of ICT are ambiguous because they are influenced by the complex and dynamic institutional setting in which it is developed, introduced and used. Moreover, they tend to reinforce existing practices, frames of reference and power positions.

2.3   The Information Ecology Approach: A Reformulation

The idea that technology should be seen as a set of tools and applications that can be put in practice in order to achieve well-elaborated goals in order to reinvent government is seen by Davenport [37] as a machine engineering approach. Inherent to such a view is that information is something that is easily modelled and stored on computers, is uniform (must be consistent and common throughout the full domain of the system) and in order for it's accessibility and use to be improved, the focus must be on technological innovation.

This, however, is not the only possible view on technology, as we have seen in the previous section. Davenport [37] and Nardi and O'Day [38] introduce another metaphor to understand the use and effects of ICTs as a contrast to the machine metaphor. In their view, the development, introduction and use of ICTs in and between organisations should be seen from the perspective of an eco-system or of mutually adapting complex systems. The metaphor of an information ecology stresses the fact that information is not unequivocal, that it can have different meanings for various stakeholder groups and can be disputed. An information ecology can be described as the evolving interactions and relations between a diversity of actors, their practices, values and technology within a specific and local (thus unique) environment. It is important to stress that social and technological aspects of an environment co-evolve [37, 38].

In Table 1, we compare the main characteristics of the machine engineering approach with the information ecology approach.

Table 1: Machine Engineering Versus Information Ecology (adapted from [37])

Machine engineering approach	Information Ecology approach
Information is easily stored on computers	Information is not easily stored on computers (it is not 'data')
Data modelling is the only way to master information complexity	The more complex a data model is, the less useful it will be
Information must be common throughout an organisation	Information can take on many meanings in an organisation
Technological change will improve the information environment	Technology is only one component of the information environment and often not the right way to create change

Davenport refers to an information ecology not so much as a static information inventory that is modelled and stored in information systems, but rather to beliefs and values about how information is stored, accessed and used by stakeholders. The concept of information ecology thus raises issues concerned with information culture (information sharing behaviour); information politics (the pitfalls that can interfere with information sharing among governments and between governments on the one hand and citizens on the other hand) refers to the internal information environment within an organisation comprising many interdependent social, political and cultural systems that impact the creation, distribution and use of information [37, 49]. According to Nardi and O'Day [38] the notion of an information ecology shows us that the development, introduction and use of technology in organisations refers to a complex system of parts and relationships. "It exhibits diversity and experiences continual evolution. Different parts of ecology co-evolve, changing together according to the relationship in the system. Several keystone species necessary to the survival of the ecology are present. Information ecologies have a sense of locality" [38: 51].

3.   Exploring the Notion of an Information Ecology

Although the concept of information ecology is intuitively rather attractive, further elaboration is needed. We make the first attempt in this section. First, we try to decompose the information ecology notions as used by Davenport [37] and Nardi and O'Day [38]. Second, we assess their approach in terms of strengths and weaknesses, and third, we reformulate the notion of an information ecology by adding some elements to it.

3.1   Decomposition

In Nardi and O'Day's [38: 51-56] conception of the information ecology, several key elements are put forward. First, like a biological ecology, an information ecology is viewed as a system that is marked by strong interrelationships and dependencies among its different parts. When one element is changed, effects can be felt throughout the whole system [38: 51]. However, Nardi and O'Day are quite vague about the nature of the parts and relationships that constitute the system. Davenport [37] is more specific. He discerns three environments that interact with one another: the external environment, the organisational environment and the information environment. Within the information environment, he distinguishes the following components: strategy, process, staff, culture and behaviour, architecture and politics. This model of intertwined environments and interrelated components in the information environments helps us to understand the overall landscape in which information is used. The functioning of the information environment is influenced by elements of the organisational environment, which in turn is influenced by the external environment.

The second feature relates to the notion of diversity [38: 51-52]. In a biological ecology, different species take advantage of different ecological niches, which provide natural opportunities to grow and to succeed. In an information ecology, there are different kinds of people and different kinds of tools. Sometimes an information ecology is a rather closed system or a community in which a certain technology is dominant. Sometimes an information technology is rather open and diverse in which people use different kinds of technologies. However, the interesting question is whether an information ecology is able to adapt to changing needs in the ecology itself and outside the ecology. The fact that each information ecology has its own adaptation process and selection process of the technology it wants to use shows the importance of looking at the local differences. Diversity is seen as necessary for the health of the ecology itself in order to permit the system to survive. That is why information ecologies should be teeming with different kinds of people and ideas and technologies.

The third element is the idea of co-evolution. A natural environment offers many toeholds for life of various forms. With tenacity and vigour, species migrate and change to fill the available niches in order to survive. Similar dynamics are at work in information ecology. Organisations but also schools and home settings will continue to be confronted with newer, faster and different tools and services – not once, but repeatedly. Information ecologies evolve as the news ideas and tools arise and people respond to them. They learn and adapt, create and re-create. Hence, there is a continuous process in which elements of the social and technological environment co-evolve [38: 52-53].

The fourth component consists of keystone species. An ecology is marked by the presence of keystone species whose presence is crucial for the survival of the ecology. When we ad new technologies to our own information ecology, we sometimes try to work in the absence of essential keystone species. Often such species are skilled people, whose presence is necessary to support the effective use of the new and old technologies [38: 53].

The last element is the notion that technology should have a local habitation and a name [38]. The name of a technology identifies what it means to people who use it. How do people understand the place its fills? The habitation of a technology refers to its location within a network of relationships. To whom does it belong? To what and whom is it connected and through what relations? In essence, the element refers to the meaning and the identity of technology as they are attached by people.

In sum, Nardi and O'Day find the ecology metaphor powerful for understanding the development, introduction and use of ICT because "it includes local differences while still capturing the strong interrelationships among social, economic and political contexts in which technology is invented and used. When autonomous technology is observed at the systematic level, its effects can be overwhelming. But in individual local settings, we see a more and varied texture of experience, than from distant vantage point" [38: 47].

3.2 Strengths and Weaknesses of the Biological Metaphor

An ecological approach of the use of ICTs in organisations has some major advantages (see e.g. [50]). First, it emphases that the technology is not given, but that is influenced by the characteristics and dynamics of the environments in which it has been developed, introduced and used. No, technology, however autonomous it may be, can develop outside a given economic, political, and intellectual context [51]. But the converse also applies: characteristics of the technology also influence the environment. So, it is important to pay attention to the interactions between technology and its environment. Secondly, it recognises the relationships between the technology itself (as a part of the technological system) with other parts of the technological system, like the components Davenport has distinguished. The relationships and interactions between these parts or subsystems illustrate that the successful introduction and use of technology in organisations depends on a wide range of interplaying factors. So, the interrelations between the several parts of the technological system and between the system and its environments say something about the 'health' of the technological system. Understanding the evolution of technology implies that we have to analyse the functioning of the interrelationships and look at the internal world of technological system, its external world and the interactions between (parts of) those two worlds. Third, the ecological metaphor shows us that because there are 'species of technologies', we should be alerted to the fact that we always have a range of choices in developing and using ICTs. This explains the variety in using technology. Fourth, in traditional organic approaches to organisation and technology, there is this idea that organisations and technologies need to adapt to their environment, or that environments select the organisations and the technologies that are to survive. The interesting point of the ecological approach as Nardi and O'Day present it, is that we should be aware of the fact that the technological environment and other environments mutually shape each other. The notion of co-evolution tries to express this.

However, we can also look at some weaknesses that are related to the conceptualisation of ICT as information ecology [50]. The first point of criticism is the fact that the technological system and its parts are presented as a functional unity and operate according the principles of functional interdependence. It is a rather harmonious concept of the technological system in which there is hardly any place for the role of interests and conflicts.

The second point of criticism, closely related to the former point, is that in the information ecology approach, an actor perspective is missing. Notions like power, interests and stakeholders who influence the selection and adoption process of ICT are missing, although Davenport [37] introduces the element of information politics in his information ecology model. In his work, the information politics component refers to the power information provides and the governance responsibilities for its management and use. As presented in the previous section, research shows that it is important to pay attention to power, interests and stakeholders 1) because the introduction of ICT in and between organisations is an important intervention, 2) because it influences the access, distribution and use of powerful and scarce resources in and between organisations, like information, knowledge, people and experience, and 3) because it touches upon existing interest and power relations and it can challenge existing practices, routines, procedures and information systems [25]. The development, introduction and use of ICTs should therefore be seen as resource politics which can favour the position, interests and values of certain actors, while other actors will see it as a threat [52]. In order to understand the interests that are at stake, it is important to look which actors and interests are involved in the development, introduction and use of ICTs, how (inter)dependent they are from one another, what strategies they use to protect their interests and what kinds of games emergence in relation to the use of ICTs [43]. The selection and use of specific technologies are intrinsically interwoven with the institutionalised and vested interests and values in an organisation, in a policy sector or in society. Technologies are inherently political technologies [53]. This is why Winner asked himself the question: Do artefacts have politics?

The third point of criticism is that is important to look at the meanings that different actors attach to the use of technology. Davenport and Nardi and O'Day look beyond the technology itself (as a tool) and see all kinds of relations with other elements in its environment that give meaning to the technology itself, but the technology itself is still seen as black box. For instance, they recognise the human resources that are necessary to use and maintain it and the meanings that can be derived from it. However, they do not recognise the meanings that are embedded in the technology itself. The meanings, which are embedded in the technology can be addressed from two perspectives.

First, there is the socio-constructionist perspective, which is organised around the following juxtaposition as Pinch, Bijker and Hughes have formulated it: "in deciding which problems are relevant, the social groups concerned with the artefact and the meanings that those groups give to the artefact play a crucial role. A problem is defined as such only, when there is a social group for which it constitutes a problem (....) We think that our account – in which the different interpretations by social groups of the content of the artefact lead by means of different chains of problems and solutions to different developments – involves the content of the artefact itself" [54: 30, 42]. The consequence is that technology is being developed, introduced and used in a continuous process of interactions in which actors produce, exchange and select meanings in order to create or impose a dominant definitions of the solution that technology will bring in relation to a specific definition of a problem or challenge. Hence, Pinch, Bijker and Hughes [54] talk about the rhetorical closure of the debate. Closure in technology involves the stabilisation of an artefact and the disappearance of problems or the redefinition of a problem so that the controversy can disappear. In order to understand the dynamics and selection process in this debate, it is important to look at the sociological, technological, political and economic argumentations that are permanently interwoven in a seamless web or network of actors and interest [55].

The meaning of technology is not only the result of the interactions between actors, which come from outside the technology itself and which constitute the dominant meaning of technology as an actor will perceive this later on. Technology itself is a cultural artefact and can be seen as the product of a process of cultural modernisation. Technology can be seen as the embodiment of the functional rationality which accompanies this process of modernisation and which is also has a very dominant pattern of meaning in the bureaucratic organisation of government [56]. There is a 'Wahlverwandschaft' between the cultural meaning which is embedded in the technology itself and the central meaning of bureaucratic organisations: the meaning to control and to discipline [56]. This meaning is always present in technology (see also [57]). This control potential was quite obvious in computerisation processes that were applied in the pre- Internet period. Computer technology forced organisation to look at their processes and could only be used if these processes were standardised and formalised. But also in the Internet period, network technology offers the possibility to overcome i.e. to control, the traditional limitations of effective ways of organising: the concentration of people, communication and the sharing of information and knowledge resources in time at one location is no longer a necessity for effective organising.

The notion of 'presence availability' acquires another meaning because network technology disciplines the functional, temporal and geographical boundaries and barriers. In her book 'The Age of the Smart Machine', Zuboff [39] illustrates   that ICT differs from other technology in that intelligence is added to it. She calls this the "informating" capacities of ICTs. Using ICT implies that new information is added to the existing information that is stored in the technology, and that can be used in such a way that new knowledge can be provided; knowledge and information that enables people and organisations to improve and fine-tune their existing business processes or to enable a broader use of the same technology in relation to additional or new goals. The informating capacities of ICT can also be seen as way of producing new and more intelligent ways of controlling those business processes in which ICT plays an important role, and Zuboff sees these capacities as 'given with and by the technology'. In the eyes of Frissen [56], these informating capacities and their control potential can be seen an patterns of meaning which is embedded in ICTs.

3.3   Redefining the Notion of the Information Ecology

Looking at Davenport's [37] and Nardi and O'Day's [38] elaboration on the information ecology concept and taking into account the strengths and weaknesses of the biological or ecological metaphor of ICT development, we want to redefine the original notion of the information ecology. In our view, the notion of information ecology of ICTs tries to express and to combine the following ideas.

First, the idea that ICTs are developed in interaction with actors who operate in the environment of technology. These actors have specific positions, roles, values, beliefs and interests that influence how they view ICTs as a solution for a specific problem. The definition of the problem itself as well as the solution which ICTs should produce is the result of complex interactions in which different meanings are exchanged, discussed or enforced. Power, dependency, interdependency, strategic behaviour, the existence of several games and playing rules plays an important in the selection and adaptation of ICTs in organisations.

Second, the meaning that is attached to the use of ICTs is not only in the products of the interactions between relevant stakeholders. At the same time, it is important to recognise the idea the technology itself is an embodiment of the potential to control and to discipline; a potential which is rather autonomous.

Third, the meaning that stakeholders attach to the technology and the meaning that is embedded in the technology itself are brought together in the complex interactions between stakeholders. This process can be seen as a dialectical process of mutual shaping, which is can also be made understandable by the notion of co-evolution. An interesting example which makes the dialectics quite clear is the tension between centralisation and decentralisation in relation to ideas about governance at a distance [58]. Although new paradigms of governance proclaim that government should only focus on certain headlines and parameters in order to steer more effectively, i.e. more decentralisation, the use of ICTs in these new governance arrangement shows us that the proclaimed distance is reduced by the capacity of ICT to monitor the activities of the decentralised agencies rather closely: the transparency that ICTs bring by processing more information and combining the information in a more intelligent way, opens the door for new ways, and more sophisticated ways of control. In practice, we see that governance at a distance more resembles a dialectical process of centralisation in the framework of decentralisation.

Fourth, the interactions between these stakeholders do not occur in a vacuum. They are embedded in a specific cultural, political, intellectual and economic environment in which specific 'rules' guide the behaviour and interactions between these stakeholders as well as the meaning that will be attached to the use of ICTs. Therefore it is important to look at the institutional context or several institutional contexts in which these actors operate [59, 60]. Hence, in the process of co-evolution as we have described it, another element should be added: the element of the institutional context in which actors operate and technology choices are made.

The fact that the development, introduction and use of ICTs is the result of complex interactions underlines the idea that these interactions are always local, that they are situated in a local organisational and institutional context. So the fifth important feature of the information ecology is the idea of variety, contextuality and contingency.

The sixth and last quality of the information ecology is the idea that interactions are not only local, but also unpredictable. This has important implications because it challenges the idea of a linear development of stages in the use of ICTs.

4.   The Information Ecology Perspective on E-Government

The re-conceptualisation of the information ecology opens new ways for understanding of e-government.

First, it is important to look which interests and central values are served by e-government and how these interests and values are shaped and re-shaped through the use of ICTs. In relation to these interests and values, it is important to analyse the network of actors or stakeholders that are involved in the introduction of e-government and what strategies they imply to stimulate or even to obstruct the introduction of e-government. For instance, is e-government primarily seen as a way to improve the quality and efficiency of public service delivery, or is it seen as a way of improving 'strong democracy'? Who benefits from the specific e-government services that are being developed? Do civil servants assess the potential of e-government in a different way then politicians?

Second, the different meanings these stakeholders attach to e-government is not only based upon the interests that are at stake, but they are also influenced by the meanings that other relevant environments produce; meanings that often reflect the dominant 'rules' in these environments. For instance, what does e-government imply for the discretion (as a rule or established practice) of street level bureaucrats who play an important role as 'broker' in boundary spanning process between government and society? Does e-government diminish the role of these brokers? If we consider it from a public management angle, do we assess the strengths and weakness of e-government in another way than from a public policy perspective?

Third, it is important to look at the autonomous control potential if ICT interferes with the interests and values of those actors who are engaged in e-government activities. Does e-government imply that the existing information and communication exchange relations with client groups can better be controlled, that their information behaviour can be disciplined in a more sophisticated way?

Fourth, it is important to recognise the fact that the practice of e-government is miscellaneous. E-government has a local flavour although all these flavours foster the idea of a better and new government. E-government in New York has a different blend than e-government in Amsterdam, Copenhagen or Brussels. The local habitation of e-government makes it rather difficult to assess the success and failure of e-government, because this is rather contingent.

Fifthly, the local colour and meanings that actors attach to e-government as a solution implies that local choices and strategies shape the nature of e-government that do not always have to follow a linear process of specific steps to be taken in order to achieve more sophisticated e-government services.

From these characteristics, we have gathered a number of contributions that help us to understand the complex nature of e-government and that looks beyond a technological perspective on e-government. E-government is seen as the result of a process of co-evolution of different kinds of (technological, political, economic, social and institutional) environments, in which the specific meanings these environments mutually shape the specific, and thus the local flavour, of e-government.

5. The Structure of the Book

This book is divided in twelve chapters, in which both conceptual as well as managerial considerations about e-government (conceived as information ecologies) are addressed.

In the second chapter ('The Locus and Focus in E-Government'), Zouridis and Thaens examine the concept of e-government and explore and position various potential uses of e-government applications from a public administration point of view. Using an information ecology perspective, Janssen and Rotthier critically examine the development and manifestation of e-government initiatives using a comparative study encompassing developments in seven OECD countries. Victor Bekkers elaborates on organisational phenomena in information ecologies (such as boundary crossing information exchange) and reflects on political, philosophical and juridical considerations of changing jurisdictions in the fourth chapter ('E-Government, Boundary Management and Changing Jurisdictions'). The fifth chapter (authored by Victor Bekkers) consists of an exploration of various types and patterns of virtual organisations. Victor Bekkers and Vincent Homburg examine back offices in e-government in the sixth chapter, and analyse processes of interorganisational information exchange as political economies. In the seventh chapter ('Digital Visions: The Role of Politicians in Transitions'), Birgit Jæger focuses on how politicians conceive and deal with technologies in order to reflect on the notion of technology in e-government initiatives. Arthur Edwards examines the democratic potential of information ecologies in chapter eight. He demonstrates how traditional political intermediaries use information and communication technologies to consolidate or even strengthen their position. In the ninth chapter, Miriam Lips and Hein van Duivenboden ('Responsive E-Government Services: Towards 'New' Public Management') discuss roots and characteristics of responsiveness in the context of e-government information ecologies. The tenth chapter is devoted to the combination of New Public Management (NPM) and e-government. Vincent Homburg and Victor Bekkers examine various trajectories of organisational and interorganisational change that emerge from the application of e-government technologies and explores the consequences of various changes for public and political accountability. In chapter eleven, Albert Meijer and Mark Bovens discuss the nature of public accountability in the information age. In the final chapter, Victor Bekkers and Vincent Homburg discuss, conceptualise and evaluate the information ecology perspective on e-government.

References

1.   Grönlund, A., *Emerging Electronic Infrastructures (Exploring Democratic Components)*. Social Science Computer Review, 2003. **21**(1): p. 55-72.
2.   Chadwick, A. and C. May, *Interaction Between States and Citizens in the Age of the Internet: E-Government' in the United States, Britain and the European Union*. Governance, 2003. **16**(2): p. 271-300.
3.   Moon, M.J., *The Evolution of E-Government among Municipalities: Rhetoric or Reality?* Public Administration Review, 2002. **62**(4): p. 424-433.
4.   Hague, B.N. and B. Loader, *Digital Democracy: Discourse and Decision Making in the Information Age*. 1999, London: Routledge.
5.   Bekkers, V.J.J.M. and S. Zouridis, *Electronic Service Delivery in Public Administration*. Electronic Service Delivery in Public Administration, 1999. **65**(2): p. 183-195.
6.   Barber, B.R., *Strong Democracy: Participatory Politics for a New Age*. 1984, Berkeley: University of California Press.
7.   Osborne, D. and T. Gaebler, *Reinventing Government: How the Entrepreneurial Spirit is Transforming the Public Sector*. 1992, Reading, MA: Addison-Wesley.
8.   Hammer, M. and J. Champy, *Don't Automate, Obliterate!* Harvard Business Review, 1990. **68**(4): p. 104-113.
9.   Thaens, M., V.J.J.M. Bekkers, and H.P.M. van Duivenboden, *Business Process Redesign and Public Administration. A Perfect Match?*, in *Beyond BPR in Public Administration. Informatization Developments in the Public Sector*, J.A. Taylor, I.T.M. Snellen, and A. Zuurmond, Editors. 1997, IOS Press: Amsterdam.
10. Kickert, W.J.M., J.F.M. Koppenjan, and E.H. Klijn, *Managing Complex Networks: Strategies for the Public Sector*. 1997, London: Sage.
11. Heeks, R., *Reinventing Government in the Information Age: International Practice in IT-Enabled Public Sector Reform*. 2001, London: Routledge.
12. OECD, *The E-Government Imperative*. 2003, Paris: OECD.
13. National Performance Review, *Conversations with America*. 2000, National Performance Review. p. http://npr.gov/converse/converse.htm.
14. Minister for the Cabinet Office, *Modernising Government*. 1999, Minister for the Cabinet Office: London.
15. National Audit Office, *Better Public Services through E-Government*. 2002, National Audit Office: London.
16. Hood, C., *Paradoxes of Public-Sector Managerialism, Old Public Management and Public Service Bargains*. International Public Management Journal, 2000. **3**(1): p. 1-22.
17. Hood, C., *A Public Management For All Seasons?* Public Administration, 1991. **69**(1): p. 3-19.
18. Rhodes, R., *The New Public Management*. Public Administration, 1991. **69**(1).
19. Pollitt, C.P. and G. Bouckaert, *Public Management Reform (A Comparative Analysis)*. 2000, Oxford: Oxford University Press.
20. Ling, T., *Delivering Joined-Up Government in the UK: Dimensions, Issues and Problems*. Public Administration, 2002. **80**(4): p. 615-642.
21. Behn, R.D., *Rethinking Democratic Accountability*. 2001, Washington D.C.: The Brookings Institute.

22.   PIU, *Wiring it up. Whitehall's Management of Cross Cutting Policies and Services*. 2000, London: PIU.
23.   Fountain, J., *Building the Virtual State*. 2001, Washington DC: The Brookings Institute.
24.   Homburg, V.M.F. and V.J.J.M. Bekkers. *The Back-Office of E-Government (Managing Information Domains as Political Economies)*. in *HICSS*. 2002. Waikoloa Village, Waikoloa, Hawaii: IEEE Press.
25.   Homburg, V.M.F., *The Political Economy of Information Management (A Theoretical and Empirical Study on the Development and Use of Interorganizational Information Systems),*. 1999, Groningen: SOM.
26.   Venkatraman, N., *IT-Enabled Business Transformation: from Automation to Business Scope Redefinition*. Sloan Management Review, 1994(Winter): p. 73-87.
27.   Bimber, B., *Information and American Democracy*. 2003, Cambridge: Cambridge University Press.
28.   Andersen, K.V. and J.N. Danziger, *Impacts of IT on Politics and the Public Sector: Methodological, Epistemological, and Substantive Evidence from the "Golden Age" of Transformation*. Public Administration, 2001. **25**(5): p. 591-627.
29.   Bellamy, C. and J. Taylor, *Governing in the Information Age*. 1998, Buckingham: Open University Press.
30.   Snellen, I.T.M. and W.B.H.J. van de Donk, *Public Administration in an Information Age. A Handbook*. 1998, Amsterdam: IOS Press.
31.   European Commission, *Government Online*. 2000, European Commission. p. http://europe.eu.int/comm/information_society/eeurope/actionplan/index_en.htm.
32.   Bekkers, V.J.J.M., *Voorbij de virtuele organisatie? Over de bestuurskundige betekenis van virtuele variëteit, contingentie en parallel organiseren*. 2001, Den Haag: Elsevier Bedrijfsinformatie.
33.   UN-ASPA, *E-Government: A Global Perspective. Assessing the Progress of the UN Member States*. 2002, New York: United Nations / ASPA.
34.   Homburg, V.M.F., *The Political Economy of Information Management*. 1999, Groningen: SOM.
35.   Minister for the Cabinet Office, *E-Government: A Strategic Framework for Public Services in the Information Age*. 2000, London: Minister for the Cabinet Office.
36.   Teicher, J. and N. Dow, *E-Government in Australia, Promise and Progress*. The Information Polity, 2002. **7**: p. 231-246.
37.   Davenport, T.H., *Information Ecology: Mastering the Information and Knowledge Environment*. 1997, Oxford: Oxford University Press.
38.   Nardi, B.A. and V.L. O'Day, *Information Ecologies: Using Technology with Heart*. 1999, Cambridge (MA): The MIT Press.
39.   Zuboff, S., *In the Age of the Smart Machine: The Future of Work and Power*. 1988, New York: Basic Books.
40.   Bijker, W.E., T.P. Hughes, and T.J. Pinch, *The Social Construction of Technological Systems: New Directions in the Sociology and History of Technology*. 1987, Cambridge: MIT Press.
41.   Kraemer, K.L., et al., *Datawars: The Politics of Modeling in Federal Policymaking*. 1987, New York: Columbia University Press.
42.   Homburg, V.M.F., *Politics and Property Rights In Information Exchange*. Knowledge, Policy and Technology, 2000. **13**(3): p. 13-22.

43.   Dutton, W.H. and K. Guthrie, *An Ecology of Games: The Political Construction of the Santa Monica's Electronic Network.* Informatization in the Public Sector, 1991. **1**: p. 279-301.
44.   McLoughlin, I., *Creative Technological Change.* 1999, London: Routledge.
45.   Bekkers, V.J.J.M., *Wiring Public Organizations and Changing Organizational Juridisctions.*, in *Public Administration in an Information Age*, I.T.M. Snellen and W.B.H.J.v.d. Donk, Editors. 1998, IOS Press: Amsterdam. p. 57-77.
46.   Taylor, J.A. and E. Hurt, *Parliaments on the Web: Learning through Innovation*, in *Parliament in the Age of the Internet*, S. Coleman, J. Taylor, and W.B.J.H. van de Donk, Editors. 1999, Oxford University Press: Oxford. p. 141-155.
47.   Coleman, S., J. Taylor, and W.B.J.H. van de Donk, *Parliament in the Age of the Internet.* 1999, Oxford: Oxford University Press.
48.   Bellamy, C. and C.D. Raab, *Wiring-up the Deck-chairs?*, in *Parliament in the Age of the Internet*, S. Coleman, J. Taylor, and W.B.J.H. van de Donk, Editors. 1999, Oxford University Press: Oxford. p. 156-172.
49.   Detlor, B., *The Influence of Information Ecology on E-Commerce Initiatives.* Internet Research, 2001. **11**(4): p. 286-295.
50.   Morgan, G., *Images of Organizations.* 1986, Thousand Oaks: SAGE.
51.   Ellul, J., *The Technological Society.* 1964, New York: Vintage Books.
52.   Kraemer, K.L., et al., *Datawars: The Politics of Modeling in Federal Policymaking.* 1985, New York: Columbia University Press.
53.   Winner, L., *Do Artefacts Have Politics?*, in *Technology and Politics*, M.E. Kraft and N.J. Vig, Editors. 1988, Durham University Press: London. p. 33-53.
54.   Pinch, T.J., W.E. Bijker, and J.E. Hughes, *The Social Construction of Technological Systems: New Directions in the Sociology and History of Technology.* 1987, Cambridge: MIT Press.
55.   Callon, M., *Society in the Making: The Study of Technology as a Tool for Sociological Analysis*, in *The Social Construction of Technological Systems*, T.J. Pinch, W.E. Bijker, and J.E. Hughes, Editors. 1987, MIT Press: Cambridge.
56.   Frissen, P.H.A., *Politics, Governance and Technology. A Postmodern Narrative on the Virtual State.* 1999, Cheltenham, UK: Edward Elgar.
57.   Beniger, J.R., *Conceptualizing Information Technology as Organization and Vice-Versa*, in *Organizations and Communication Technology*, J. Fulk and C. Steinfield, Editors. 1990, SAGE: Newbury Park.
58.   Bekkers, V.J.J.M., *Grenzeloze overheid. Over informatisering en grensveranderingen in het openbaar bestuur.* 1998, Alphen aan den Rijn: Samsom.
59.   DiMaggio, P.J. and W.W. Powell, *The New Institutionalism in Organizational Analysis.* 1991, Chicago: Chicago University Press.
60.   March, J.G. and J.P. Olsen, *Rediscovering Institutions. The Organizational Basis of Politics.* 1989, New York: The Free Press.

[handwritten annotations across top of page: "Mostly ill-informed + not clear + wrong And", "no evidence to support", "w/ virtually no conclusions", "(esp re Taylorism)."]

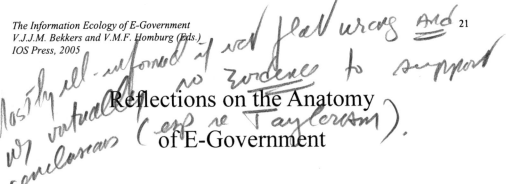

Reflections on the Anatomy
of E-Government

Stavros ZOURIDIS

Centre for Law, Public Administration, and Informatization, Tilburg University,
PO Box 90153, 5000 LE Tilburg, The Netherlands

Marcel THAENS

Ordina Public, PO Box 3069, 3502 GB Utrecht

Abstract. In this chapter, the phenomenon of e-government is analyzed from a
public administration point of view, as opposed to an information management point
of view. It is argued that many e-government programmes are based on an often
implicit informational Taylorism. This could endanger the societal foundations upon
which public administration rests and the legitimacy of government in the long run.
However, e-government programmes do not necessarily have to step into the pitfalls
of a Tayloristic approach. If e-government departs from a public administration
perspective, and takes various roles of citizens and rationalities into account, it could
avoid a tunnel vision that blinds the real nature of public administration.

1. Introduction

The rapid diffusion of information and communications technologies (ICT) within
government has stimulated both utopias and distopias. The concept of e-government is
usually seen as a desirable idea, and e-government has become a key word in many policy
proposals. Processes of change and renewal have been based upon e-government for
improving the organisation, the effectiveness and the efficiency of public administration. E-
government seems to have further stimulated processes of administrative reform and new
public management worldwide. Along with the schools and universities (e-learning) and the
private sector (e-commerce and e-business), governments had to prepare for the new
millennium. The advocates of e-government suggested that only governments 'online' or e-
governments would survive. Although the e-government trend has been widely studied, the
research primarily concentrates on the pace of change. The most important question seems
to be which government wins the gold metal for being the most e-government this year.
Conferences and books are filled with case studies that tell us how a specific national or
local government has been transformed into e-government. Although this research is
valuable, we believe that we also need a better theoretical understanding of e-government.
We know what e-government means from an IT perspective, but what does this mean from
the perspective of public administration theory? One of the most important trends in public
administration does not even seem to be on the radar screen of the scientific public
administration community. As such, e-government seems to imply that governance and
governments as we know them will become electronic or online. In the past, we had
government and governance, but the future will be characterised by e-government and e-

governance. Although the IT cowboys promise that these changes will only make government and governance more effective and efficient, the vast literature on technological change tells another story. Several decades ago, early research demonstrated that information and communication technology not only make society more efficient and effective, but it also fundamentally affects our world views and the social, organisational, and political foundations on which society is built (see, for example, [1-4]). Therefore, it is important to search for the transformations that are resulting from the current trend toward e-government. Following the argument of Nardi and O'Day [5], we do not uncritically accept or condemn ICT. We are primarily interested in how new ICT affects a given information ecology. This is primarily an empirical issue. We deal with it by looking at the worldwide trend towards e-government in two ways. First, we describe this trend and some leading practices and initiatives (Section Two). We then analyse these initiatives by looking at the objects of e-government (Section Three). Where are the e-government initiatives located in public administration? Which parts of government become e-government? Then, we analyse how the current initiatives define governance and public administration (Section Four). How do these initiatives approach government and governance? The empirical issue of the transformations caused by e-government as such may be interesting, but it does not tell us how to evaluate them. Saying that ICT changes public administration is meaningless if we cannot assess the nature and the impact of these changes. Therefore, we explore how these changes can be evaluated from a public administration science perspective. We also use the public administration perspective to find some clues and leads for the future of e-government (Section Five).

2.   E-Government: Exploring the Phenomenon

2.1   E-Government as a Global Phenomenon

The transformation of government into e-government turns out to be a global phenomenon. Many countries have formulated their dreams, visions and plans for introducing at least some form of electronic government. Consequently, many governments are also working hard on realising their visions and plans. A global e-government survey, carried out by the UN-ASPA in 2002, concludes that change is the only constant [6: 4]. Numerous barriers have to be overcome in this process. Organisational and financial barriers especially hinder the development towards e-government [7]. All surveys indicate that government institutions are the main bottlenecks. Implementing e-government is not technically, but institutionally restricted. While the sky seems to be the limit from a technical perspective, only some initiatives are actually being carried out. According to a Gartner Group survey [8], the transition from government to e-government can be characterised by four stages.

First, there is the presence of government on the Internet. After the presence stage, government is able to interact with its citizens via the Internet. The interaction stage is succeeded by a transaction stage in which communication between government and its citizens via the Internet is connected with public service delivery. Finally, because of the electronic service delivery, government will transform its organisations and institutions.

The first three stages focus on improving the form of government and establishing much of the basic e-infrastructure. The fourth stage focuses on designing a new form of government [8]. Various international research companies closely monitor the e-government efforts in many countries. A recent example of such a benchmark is a study carried out as part of a programme that assesses the progress of the e-Europe initiative launched by the European Commission to bring the benefits of the information society to all Europeans. This particular benchmark focuses on the availability of the public services on the Internet [9]. Accenture produced a well-known and widely used benchmark study [10]. In their third annual survey, they concentrated on how governments in 23 countries are realising their vision for online government. One of the objectives of the survey was to find out which countries were making the greatest progress and what factors could explain progress. The benchmark also highlighted emerging e-government trends [10]. The study showed that there are three 'Innovative Leaders' (Canada, Singapore and the USA), followed by a large group of 'Visionary Challengers' (for example, Australia, the Netherlands, Germany, Hong Kong and France). The third group is a smaller group of 'Emerging Performers' (New Zealand, Spain, Belgium and Japan) followed by a group of 'Platform Builders' (among others, Brazil, Italy and South Africa). The study concluded that the Visionary Challengers made the greatest progress in 2001. It also concluded that the imprecise, ambitious vision statements of governments are being replaced by a broader approach that focuses on how benefits can be delivered. One of the e-government trends is the growing tendency to treat citizens and businesses as customers and to introduce the techniques of Customer Relationship Management (CRM) to government service delivery. Another global benchmark study aimed at assessing the progress of the 190 UN Member States. This study developed an e-government index to rank the countries [6]. A major conclusion of the study was that national e-government programmes development among the UN Member States advanced substantially in 2001. The sophistication with which countries use the Internet to deliver quality information varied. In 2001:

- 89 per cent of the UN Member States used the Internet to deliver information and services;
- 30 per cent of the UN Member States offered interactive online services; and
- 9 per cent of the countries offered the capacity to conduct transactions online.

The e-government index showed that North America, Europe, South America and the Middle East scored above average, while Asia, the Caribbean, Central America and Africa remained below average. The score was based on a country's official online presence, an evaluation of its telecommunications infrastructure and an assessment of its human development capacity. Almost every public administration worldwide has taken at least some initiative for realising a certain degree of electronic government.

2.2 Shaping the Conditions for E-Government

In order to transform into e-government, a government has to meet certain conditions. These conditions refer to ways for realising applications in order to actually improve the relation between government and citizens/companies. Some of the initiatives undertaken by governments in shaping the conditions for realising e-government at this moment are:
- *Providing access to laws and regulations.* Databanks containing legal texts have been made accessible on the Internet to citizens and companies. For example, in the USA the Library of Congress provides legislative information online at www.thomas.loc.gov.
- *Streamlining basic data.* Some governments connect the personal data of their citizens and use this information for basic services. They are currently developing unique registrations to monitor the quality of the information (for example, is the information correct and up-to-date?). These registrations contain personal data of citizens. By connecting them, the same data do not have to be registered in different information systems.
- *Securing confidential transactions.* In order to increase the security of ICT-usage, governments are launching programmes to develop electronic signatures, electronic identity cards and a Public Key Infrastructure (PKI). Singapore took the lead in 1998 as one of the first countries to enact an Electronic Transaction Act (ETA) to provide legal

recognition of electronic signatures through the use of digital certificates. At present, some governments, for example the Dutch Government, are piloting projects to incorporate biometric characteristics in travel documents or identity cards in order to improve their security. Experiments with iris scans and face recognition have been carried out in the United States and many Western European countries.

- *Creating ICT awareness and developing ICT skills.* For citizens to be able to make use of the possibilities offered by e-government, they have to know the benefits and they also have to be able to use the necessary technology. One example of an initiative aimed at creating awareness is the development of the digital 'playing fields' in the Netherlands. Digital playing fields are easily accessible experimental free zones in problem districts in thirty Dutch cities.
- *Establishing e-government support organisations for the implementation and coordination of the initiatives.* This organisation would coordinate different aspects of e-government, stimulate the role of ICT by public administration, and initiate necessary cultural changes within the government. An interesting example of such an organisation is the e-government Coordination Office in Hong Kong.

2.3   Improving Government Operations: Leading Edge Practices[1]

Human Services

An analysis of some of the leading edge e-government practices might further illustrate what e-government is about. On a national level, e-government is deployed in several areas of public policy. In the *Human Services* Area the leading initiatives primarily focus on employment. These initiatives concern the development of websites on the Internet that allow people searching for a job to create a resume by using a resume-builder feature. Both the United States and Australia have developed online job search services (see www.ajb.org for America's Job Bank and www.jobsearch.gov.au for the Australian job search service).

The Canadian online service even goes one step further by enabling its citizens to register online as unemployed in order to apply for a unemployment insurance. In addition, a service is being tested through which Canadians can apply online for employment insurance benefits.

Revenue and Taxes

Revenue is identified as the most sophisticated and mature online government sector. There are many leading edge Revenue websites. Most of these websites focus on the electronic payment of taxes. For example, the Irish Revenue Online Service (www.ros.ie) facilitates voluntary compliance since taxes can be filed and paid rapidly online. Customers using the service are supplied with digital certificates to enable them to digitally sign enforceable tax returns. The Integrated Management of Wealth and Income Tax was initiated by the Spanish Tax Agency (www.aeat.es) in 1999. This project covers the entire tax process (information, electronic tax return filling and payment, certifications, et cetera) for all types of taxpayers. Tax declarations are submitted online and tax payments can be transferred through online banking facilities. With a Digital Certificate from the Spanish Federal Reserve, citizens can apply for a tax return. Companies can handle their corporate tax and VAT via AEAT's Website [9].

---

[1] Based on the 2002 Accenture Report (p. 20-33) unless indicated otherwise.

Education

An illustrative example of e-learning is the EdNA Online Service from the Education Network Australia (www.edna.edu.au). Edna Online is an information service that provides two key functions. First, it offers a directory that contains all educational and training programmes in Australia and a database of web-based resources useful for teaching and learning. Second, it serves as a communications service aiming to promote collaboration and cooperation throughout the Australian education and training sector. Other practices in the education field are aimed at completing applications online, for example for financial aid (www.fafsa.ed.gov) or for admission to the first year of undergraduate courses (www.cao.ie).

Justice and Public Safety

In several countries, the police, courts and prisons are exploring the possibilities of the Internet for transforming and redesigning traditional methods and procedures. Three leading *Justice and Public Safety* sites were identified by Accenture's research; one relating to online filing of court applications (The Federal Court of Australia, www.fedcourt.gov.au) another to online payment of fines (the Belgian Ministry of Justice, www.just.fgov.be) and a third to filing claims online (the Subordinate Courts of Singapore, www.smallclaims.goc.sg).

Democracy

Although using the Internet to promote participation and *democratic processes* is relatively under-explored, there are some examples of national governments reaching out to citizens in this manner. British Parliament webcasts its parliamentary debates (www.parliamentlive.tv). An Internet pilot for military and overseas civilian voters was implemented during the 2000 presidential election in the United States. The pilot concerned a very small population (84 voters who actually voted over the internet), but it illustrates that governments are seriously exploring the potential of online voting in national elections. Another example can be found in Finland's Otakantaa (www.otakantaa.fi/kaynnissa.cfm). This initiative refers to an interactive service for public discussions (including online debates) on highly topical issues. One ministry hosts and facilitates this service each month.

Social Security

In the field of *social security benefits*, an interesting practice is taking place in France (www.ameli.fr) concerning the reimbursement of medical costs by the medical insurance. On a local level, the insurance funds are responsible for the registration of the insured and day-to-day management. They have created a service in which citizens can consult their files and reimbursement status from a single access point [9]. Belgium has an interesting practice for the social contribution of employees. The website of the social security administration in Belgium (www.sociale-zekerheid.be) is a good example of the combination of back-office integration and an e-portal solution. This website is a front-office result of a long-term effort that the Belgian government has made in recent years to link different databases. The portal site has been designed in such way that each citizen or employer can easily find answers to his questions concerning Belgian social security. Employers can handle several transactions online (such as the social contribution for employees) by means of electronic forms. In the course of 2003, the website was to be extended to enable electronic transactions for citizens as well [9].

3. The Locus of E-Government

Although the pace may differ, the developments we have described point in the same direction. Little by little, government agencies are connecting their operations with the online world of the Internet. The advantages seem obvious. First, e-government aims to be more customer-oriented. Governments can get rid of a lot of red tape by using computers. Instead of going to a tax office or a municipal bureau, citizens can download the necessary brochures and forms immediately, 24-hours a day and 7 days a week directly from the Internet. Second, public administration becomes more efficient with e-government. Second, both money and paper can be saved when public administration connects to the Internet. Procedures and routines are automated in order to save on expensive civil servants. Third, e-government modernises public administration. This is one of the major attractions of e-government; which public administration does not want to be modern? After all, the opposite (old-fashioned) cannot be seriously regarded as an alternative. Because society is increasingly becoming an information society (e.g. [11]), our governments should adapt and become e-governments. The trend towards e-government is then seen as part of a broader process of worldwide public sector reform (e.g. [12]). Although these advantages of ICT may be valid for an information ecology in the private sector, this line of reasoning seems too simple to account for public administration. Can we simply compare selling books or insurances via the Internet with electronic government? And if not, how should we understand e-government? To gain an understanding of how new ICTs affect the information ecology of government, we use two analytical dimensions. First, we analyse the locus of e-government. Which parts of the organisation are being replaced by information technology? Which phases of the policy process are being carried out by means of computers? How do political actors use computers? Which relationships between government and citizens become digitalised? Second, we analyse the focus of e-government. How does it approach the processes, procedures, routines and departments that become electronic? Let us first take a look at the locus of e-government.

Organisation

Public organisations are multiple entities *par excellence* (for example [13]. Although the organisational structure may not tell us a lot about the organisational reality, looking at their structure is a common way of approaching (public) organisations. To find out where e-government is located in public organisations, we can use Mintzberg's [14] conceptual map of the organisation. He distinguishes between five parts: (1) operating core, (2) strategic top, (3) executives, (4) technostructure, and (5) support staff. If we take a look at e-government, we can conclude that a substantial amount of attention is given to supporting the implementation of services. This is a spearhead in every country. Almost every leading edge practice is focused on service delivery. E-government primarily concerns the operating core, but the technostructure is also being affected by e-government. The technostructure has to create the conditions for e-government (for example PKI and the electronic signature). The e-government support organisation belongs to the technostructure of public administration. None of the identified activities have focused on targets and strategy yet, so there has been no affect at the strategic level within government organisations.

Policy

Policy is a key concept of public administration science. Like organisation, there are numerous ways of approaching public policy. Although all analytical tools in the policy sciences seem to be essentially contested, a rather common analytical tool is the policy process based upon systems theory [15]. From a systems approach, the policy process analytically consists of the following phases: problem acknowledgement and agenda setting, policy development and decision making, policy implementation and managerial control. The evaluation phase loops implementation with new processes of agenda setting. This process approach may not tell us how policies develop in practice, but it is a helpful analytical tool for finding the locus of e-government. An analysis of e-government initiatives worldwide demonstrates that e-government primarily concerns the implementation of formulated policy. The principal issue is improving citizen-focused services and getting government authorities online (digital transactions). A trustworthy and secure infrastructure can be considered part of this principal issue. Many of these initiatives concern the improvement of managerial control of the policies that are being implemented. As examples, we can mention the access to laws and regulations, the streamlining of basic data, the development of the electronic signature and biometry. Few or none of the identified initiatives are geared towards the acknowledgement and agenda setting or the formulation of public policy and decision making. One of the few exceptions perhaps is the described interactive service for public discussions in Otakantaa in Finland.

Politics

Politics is essentially connected with public administration. It is one of the reasons e-government cannot be compared with e-Business. Public administration is not just another branch of industry, but a different type of institution. Citizens are not just shareholders who want to make profit, but constituents of a polity that is democratically organised. Therefore, politics is part and parcel of public administration and e-government. When we look at representative bodies in Western democracies, politics comprises four activities. First is representation: the choice of a representative body that can make decisions on behalf of the people [16, 17]. Second, politicians select and define social problems that qualify for policymaking (idea-generation and consideration). Decision making and deliberation in Parliament is a third political activity. According to the principle of checks and balances, democratic supervision is the fourth and last type of political activity. Although the design may depend on the specific state system, representative bodies supervise governments.

The e-government initiatives carried out so far seem particularly aimed at supporting democratic supervision. For example, we can mention online public access to laws and regulations. Access to government information aims to increase the transparency of public administration for citizens and interest groups. Therefore, it enables them to assess and criticise government's actions and its policies. For the time being, e-government has little bearing on other political activities. An exception however, is e-Voting in the USA. This pilot had a very small population (84 voters). This initiative mainly focuses on representation. In terms of shaping the conditions for stretching e-government to the collective decision-making processes, the developments occurring around PKI are interesting because this infrastructure could support direct democracy in the long-term. Ad hoc, many government authorities in various countries also use Internet for chatting and discussion platforms.

Citizens

In Western democracies, citizens and public administration are connected in several ways. A defining characteristic of a republic is that citizens are both rulers and ruled (for example [18]). Citizens rule in at least two ways. First, the representative democracy allows citizens to choose their representatives (citizens as *voters*). Second, citizens are connected with everyday practices of policymaking and decision making. Sometimes government consults citizens to hear what they think about a specific policy proposal, but generally citizens as *citoyen* make up the building blocks of civil society. As people being ruled, citizens are addressed by public administration in at least two ways. First, they are *subjected* to the authority of government. Penal law is an example of this relationship between citizens and public administration. Second, citizens are increasingly defined as *consumers* of the products and services that are being supplied by government.

At present, the majority of e-government initiatives concerns citizens as consumers. This is because there is a keen interest in the development of customer services. Streamlining basic data also falls under this category; in fact, this concerns a type of government Customer Relationship Management. The government's interest in the citizen as a subject is less prominant although there are initiatives such as securing the confidential transactions and biometry. Initiatives concerning the citizen as citoyen are still scarce. The e-voting initiative in the USA is a clear example of the perspective in which the citizen is seen as a voter.

Conclusion

By means of common public administration concepts, we have found the location (or locus) of e-government within public administration. First, it can be concluded that e-government mainly concentrates on the operational core. This is the result of the focus on customer services. The initiatives give little attention to the executive, strategic, and supporting parts of public organisations. In the policy process, e-government primarily concerns policy implementation and, to a certain degree, the managerial control of this policy. At present, e-government plays no role in the phases of acknowledgement and agenda setting or in the formulation of policy and decision making. In the realm of politics, e-government is used to support democratic supervision and representation. It has little or no affinity with propagation and consideration of ideas and political decision making. Finally, e-government is particularly geared to citizens as consumers of the products and services of public administration.

4. The Focus of E-Government

A Limited Locus, but also a Limited Focus

Because of e-government's rather narrow locus in public administration, E-services (or: I-services) would be a better name for the current trend towards e-government. But this trend is not only limited in its locus; it is also limited in its approach towards public administration (the focus). At first sight, the issue at stake does not seem to be very important. After all, e-government only appears to improve government services. It takes a specific activity of a government agency as a starting point (for example, social security benefits, the openness of government, finding a job, etc.), and then changes it into e-government by putting the process into computers and connecting it to the Internet. As the advocates of e-government tell us, only the instruments are being replaced. What used to be done manually is now being carried out by computers. Through technology, government services merely become more efficient, more modern and more reliable.

In his book *Understanding Media*, Marshall McLuhan [3] demonstrates that such a socially and culturally neutral replacement of technology is impossible. He argues that new technologies will never be neutral with regard to their social and cultural context. McLuhan illustrates his argument with numerous examples. The Graeco-Roman alphabet is not just a written reflection of the spoken word, but a specific form of writing with its own bias. Because of the fact that our alphabet detaches the symbols and sounds from their semantic and verbal content, it has proved to be the most radical technology for the homogenisation of diverse cultures. Hieroglyph, which connects symbols with their semantic content, would never have had such an enormous impact on different cultures because is serves a specific culture and distinguishes it from other cultures.

Technology's Ideology

McLuhan demonstrates that we should not only look at the content of the message, but also at the content of the medium. This is expressed by the famous phrase 'the medium is the message'. Neil Postman argues that a specific ideology is hidden behind every technology. Every seemingly neutral technical instrument is tied up with (hidden) ideological bias. Although one is able to use a hammer in numerous ways, to a man with a hammer, everything looks like a nail. Postman proceeds:

> "To a man with a pencil everything looks like a list. To a man with a camera, everything looks like an image. To a man with a computer, everything looks like data. And to a man with a grade sheet, everything looks like a number" [19].

Only by exploring and revealing the (hidden) ideology behind a technology is one able to get a grip on its social and cultural implications. Which ideology is hiding behind the physical things? In what way do these objects or instruments change people's worldview and their perception of reality? The attention should therefore be shifted from the content of what is processed by computers to the ideology behind computer processing because only then will the real transformations be uncovered that are caused by a specific technology.

Government as Information Management

So what is the ideology behind e-government? A clue can be found in Postman's quote, namely that 'for a man with a computer everything looks like data'. According to e-government's ideology, governance is a matter of information collection, information processing and information dissemination. For e-government, information is the core of public administration. When we believe in this e-government ideology, government essentially becomes a matter of information. Whether this is done manually or by computers, it will be the same process. Because people are imperfect, so will the information be when people process it. Therefore, citizens are better served when the computers process the information because they are more efficient and more reliable.

The ideology behind e-government can thus be characterised as an information ideology. In its core, public administration is a matter of information. We do not want to criticise this ideology, although it seems a vulnerable one. Brown and Duguid [20] demonstrate the consequences of the 'infologic' that sometimes seems to replace the logic of humanity:

> "Thus you don't need to look far these days to find much that is familiar in the world redefined as information. Books are portrayed as information containers, libraries as information warehouses, universities as information providers, and learning as information adoption. Organisations are depicted as information coordinators, meetings as information consolidators, talk as information exchange, markets as information-driven stimulus and response" [20: 20-21].

Like Procrustes' bed, Brown and Duguid define the dominance of the information ideology as 'infoprefixation'. This results in a tunnel vision that tends to be blind for the richness of the institutions that are being transformed into something informational. Besides being a tunnel, Lash has demonstrated that information tends to function as a prison from which it is difficult to escape [21]. The information ideology is not only a perspective or a worldview; when it is being applied, it tends to become a 'social bulldozer' that transforms practices into 'infopractices'. When a meeting is defined as an information consolidator, it will probably be designed as such. While the social consequences of this design may be disastrous, from a scientific point of view it is merely interesting to understand the transformation. Because public administration is a socially rich institution, the reductive focus of information should arouse scientific interest from public administration scholars.

The limited focus of e-government uncovers the bias that this ideology creates. When information management becomes the dominant approach, every issue concerning government and public administration will be defined as an information issue or an issue relating to the organisation of information. The ideology of e-government can be labelled as an informational Taylorism. If it is applied to public administration, it will ignore other meanings of government. But what exactly will we lose with e-government? Snellen [22] offers an interesting and useful conceptual framework to understand the richness of public administration as a web of information ecologies. He distinguishes four different paradigmatic approaches toward public administration. These approaches can be empirically regarded as institutional pillars upon which public administration rests. Therefore, Snellen speaks of four different rationalities.

First, there is *political rationality*. Democratic governance always results from conflict between proponents and opponents. The disputes concerning government policy may be regarded as the essence of politics. These disputes are settled by debate, voting, and ultimately the use of power (sometimes even force). Conflict, power, force and political decisionmaking are always connected with (democratic) public administration. Second, there is *legal rationality*. Every action of government needs to be legal, both in its form and in its substance. Usually, government moulds its activities in a legal form. Legal security, legal equality and the obligation to motivate government decisions are requirements that government's actions and structures must meet. Third, *economic rationality* underlies public administration. Efficiency is a typical requirement relating to this rationality. Even when the economy flourishes, government is confronted with economic scarcity. The means are never sufficient for society's demands. Economic rationality also requires a rational organisation of public administration. Fourth, there is *professional rationality*. Effective government policy requires a valid policy theory. Professional rationality requires scientific knowledge with regard to the effects of government's interventions.

Implications of E-Government's Bias

Snellen's rationalities can be used to analyse the e-government initiatives described above. We then see that e-government as an information ecology primarily relates to economic rationality of public administration. It aims at creating a rational organisation of public administration. It enhances the economic rationality of public policy and the efficiency and the effectiveness of government agencies. E-government also (un)consciously contributes to some other requirements and rationalities. As far as it concerns professional rationality, it enhances the internal consistency and harmony of public policy. With regard to legal rationality, only a specific interpretation of this rationality is enhanced by e-government. It departs from a formalistic, positivist conception of law and it serves a formal ideal of legal security and legal equality in practice. Political rationality is largely ignored by e-government. Because of its bias, the implementation of e-government causes at least four transformations.

1. E-government solidifies political and power relationships by stabilising data definitions and the informational architecture of public administration [23]. The existence of different definitions does not always express the laziness and

sloppiness of public administration, but each definition reflects a specific interest. A variety of definitions may be required by political, professional or legal rationality. By solidifying specific definitions, and thus specific interests, e-government also solidifies a certain distribution of power. When e-government has actually been realised, we may expect fewer conflicts and bureaucratic struggles within public administration. Although bureaucratic politics will likely flourish during the development of the necessary software and information architecture, it will decrease after the e-government initiatives have been implemented. The informational Taylorism may be efficient, but it does not create counter-power and checks and balances because these are seen as inefficient.

2. E-government rationalises public policy from the point of view of professional rationality (see for example [24, 25]). Almost all research into the effects of information and communication technology has led to the conclusion that both the policy process and the policy itself become more rational. Effectiveness and efficiency become the primary values for assessing policy processes and policy proposals. The possibilities for political conflict are channelled and sometimes reduced because of this rationalisation process.

3. E-government transforms legal processes into administrative-technical processes. For many years, legal informatics and artificial intelligence have debated whether legal reasoning could be automated (for example, [24]). Although the theoretical debate has not reached a final conclusion, practice has already found a bypass. It accepted that if individual situations are brought under the rule of law, legal reasoning is never completely unilinear (from general rule to individual situation). Legal decision making always jumps from the general rule to the individual situation *and back*; each individual case tests the tenability of the rule as such and the justification of the application. Computers do not and cannot jump back. Therefore, public administration practice does not try to automate legal reasoning. Instead, it transforms legal processes into administrative-technical processes. Administrative processes can be automated easily. This process has only recently been discovered [26]. It affects the openness of law fundamentally and raises some new issues with regard to democratic guarantees (see [26]).

4. E-government transforms citizenship into 'consumership'. It aims at providing services proactively (for example, [27]). Citizens no longer have to fill in numerous forms, but the information that is already possessed by government agencies is taken as a frame of reference for government services. Active government that does not wait for citizens to apply for services could have counterproductive effects from a democratic point of view. Instead of expecting them to contribute to the public interest, citizens are forced to behave as consumers. It only communicates 'ask what your country can do for you'. It tends to forget that public administration is also built on active citizenship ('ask what you can do for your country).

Although the transformations may be desirable, they require further reflection. E-government affects the fundamental character of public administration and the basic structure of its institutions [28]. Therefore, it may also affect the legitimacy of public administration and government's societal position. In practice, these questions are seldom posed. Instead, we are hypnotised by the information ideology of e-government's advocates.

5. Towards a Public Administration Approach to E-Government

The final question we want to take up is whether e-government can be enriched from a public administration point of view. Can we imagine a concept of e-government that does justice to the richness of public administration institutions? If we use the locus and focus dimensions, we might find some clues.

Enriching the Locus of E-Government

At the moment, e-government primarily aims at the implementation of public policy, democratic control, the operational core, and consumership. We can enrich the locus of e-government by using ICT in other parts of public administration and using it for other activities as well.

1. ICT can be deployed for the development of new policy proposals to mobilise the support and creativity of citizens. Currently, a typical process for new policy proposals is characterised by three core aspects. First, government works towards a single and tangible product (a policy paper). Second, public administration manages both the policy proposal and the policy process. Government decides what topics will be handled in the policy paper, what the policy agenda will be, and so on. Moreover, government agencies decide who will participate and at what moment. Third, the process is rather restricted and sophisticatedly managed. Although this way of preparing policy proposals seems logical, the question can be posed of whether the use of computers and the Internet opens some new possibilities. The development of the Linux operating system offers a famous example of 'product development' on the Internet (see for example [29]). The Linux story and the open source movement inspire us to think about these characteristics because they completely differ from the 'product development process' of a policy proposal.

    First, the Linux process does not require one single and tangible product. Many versions and modules of Linux exist, and users are able to build their own system. There is no single final product but everyone is able to select and combine the functions he or she needs. If this principle is translated to the realm of policymaking, the Linux model could mean that government agencies connect their policies with the development of a specific policy field and the actors in this field. Instead of enforcing a policy, it could be co-created with the involved actors.

    Second, the Linux process is not managed by anyone. Nobody manages what people do with Linux, how they improve the existing versions, and what new modules people add to the existing versions. Neither the content nor the process is centrally managed. Everyone manages his version of Linux, but there is no overall management. This stimulates people both to use the system and to add something to it or adapt it to their preferences.

    Third, the system is entirely open. The Internet facilitates both the openness and the free dissemination of Linux and also the community structure for the development of the system.

    As a metaphor, the example of Linux may be interesting for the way we think about policy processes. Could policy proposals also be co-created by communities on the Internet? Could ICT be used to create platforms and communities that are built around specific policy issues? A Linux model of policymaking may improve both the effectiveness and the societal support for new policy proposals. Moreover, it appeals to active republican citizenship (citoyen).

2. ICT may also be directly deployed for the interventions and steering attempts of government. Right now, government uses legal regulations (the 'stick'), money (the 'carrot'), and communication (the 'sermon') to influence societal processes. It could also use ICT for the purpose of influencing these processes. According to Kevin Kelly [30], all our networks for the production, distribution, and consumption will become 'intelligent' rather soon. This means that every physical thing will be equipped with a chip. Although the capacity of the chip may be limited, it makes it possible to connect the object involved with an entire network. When all of these pieces of intelligence are connected to each other, the networks and chains for the production, distribution and consumption as a whole become 'intelligent'. It could be that the technological interventions governments enforce in these chains by means of ICT are much more effective than the current steering attempts. Think of the possibilities of this kind of e-government for the implementation of environmental policy or the collection of taxes.

3. ICT can be used by the organisation to support the strategic process. For example, without much effort an organisation can organise a digital debate with stakeholders regarding its own goals. The question can even be asked whether a certain policy carried out by a specific organisation is still necessary, considering the societal developments nowadays. An organisation can also use the possibilities offered by group decision rooms to internally reassess its goals and strategy or to develop new goals or strategies. Moreover, ICT makes benchmarking a more feasible option. Due to modern technology it is possible to easily compare the performance of an organisation to other organisations, whether it be in the same policy field in another country or in another policy field in the same country. The results of benchmarking can be used to redirect the chosen strategy.

4. The political domain could also enrich the locus of e-government. The literature on E-democracy is too extensive to summarise in this contribution (for example, [31, 32]). If we look at the activities of politics, the possibilities of ICT are numerous. When it concerns representation, ICT could be used to interactively connect the elected representatives with constituencies and citizens in their voting roles. Communities of voters may generate and deliberate new ideas. These can be connected digitally with processes of democratic control by Parliament. How to think of the use of ICT to support Parliament by means of specific parliamentary information systems? Why not enrich e-government with e-democracy?

Enriching the Focus of E-Government

Enriching the focus of e-government means that we have to look at the bias with which the current initiatives have been designed. A number of design requirements can be derived from the rationalities that underlie public administration.

1. We have concluded that e-government aims at solidifying and stabilising public policy. To some extent, political rationality requires vagueness and volatility. For e-government, these requirements mean that ICT has to be designed flexibly. If it is not flexibly designed, its practice will be limited to rather trivial initiatives like a digital passport. Moreover, if the more complex initiatives are being realised in practice, they will be rather vulnerable if their design is not flexible. This may explain why a substantial amount of money has been wasted in the past on ICT projects in public administration. It can be expected that a system for social security benefits has to be continuously adjusted due to changing political preferences.

2. Political rationality also requires that a certain amount of bureaucratic politics be embedded in e-government's design. Right now, e-government aims at dissolving bureaucratic politics. 'Joining up government' is its primary goal and a lot of bureaucratic energy is being devoted to creating the conditions under which government agencies can be joined up. Joining up government agencies may bring the undesirable forms of bureaucratic politics to an end, but it also throws the bureaucratic baby away with the bathwater. To a certain extent, bureaucratic politics create the necessary context for second-loop learning processes.

3. Among others, legal rationality requires some institutional barriers for joining up government. To prevent government from invading our freedom, it is provided with a number of checks and balances. The adage that every power has to be supplied with a countervailing power is one of the foundations of the modern state. If we take criminal law as an example, the organisational chain of police organisations, the Public Prosecutor, and the judges has been explicitly created as a system of checks and balances. Every succeeding organisation has to reassess what the preceding organisation has done. When this chain is being joined up through ICT and electronic networks, every link uses the same information. This may threaten institutional cleavages. Therefore, e-government should not only be designed from the perspective of rational organisation, but also from a legal perspective.

4. We have defined government services as legal processes. As we have seen, legal decision making always mixes the general rule with the individual case. It may depart from a general rule stated by law, but it always jumps from the general rule to the individual case and back. E-government transforms these processes into administrative processes of bringing an individual case under the general rule. Judged by legal rationality, the design should also allow the technology to jump back. Therefore, e-government requires reflexive technologies to meet the requirements of legal rationality.

6. Concluding Remarks

The concept of e-government seems to suggest that it merely adds electronic devices to government. By using concepts derived from public administration science, we have demonstrated that this is not a valid line of reasoning. First, e-government only touches some parts of public administration: the operating core, the implementation of public policy, democratic supervision by Parliament and citizens as consumers. Second, e-government redefines these parts by means of the 'infologic'. It then transforms these processes into informational processes.

We have thus revealed the underlying information ecology of e-government by analysing its locus and focus. It appears that informational Taylorism is the fundamental information ecology of current e-government programmes. We believe that this bias does not exploit the possibilities of the concept. Moreover, informational e-government could very well transform public administration into an effective information-processing machine. This could endanger the societal foundations upon which public administration rests and the legitimacy of government in the long run.

The final section of our contribution argues that e-government does not necessarily have to step into the pitfalls of the information management approach. If e-government departs from a public administration perspective, it could avoid a tunnel vision that blinds the real nature of public administration.

References

1. Mumford, L., *Technics and Civilization*. 1934, New York: Hartcourt Brace and Company.
2. Ellul, J., *The Technological Society*. 1964, New York: Vintage Books.
3. McLuhan, M., *Understanding Media. The Extensions of Man*. 1964, London: Routledge.
4. Winner, L., *Technology: Technics Out-of-Control as a Theme in Political Thought*. 1977, Cambridge: Cambridge University Press.
5. Nardi, B.A. and V.L. O'Day, *Information Ecologies: Using Technology with Heart*. 1999, Cambridge (MA): The MIT Press.
6. UN-ASPA, *E-Government: A Global Perspective. Assessing the Progress of the UN Member States*. 2002, New York: United Nations / ASPA.
7. Forrester, *Sizing US E-Government*. 2000, Cambridge: Forrester.
8. Gartner, *Western Europe Government Sector: IT Solution Opportunities*. 2000: Gartner Group.
9. Cap Gemini Ernst and Young, *Online Availability of Public Services: How does Europe Progress? Web based survey on electronic public services*. 2003, Brussels: Cap Gemini Ernst and Young.
10. Accenture, *E-Government Leadership - Realizing the Vision*. 2002: Accenture.
11. Castells, M., *The Information Age. Economy, Society and Culture*. 1996, London: Blackwell.
12. Heeks, R., *Reinventing Government in the Information Age: International Practice in IT-Enabled Public Sector Reform*. 2001, London: Routledge.
13. Morgan, G., *Images of Organizations*. 1986, Thousand Oaks: SAGE.
14. Mintzberg, H., *Structure in Fives: Designing Effective Organizations*. 1983, Englewood Cliffs: Prentice Hall.
15. Easton, D., *The Political System*. 1953, Chicago: Chicago University Press.
16. Manin, B., *The Principles of Representative Government*. 1997, Cambridge: Cambridge University Press.
17. Pitkin, H., *The Concept of Representation*. 1967, Berkeley: University of California Press.
18. van Gunsteren, H., *A Theory of Citizenship: Organizing Plurality in Contemporary Societies*. 1998, Boulder: Westview Press.
19. Postman, N., *Technopoly. The Surrender of Culture to Technology*. 1993, New York: Vintage Books.
20. Brown, J.S. and P. Duguid, *The Social Life of Information*. 2000, Boston: Harvard.
21. Lash, S., *Critique of Information*. 2002, London: SAGE.
22. Snellen, I.T.M., *Conciliation of Rationalities: The Essence of Public Administration*. Administrative Theory and Praxis, 2002. **24**(2): p. 323-346.
23. Zuurmond, A., *From Bureaucracy to Infocracy: Are Democratic Institutions Lagging Behind?*, in *Administration in an Information Age. A Handbook*, I.T.M. Snellen and W.B.J.H. van de Donk, Editors. 1998, IOS Press: Amsterdam.
24. Bing, J., *Three Generations for Computerised Systems for Public Administration and Some Implications for Legal Decision Making*, in *25 Years' Anniversary Anthology in Computers and Law*, J. Bing and T. O, Editors. 1995: Oslo.
25. Van de Donk, W., *De arena in schema*. 1997, Lelystad: Koninklijke Vermande.
26. Bovens, M. and S. Zouridis, *From street-level bureaucracy to system-level bureaucracy: How information and communication technology is transforming*

administrative discretion and constitutional control. Public Administration Review, 2002. **62**(2): p. 174-184.

27.   Lips, A.M.B., *Public Service Delivery in an Information Age*, in *Public Administration in an Information Age. A Handbook*, I.T.M. Snellen and W.B.J.H. van de Donk, Editors. 1998, IOS Press: Amsterdam. p. 325-340.

28.   Zouridis, S., *Information Technology and the Organization Chart of Public Administration*, in *Public Administration in an Information Age. A Handbook*, I.T.M. Snellen and W.B.J.H. van de Donk, Editors. 1998, IOS Press: Amsterdam. p. 245-258.

29.   Kollock, P., *The Economies of Online Cooperation. Gifts and Public Goods in Cyberspace*, in *Communities in Cyberspace*, M.A. Smith and P. Kollock, Editors. 1999, Routledge: London / New York.

30.   Kelly, K., *New Rules for the New Economy: 10 Ways the Network Economy is Changing Everything.* 1998, London: Fourth Estate.

31.   Van de Donk, W.B.J.H., I.T.M. Snellen, and P.W. Tops, *Orwell in Athens. A Perspective on Informatization and Democracy.* 1995, Amsterdam: IOS Press.

32.   Hague, B.N. and B. Loader, *Digital Democracy: Discource and Decision Making in the Information Age.* 1999, London: Routledge.

The Information Ecology of E-Government
V.J.J.M. Bekkers and V.M.F. Homburg (Eds.)
IOS Press, 2005

Trends and Consolidations
in E-Government Implementation

Davy JANSSEN
University of Antwerp, Department Political Science (Public Management),
Korte Sint-Annastraat 6, B-2000 Antwerpen, Belgium

Sabine ROTTHIER
Policy Research Centre – Governmental Organization Flanders,
Hogeschool Gent, Voskenslaan 270, 9000 Gent, Belgium

Abstract. The promise of e-government is to offer citizens higher quality service delivery and to engage them more closely in policymaking. The individual citizen is central to the e-government discourse. This seems to imply that citizens, as stakeholders, are involved in the development and refinement of an electronic government. Technology is not neutral, but it develops and is used in specific environments by different people in different ways. These environments are characterised by Nardi and O'Day as 'information ecologies'. However, the findings of a comparative e-government study of seven OECD countries revealed an e-government that is being shaped by (international) organisations and countries in a top-down manner. Citizens do not have a real say in how applications are developed for them, and this leads us to believe that the human component of information ecologies is unjustifiably neglected in e-government development.

1. Introduction

ICT developments have pervaded the social environments of citizens. We make purchases with our bankcards, we make calls with our cellular phones to say we are late, we find directions with route planners available on the internet at no charge. We send e-birthday cards; we order and purchase concert tickets online; and we hold conversations via SMS and in chat rooms. Underlying consumer wants and needs are recognised by a private market that continues to develop the desired applications. The success of a new application is tied up with the degree to which it fits in with consumers' social environments. Consumers seem to know what they want and appreciate (consider the success of SMS), and thus steer the development of technology in a certain direction by the elusive power of consumer choice. A similar, albeit modified, dynamic should apply to government service delivery as well. The critical consumers of the market are also the demanding 'customers' of government services. And while governments hold the monopoly in the delivery of certain services, there is definitely consumer choice (especially the negative choice not to use it) in the case of electronic service delivery. A logical consequence then, would be that citizens have a say in how these electronic services are modelled and tailored. Before we deal with this issue in the rest of this chapter, it is important define e-government as we see it. We choose to use a definition by Bekkers and Homburg who view e-government as *"the use of ICT, especially internet and web technology, by a public organisation to support or*

Normative

redefine the existing and/or future relations with stakeholders in the internal and external environment in order to create added value". We like this definition because of its focus on value creation instead of on technology.

2. The E-Government Ecology

Citizens contact government for two main reasons, i.e. to enjoy government service delivery and to participate in democratic processes. Zuurmond [1] frames these different citizen's roles in his democratic triangle, where citizens are typified either as 'clients' of service delivery or as 'citoyens' participating in the workings of democracy (Figure 1).

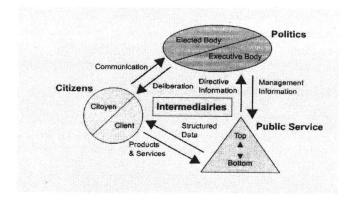

Figure 1: Zuurmond's Democratic Triangle [1]

These client/customer and citoyen roles are central to the e-government discourse as well. If one takes the various national e-government strategy documents to be a good indication of the relative development of e-government, it would seem that the desired e-government is 'customer focused', 'tailored to the individual citizen', 'built around the logic of the citizen (and not that of the administration)'. The surrounding discourse is indeed very human-centred so there would seem to be no need to heed Nardi and O'Day's [2] warning of a too narrow focus on technology. These authors' research on the concept of an 'information ecology' provides an illustrative framework for interpreting human activity in its relation to technology. The authors acknowledge the fundamental impact of technology on our lives but do not succumb to utopian or dystopian (deterministic) accounts based on deep-seated hopes or fears. Rather, they argue that technological progress in one or other direction is never inevitable: people do have a say as to how their technologies develop.

In order to develop their argument, Nardi and O'Day move away from systemic conceptualisations of technology and bring in local habitation as an explanatory context in which technology 'grows'. The local habitation includes those settings *'in which the individual has an active role'* because he possesses *'knowledge and authority'*. The information ecology then, is *'a system of people, practices, values, and technologies in a particular local environment'*. Davenport [3] uses the same metaphor and defines it (at organisational level) as follows: "*It addresses all of a firm values and beliefs about information (culture); how people actually use information and what they do with it (behavior and work processes); the pitfalls that can interfere with information sharing (politics) and what information systems are already in place (yes, finally, technology)*". If we apply the concept of the information ecology to the domain of e-government, there are basically four e-government ecologies:

1. Self-service e-government using some device (PC, television, PDA) at home
2. Self-service e-government using some device (PC, terminal, kiosk) in a public space (library, supermarket, government office)
3. Mediated e-government in a 'service centre' (physical)
4. Mediated e-government in a 'call centre' (telephone)

Ecologies 1 and 4 consist of person X contacting government from the home. In ecology 1, person X manipulates some form of online technology to get what he wants, whereas in ecology 4 he talks to person Y at the other end of the phone. Person Y is situated in a call centre where she is using technology to help person X (possibly the same technology person X would use himself in ecology 1). Ecologies 2 and 3 are both situated outside the home in some public space, possibly a government office. In ecology 2, person X approaches some technological device and manipulates it (no mediation), whereas in ecology 3, person X approaches a counter and asks person Y to help him. Again, Y would have technology at hand to perform the request. Thinking about e-government in terms of information ecology has the merit of moving the focus to the users of technology and to how they interact with it. As suggested in the introduction, it would seem that the e-government discourse fits in quite well with this view, as it is also centred on the user of technology, illustrated by terms such as 'client-centred' or 'customer focussed'.

In the remainder of this chapter, we compare the e-government rhetoric with our research on actual e-government implementation in seven OECD countries; but we would like to hint at a possible divergence of rhetoric and practice in advance. Take the notion of 'life events', the widely celebrated *best practice* of portal site development. Citizens are supposed to find information in an intuitive way with the help of a decision tree that consists of life events such as being born, study, work, moving, dying, etc. The truth of the matter is, that if you are actually looking for specific policy documents, government forms, or coordinates on any of the existing national portal sites, you are bound to get into trouble. At one defining moment in the decision tree, the logic of the administration will probably appear again, and information is again structured according to their terms. Some portal sites even offers a box in which you can just type your question in full, with an absolute guarantee of never finding anything even remotely relevant.

The implication of looking at e-government development from the information ecology perspective would be that the individual (in her relation with technology) is the focus of attention. Governments would constantly involve citizens in the further refinement of e-government applications by allowing them to provide feedback on their experiences with these applications. The reality is somewhat different though: e-government development is organised centrally, at the national or international level, with little user involvement. Governments are faced with a shortage of IT knowledge and with a globalised IT industry in the business of selling standardised IT solutions. The focus of attention often shifts from solving real problems to the challenge of integrating large-scale IT systems. This situation in which the focus is once again on technology is far removed from the ideal of a balanced e-government ecology. It needs to be mentioned though, that this shift of attention to a 'technology fix' has been recognised as one of the challenges for e-government, also for instance by Lau, project leader of the OECD e-government project, who stated that *"Technological advancements and the search by suppliers for new markets have resulted in a bewildering array of technical solutions in search of problems to fix"* [4].

3.   E-Government in Practice: So Far Neglecting the Information Ecology?

This part is based on the results of an international study on e-government started in 2002 and completed in 2003 [5]. For 2002 our task was to set up an international comparative study. The Flemish government commissioned the study because it wanted to know how other countries' e-government was proceeding. Seven countries were taken into consideration: Canada, Finland, the Netherlands, France, Germany, the UK and Ireland. The research was mainly based on documentary analysis and informal interviews of policymakers, government experts and civil servants.

By comparing the findings of the different country studies, we have observed significant similarities in the national e-government agendas [6]. These similarities once again illustrated the steering role of governments in getting e-government implemented throughout all government organisations. It appears that the 'how' questions of e-government implementation are central and that the answers to them are rather similar, while the 'why' questions keep on disappearing into the background. In what follows, we move away from the information ecology theme and present the empirical results of our comparative research.

In order to frame the findings, we have been working with theories of policy transfer and policy convergence as an interesting explanatory framework for our findings. Policy transfer, as defined by Dolowitz and Marsh, is a *'process in which knowledge about policies, administrative arrangements, institutions etc. in one time and/or place is used in the development of policies, administrative arrangements and institutions in another time or place'* [7]. In the case of e-government development, there is no doubt that transfer occurs, as policymakers increasingly point to e-government developments abroad to legitimate their own initiatives. Study journeys are made by newly appointed e-government officials and forums where best practices are exchanged and are often referred to in policy documents. Whereas policy transfer can be seen as an instance of lesson-drawing [8], with no guarantee that the resulting lessons will entail an identical policy outcome, the policy convergence hypothesis assumes that processes of policy transfer have resulted in many areas in a convergence of policy goals, policy content, policy instruments, policy outcomes, or policy styles [9]. We present our findings below for the first four areas. The fifth area, i.e. policy style, was not a major focus of attention in our comparative study.

3.1   Policy Goals

Convergence of *policy goals* is defined by Bennett [9] as *'a coming together of intent to deal with common policy problems'*. The advanced industrial nations have indeed found each other on the international forum in the objective of preparing themselves for the *information society* or *knowledge economy*. The formal policies they have developed share concerns with the establishment of an electronic government, the development of a high-speed ICT infrastructure, the stimulation of the knowledge economy, and with the ICT – awareness of their population.

The 'problem' of the information society has clearly been recognised by most industrialised countries, and the policy answers to this problem seem to be similar in scope and content. All countries have drafted a formal e-government policy, as well as a broader Information Society policy (Table 2).

Table 2: E-Society Policy and Formal E-Government Policy

CAN	E-government policy	Government Online, Service Canada
	Information Society policy	Connecting Canadians
FIN	E-government policy	Programme of Action to Promote Online Government
	Information Society policy	Quality of Life, Knowledge and Competitiveness
FR	E-government policy	Pour une Administration Electronique Citoyenne
	Information Society policy	Programme d'Action Gouvernemental pour la Société de l'Information
GER	E-government policy	Bundonline.2005
	Information Society policy	Innovation und Arbeitsplätze in der Informationgesellschaft des 21. Jahrhunderts
IRL	E-government policy	ePublic Services Model
	Information Society policy	New Connections
NL	E-government policy	Aktieprogramma Electronische Overheid
	Information Society policy	Contract met de Toekomst
UK	E-government policy	UK Online Strategy

While e-government is usually defined as online service delivery, an e-Society policy is generally defined as a socially inclusive policy, aiming at ICT infrastructure and ICT skills with the intention to stimulate the knowledge economy and to prevent digital exclusion of citizens in an information society. On a more abstract level, countries basically want to 'prepare themselves' for the information society. A first prerequisite for this is that all people should have access to ICT and the Internet, and for this a country's ICT infrastructure policy is seen as crucial. This policy generally aims at the development of a high-speed (broadband) network, enabling all citizens to connect to the Internet. Governments believe this to be too important to leave it entirely to the market and therefore often intervene with public-private-partnership programmes. Another major concern of most countries involves the costs of Internet access. Internet access is increasingly seen as some form of a 'basic right' for citizens, and that is why governments often try to get a grip on the pricing mechanisms of Internet access costs. A final objective of the infrastructure component of an e-Society policy has to do with the provision of hardware. If you consider Internet access to be a basic right, you will have to provide not only a high-speed infrastructure but also access to hardware. Countries take different approaches here with some providing pcs in public areas, some providing kiosks, and some aiming at ICT-backed call-centres. In addition to infrastructure, an e-Society policy has to address ICT skills. Here the objective is to educate an ICT-literate population. Countries take different approaches to the development of ICT courses for different target groups. These diverse educational programmes are mostly embedded in a 'lifelong learning' philosophy, by which countries urge their population to continuously upgrade their knowledge in an ever changing world.

3.2   Policy Content

A second form of convergence, *policy content*, can also be found in the international e-government environment. The most significant similarity in the content of the different countries' e-government policies is the definition of e-government as e-Service delivery, quantified as a 'percentage of services online' target (Table 3).

Table 3: 'Percentage of Services Online' Target

CAN	All key government services fully online by 2004
FIN	A significant proportion of forms and requests can be dealt with electronically by 2001
FR	All administrations to provide public access to government services and documents by the end of 2000
GER	All feasible federal administrative services available online by 2005
IRL	All but most complex of integrated services by end of 2001
NL	25% of public services delivered electronically by 2002
UK	100% of public services carried out electronically by 2005

All countries deploy such a quantitative target combined with comparable progress reporting mechanisms. There are also parallels in the concepts that are used in policy documents, hinting at a reciprocal learning process by which administrations have taken over innovative ideas and concepts elsewhere. Examples of such concepts are: *multi-channel policy, gateway approaches, service delivery architectures, demand orientation* in service delivery, *life events* structuring, etc. Finally, the selection of 20 'basic public services' in the *e-Europe* framework (the EU's information society policy) has resulted in similarities in the policy domains that get priority e-government attention.

3.3   Policy Instruments

A third area of policy convergence is that of *policy instruments*. When we look at the organisational aspects of e-government implementation, we see similarities in instruments or 'tools' of e-government. The commitment to realise targets generally comes from the political top. Change processes need top-level commitments, and in the UK, Ireland and Germany it is Tony Blair, Bertie Ahern and Gerhard Schröder themselves who are responsible for the realisation of the e-government targets. The responsibility on an administrative level is often situated with an e-government 'team', sometimes with a recognisable 'Mr. e-gov' at its head. The textbook case is that of the UK, where the *Office of the E-Envoy* is headed by the *E-Envoy*, the top civil servant embodying e-government in Britain. In the Netherlands, the implementation of national e-government policy is left to a newly founded project organisation called *ICT Uitvoeringsorganisatie* and until 2002 was embodied by Roger van Boxtel, not a civil servant but a minister. In Finland, it is the civil servant of information and his team who are authorised for e-government coordination, in Germany it is the *Bundonline 2005 Project Group*, in Ireland the *Information Society Policy Unit*, in France the *Comité Interministériel pour la Société de l'information*, and in Canada the *Treasury Board Information Management Subcommittee*.

The coordinating e-government organisations predominantly monitor implementation of the national e-government strategy in the central government departments. This coordination process is quite similar in the different countries. The coordination approach in the UK and Ireland can serve as an example. As a reply to the national e-government strategies, central government departments are obliged to produce *e-Business Strategy Documents* (UK) or *e-Strategy Documents* (IRL) in which they formulate departmental e-government strategies that are compliant with the national strategy. In the UK, these documents contain the department's plan to realise the national e-government target (100% services online by 2005). The department reports progress to the *Office of the E-Envoy*, which in its turn checks the validity of this progress. During the development of the departmental e-government strategies, each department bilaterally negotiates its strategy with the *Office of the E-Envoy* and with *Her Majesty's Treasury*, the department of Finance. They can agree to provide the department with extra funding in return for extra efforts concerning the national UK online strategy. Ireland has a similar approach. The departments provide departmental strategies to realize national targets, report progress to the *Information Society Policy Unit*, and can negotiate with the Finance department for extra funding from the *Information Society Fund*.

In France and the Netherlands, the same ingredients can be found: national action plans, departmental plans, monitoring of departmental progress by a coordinating organisation, and a supporting fund. Finland takes a somewhat different approach, but there is a growing recognition of the advantages of the system of a more central administrative coordination outlined above. In a critique of Finish e-government, the *Information Advisory Board* (ISAB) claimed that Finland was be-ginning to feel the disadvantages of its decentralised approach to government IT policy (ISAB, 2001). The ISAB advises government to develop measurable targets and to oblige departments to draft strategy documents. It pleads for an increased role for the ministry of Finance in coordinating the implementation of departmental strategies.

Another similarity in policy tools is the technique of using financing as leverage. The instrument of e-government funding is a very important leverage through which central governments can try to get the national e-government policy implemented by all tiers of government. A creative use of this instrument is crucial for the realisation of an intensive change process. In most countries, government departments can be characterised by a certain degree of 'departmentalism'. Existing traditional mechanisms of financing often imply that a minister responsible for a certain department is destined, at the time of budget negotiation, to explicitly point at successes of her 'own' department in order to obtain enough financial means in the next budgetary period. This leads to a situation that is not conducive to interdepartmental cooperation. But from a citizen point-of-view, the development of an integrated e-government policy should thrive on an interdepartmental cooperation perspective: a demand oriented approach to service delivery does not stop at departmental boundaries.

Different approaches to e-government financing can provide an outcome here. Although costs for operational informatisation are financed by normal departmental budgets, different countries do deploy a supplementary form of financing to stimulate specific e-government developments. In the UK, for example, an extra budget of £1 billion was made available to facilitate the implementation of the e-government action plan in the period 2001-2004. Government departments can negotiate for a part of this budget during their bilateral negotiations on departmental e-government strategy with the finance department and the *Cabinet Office*. Apart from this budget, there are several other funds - such as the *Capital Modernisation Fund* and the *Invest to Save Budget* stimulating government modernization that can be used to finance innovative e-government projects. The main advantage of these budgets is that they are, as it were, 'floating'. This means that they are not assigned to some department beforehand, but are only assigned to government organisations that confirm to certain criteria, especially on intergovernmental cooperation.

In this way these budgets are supportive of the demand-oriented logic of integrated service delivery and can be an incentive to structural change.

Ireland also uses a 'floating' budget, the *Information Society Fund*, as a support for the implementation of its national e-government action plan. The ministry of finance manages the budget, drafts the criteria for assignment and evaluates the project proposals. The criteria for assignment are, as in the UK, aimed at interdepartmental coordination, and also at stimulating decentralised developed projects. For the period 2000-2002 the *Information Society Fund* contained €154 million. Negotiations for a continuation of the Fund are ongoing, but for 2003, €43 million has already been put aside. As in the UK, operational informatisation is financed by existing budgets. E-government financing in Finland and France is characterised by the same approach, aimed at stimulation cooperation between government organisations. The ministries of finance manage special funds, while operational investments continue to be financed from normal budgets. The Netherlands also follows this two-track policy for operational investments and specific e-government projects. The special fund supporting the implementation of the e-government action plan contains about €35 million a year.

The coordinating mechanisms described above were mostly aimed at getting central government departments to implement national e-government strategies. In this paragraph we look at how central government tries to get local government involved in its e-government strategy. In general, there seem to be two ways in which coordination of sub national governments can take place, viz. a top-down and a bottom-up approach. Countries such as Finland, the UK the Netherlands and Ireland take a more top-down approach. Finland is a unitary state with an intensive participation of central government in local government policy. The authority of local government is fairly limited for delocalized central government offices offer services that would be offered by local governments in most European states.

In the UK, the centrally drafted *e-gov@local* initiative offers a formal strategy for local e-government. It consists of a local e-government framework and it indicates which policy domains should get priority e-government attention (in return for possibilities of extra financing of local e-government policy). A third of the £1 billion e-government action plan budget is being deployed at local level. In return for an alignment with the national e-government strategy, local governments can apply for extra financing. In effect, this means that local governments are rewarded for the drafting of a local e-government strategy – the so-called *Implementing Electronic Government Statements*- with an amount of 'seed money', and can get extra financing in return for extra efforts. Local governments have the same obligation as central departments when it comes to getting 100% of services online by 2005.

In the Netherlands, a part of the national e-government budget is reserved for local government initiatives in a comparable way. Because of local government autonomy, the responsibility for providing local content lies with local government itself. Central government tries to develop other mechanisms to coordinate local government efforts. For this, they have developed a theoretical framework for the realisation, for example, of one-stop-shops. When local governments take on the framework they can get supplementary financing. Funding is used as an instrument of persuasion; trying to get local governments to align with central e-government strategies, standards and architectures. Local governments, for their part, are often willing to take part because of the possibility for economies of scale.

In Ireland, a similar form of coordination takes place. But while Dutch local governments are still somewhat hesitant to follow national guidelines, Irish local governments seem more eager to do this. They are, for example, all involved in a national project concerning 'generic forms' which local governments can personalise and use in their service delivery. France is characterised by a less top-down steering of the local level, although this might change with the recent foundation of *L'Agence pour le Développement de l'Adminstration Electronique*. This newly founded agency coordinates government reform processes on all government levels. Prior to the existence of this organisation, there was no coordination of local e-government efforts. Germany and Canada are federal countries and this is reflected in their e-government funding and coordination. The German Länder and the Canadian provinces are themselves responsible for the development of an e-government policy for their territories, including local government. In both countries, there is no national financing of regional of local e-government efforts, and local governments are free to establish their own e-government content (resulting in great differences between different local governments). In Germany, central government does try to stimulate decentrally developed e-government through the *MEDIA@komm* competition, but this is the only form of central involvement to be found.

3.4   Policy Outcomes

A fourth possible domain of convergence, according to Bennett, is that of policy outcomes. These are similarities in the actual results of policy and they can be negative (when all are making the same 'mistakes') or positive (when policy results in its intended consequences). In this paragraph we will first describe similarities in policy outcomes in the front office. In a second step we have collected issues of identification and authentication, security and privacy, and service delivery architecture under the heading of back-office similarities.

3.5   Policy Outcomes in the Front Office

One general negative policy outcome in the countries is that a too exclusive attention for front office ICT applications has lead to an oversupply and fragmentation of e-government applications in combination with low take-up rates. The e-government debate at a strategic level has recognised this problem with the introduction of the concept of e-government 'take-up'. A more positive instance of convergence in the front office is that of national portal site development. The various portal websites mainly offer online government information and (the promise of) online service delivery. The table below gives an overview of the layout of the homepages of national portal sites at the moment of the study (Table 4).

Table 4: National Portal Sites

NL	The Netherlands uses one main government portal (www.overheid.nl) offering information and services. • Target group classification: private persons, business and organisations, politicians and civil servants, young people, guests • 2nd classification: government counter (thematic classification), government organisations, government themes, official publications, laws and rules, join the conversation, news, working with the government, this is how government works
UK	The UK uses its main government portal (www.ukonline.gov.uk) for information and services. The site is structured as follows: • Citizen Space: take part in consultations • Your Life: a life-events classification for information and

services
- Do it Online: a thematic classification for information and services
- Newsroom: a news section
- Quick Link: three search engines

GER Germany goes full out for a thematic approach on its government portal (www.bund.de). There are 19 themes on the site's homepage, and these are a mix of themes and life-events.
- Themes: nature, science, culture, Germany in the world, ...
- Life-events: building, family and partnership, children, ...

FR France's government portal (www.service-public.fr) is characterized by a clear business-citizen dichotomy.
- Citizens: a mixed thematic approach with 24 themes (environment, military, elections) and life-events (work, education, retirement).
- Business: forms online, services online, FAQ section, public procurement section, a section on collective labour agreements, and a 'useful addresses' section.

IRL Ireland does not have a single portal but uses a general information site and two service delivery sites
- www.irlgovie : information on the Irish state.
- www.oasis.gov.ie : service delivery and information for citizens. This site is thematically structured and most 'themes' are life-events.
- www.basis.ie : for business. This site has a service locator section, a forms download bank, and a 'doing business online' section

FIN Finland has a central government portal that is complemented by two other websites.
- www.suomi.fi : official government portal site with government information and service delivery (thematic classification) and a body of standardised electronic government forms.
- www.julha.fi : site with contact information for government organisations and personnel
- virtual.finland.fi : English site with extensive amount of information on Finland

CAN Canada has an extensive government portal site (www.canada.gc.ca) which is structured in a demand-oriented way.
- Three access points: citizens, business, foreign visitors
- Cluster classification: life-events, themes, target groups

For the most part, the current content of national government portal sites consists of thematically organised government information, along the lines of 'life events'. All sites, however, also aspire to offer online service delivery, and countries clearly face nearly identical implementation problems that all have to do with digital authentication. Therefore much of these applications remains in the stadium of interaction (in stead of the wished for transaction/transformation phase) or remain focused on those policy domain in which an absolutely fail-safe authentication is not required.

3.6 Policy Outcomes in the Back Office

An important back office problem is the unsuccessful full-scale roll out of Public Key Infrastructure environments, complete with digital identity cards. Countries seem to face similar problems when aiming at the introduction of multi-functional electronic identity cards. The current situation is often one in which several functional smart cards operate independently of each other. In this section, we look more closely at some analogous outcomes in the back office.

Identification in the Back Office

A first prerequisite for an authentic back office integration is the possibility of unique identification of subjects. In the past, government organisations have often used incompatible computer systems. The resulting lack of links between different government files brought about a situation in which a certain citizen or company was known to government under different 'names'. Aspiring to achieve a truly integrated service delivery, however, calls for a more intense coupling of government information with government organisations using a common denominator to identify a subject. Several countries have already introduced such a denominator or are about to develop one. Canada uses a *Social Insurance Number*, Ireland uses a *Personal/Business Public Service Number*, and the Netherlands is developing a *Citizen Service Number*.

The United Kingdom is the odd man out because it does not have a central population register. There are some non-exhaustive and overlapping registers, but no single rationalised register that allows for a unique identification for each citizen. The UK E-Envoy does indeed recognise this absence as one of the most pressing back office problems. Seeing that the UK population is opposed to the introduction of a common identification document, a basic databank will be developed to allow for some use of unique denominators. In Finland, the approach is quite the opposite. The country has a very detailed population register and uses a unique denominator based on the social security number in a very proactive manner. Personal information from different kinds of databanks is regularly matched, for example in the case of its population census (where information from some 30 databanks is matched to provide citizens with a filled-out form) and in the case of its 'tax proposal' (also an already filled-out form).

When different government organisations use a single denominator for citizens and businesses, it is still possible for different databanks to contain contradictory information on that particular citizen or business. In order for this information to be rationalised, most countries adopt the 'principle of the authentic source' when storing and sharing information. The principle requires that a specific government organisation be appointed as the authentic source for a certain kind of citizen/business information. When other government organisations need this information, they will have to retrieve it from the 'owner' organisation and not from the citizen. It is also the organisation storing the personal information that is responsible for its accuracy. There are considerable advantages for citizens and even more so for businesses since they do not have to provide the same information in different formats to different organisations.

An example of an authentic source is a basic person or business register. Such a register collects all basic administrative data concerning citizens/businesses and is responsible for the further distribution throughout government. In Belgium, the central population register guards and distributes all basic personal data, and two so-called 'crossroad banks' are responsible for social security information and administrative business information. The Netherlands also use a system of authentic source, and the UK will introduce such a system as soon as the problems for unique identification of subjects are dealt with. Finland's proactive approach obviously also implies a rationalised system of authentic source organisations. The countries mentioned in the previous paragraph all use the authentic source principle in combination with a decentralised approach to data storage: different organisations store different sorts of information pertaining to the same subject.

Some countries, however, adopt a special case of the authentic source principle, i.e. that of the digital vault The digital vault is (ideally) a well-protected space on the internet or on a smart card where citizens are able to store personal information. The main difference with the approach described above is that the citizen or business is actually his/her own authentic source. A second difference is that such a vault contains different *sorts* of personal data. This means that no functional coupling of data is required to result in an appropriate data mix for a certain service application. The Netherlands has done some research on digital vaults but ultimately decided not to implement them for security reasons. Ireland, on the other hand, has given the digital vault principle a manifest role in its online service delivery architecture.

Authentication of End Users
The identification issue described above dealt with how information from different government organisations can be efficiently coupled by the use of a system of unique identification. A second, albeit related issue, is that of authentication. Authentication deals with how a person can authenticate himself/herself in an online environment. Put differently: the only situation in which government is going to pay you back some money, for example, is one in which it is absolutely sure who it is dealing with at the other end of, say, a pc-screen. All of the countries are obviously trying to tackle this issue. The technology-driven solution all of countries prefer is a full-scale Public Key Infrastructure (PKI) environment, including digital certificates or digital identity cards. The IT industry is also very much in favour of this solution, not in the least because it includes a significant hardware-component such as card readers and smart cards. The countries under consideration all have some form of PKI environment, which they are continuously trying to refine. They have also passed legislation (or are about to) that establishes the use of smart cards and provides a legal base to digital signatures.

Opinions diverge on the necessity of electronic identity cards. The major opponents can be found in the Anglo-Saxon world, where people have never liked the idea of a paper identity card, let alone a digital one. In the UK, therefore, digital certificates and even simple logins and passwords are used for online service delivery. The situation has changed quite recently, however, with central government pushing for the introduction of an electronic identity card. Irish government would like to see an increase in the use of its *Public Services Card*. To support this, it points out, as evidenced by the name of the card, that it is not an electronic identity card but merely an easy tool for public service delivery, analogous to a credit card. The Netherlands is a supporter of an electronic identity card and aims at a large-scale distribution in the near future. The distribution of electronic identity cards is a reality in Canada and Finland, but only on voluntary basis. In Canada, people can ask for the *e-Pass*, an embryonic identity card with only limited functional capabilities at present. Finland also has a voluntary, but fully functional, electronic identity card. Only France seems to have decided against any future introduction of an electronic identity card even though France has a wide circulation of different kinds of functional smart cards in the health sector. Finland also has several kinds of functional smart cards, in addition to its identity card. In conclusion, none of the countries has realised, or is aiming at, an exhaustive (obligatory) circulation of multifunctional electronic identity cards.

Security and Privacy
When the coupling of data in the back office as well as the authentication of end users is realised, the issue of making the existing systems as safe as possible arises. The safety issue

includes several aspects. The aspect of *confidentiality* concerns the prevention of access to information by unauthorised persons as well as how government uses the information. The aspect of *integrity* implies that the information has not been manipulated by the time it reaches government. A third aspect, that of *non-repudiation*, means that a person who undertook a transaction cannot deny this fact, and that a civil servant who receives a message cannot deny this fact either. The final safety aspect of *authentication* i.e. ensuring the identity of end-users, has already been dealt with. All of the countries are trying to find technological solutions to these different security aspects in the form of encryption techniques, digital signatures, PKI environments, smart cards, etc. Given that the IT industry is a global sector and the solutions to the security problem are mostly technology-driven, it is not surprising that the different countries' solutions look alike.

The issue of privacy is not so much a technological issue as it is an information issue. Fundamentally, it concerns the intensity of information coupling in the back office. From a citizen point-of-view, privacy concerns knowing which kinds of personal data will not be matched and which kinds possibly will be. The desire for an integrated government service delivery immediately calls for a debate on the meaning of privacy in the information society. ICTs are fundamentally ambiguous technologies [10]: aiming at a personalised, integrated service delivery immediately implies an intensification of the sharing of data between government organisations in the back office. A 'tax proposal', for example, is a tax form that has already been filled out for the most part. Citizens might perceive this as an excellent example of personalised service delivery or they might feel ill at ease when realising that a lot of personal information is already there on the form.

Finland takes a pro-active approach here, and it is the first country to offer a filled-out tax proposal. At regular intervals, it also presents a filled-out census form to the population. The Netherlands also tries to take a pro-active approach to data matching. Ireland plans to store different kinds of personal data in a citizen-owned digital vault. By handing over the informational control to citizens, Ireland is trying to personalise the privacy issue. Each citizen can decide how many kinds of different data are stored together. An often heard safety consideration concerning digital vaults is that it is less safe than a decentrally stored set of data where data matching only happens on a functional basis. With digital vaults, there are different kinds of data in the vault and they are therefore permanently matched.

Service Delivery Architecture
A final back office aspect being dealt with here is that of the 'service delivery architecture', an integrated solution allowing transactional e-government functions throughout the different tiers of government. The service delivery architecture of the UK is called the *Government Gateway*. This gateway allows for the routing of transactions throughout the different back office systems of different policy domains and tiers of government. It is the so-called middleware that sits between existing back office systems and the end-user in the front office. Once citizens have registered at the gateway, they are 'inside' a virtual government administration in which they are recognised and in which they can perform safe transactions. Ireland also has an integrated back office architecture, called the *Public Services Broker*. Traditionally, intermediaries have played a significant role in the Irish administration, helping people find their way in the bureaucracy. This role of 'broker' is now being virtualised in a services gateway that guides citizens throughout government. Since local government delivers a substantial amount of services in Ireland, it is especially relevant that the broker includes different tiers of government. Local government is provided the opportunity to access a system of nationally developed 'generic forms', easily adaptable to the local context. This example of a 'build-once-use-many' architecture allows for economies of scale- another advantage of integrated service delivery architecture. The final country with such a system is Canada, where it is also called the *Service Broker*. The

other countries under consideration showed less integrated approaches to transactional service delivery.

4. Conclusion

In this chapter we have been looking at how several OECD countries are implementing their e-government. We have used Bennett's definition of policy convergence in order to illustrate similarities in different country's e-government goals, policy content, policy instruments and policy outcomes. We cannot, however, draw any real conclusions as to the hypothesis of convergence. Our research was not suited for this: we primarily conducted documentary analysis and looked at e-government policy at one point in time. According to Pollitt, comparative research on the convergence of the results of policy requires "*the kind of full-scale evaluations which are expensive, time-consuming, difficult to design*" [11]. According to Bennett, convergence "*implies a pattern of development over time*". This leads him to conclude that "*comparative policy studies that are not set within a relatively explicit and extended time-frame cannot by definition test convergence theory*" [9]. Because of the Pollitt argument on methodology and the Bennett argument on time, we cannot conclude to have found a convergence of e-government policy. What we can conclude is that processes of policy *transfer* have taken place and that there are clear *similarities* between e-government policy and practice at an organisational level (Table 5).

Table 5: International Similarities Between E-Government Policy and Practice

Interpretation of E-Government	<ul><li>Priority attention for e-Service Delivery, operationalised as a 'percentage of service delivery online' indicator</li><li>Attention for e-Society policy as a *conditio sine qua non* for a successful e-government</li><li>Increasing attention for e-Democracy developments</li></ul>
Front office	<ul><li>National portal sites</li><li>Demand orientated e-Service delivery in the form of life-events or other thematic classifications</li><li>Cost-benefit approach in the prioritisation of e-government applications: especially income generating services</li><li>(At least formal) attention to digital divide: multi-channel access policy</li><li>The creation of a government supply of e-government applications in the front office has generally lead to a fragmentation of service delivery, no real integration of service delivery has taken place</li></ul>
Back Office	<ul><li>unique identification as a basic condition for an integrated service delivery</li><li>Principle of authentic source or digital vault</li><li>Authentication: PKI, no full-scale roll-out of multifunctional cards but a proliferation of smart cards</li></ul>

Implementation	• Debate: linking back office info vs. privacy
	• Presence vs. absence of e-Service Delivery Architecture
	• Two kinds of strategic documents: e-government and e-Society
	• Quantitative e-Service Delivery targets and coordination by newly established organisations
	• High level political responsibility for e-government results
	• Developments of coordinating organisations
	• Financing as important leverage
	• Trend toward more top-down treatment of lower tiers of government, esp. local government

We can further conclude that so far, governments have approached e-government implementation quite centrally. When one realises that e-government is still a fairly recent development that is not yet fully 'up and running', this is no real surprise. The infrastructure has to be set up, central building blocks (such as gateways, PKI environments, smart cards, authenticators, etc) have to be built and legacy systems have to be talking to one another. The focus is still on the first part of the Homburg and Bekkers definition: *'the use of ICT, especially Internet and web technology, by a public organisation'*. We believe that when a certain stage of maturity is reached, local habitation will come back into play. Lip service is already being paid to the idea that the 'customer' is central and that services will be tailor-made for him/her. Real refinement of ICT-enabled service delivery can only be reached when research is done in the local habitations where people meet technology. The four e-government ecologies that we have suggested in this chapter will provide the research environments for learning how to reach the objective *"to support or redefine the existing and/or future relations with stakeholders in the internal and external environment in order to create added value"* of the second part of the Homburg and Bekkers definition.

There are already indications that the focus of attention is shifting from technology to its users. E-government 'take-up' was the e-government buzzword of 2003. Attention shifts to the actual levels of usage when applications are up and running. The recent EU *Top of the Web Survey* also focused on the users of e-government applications but had to conclude that so far *"the level of use of public e-services is largely unknown to webmasters and e-service providers"*. But this will be changing soon. The demand side of e-government ('take-up') is now increasingly included in benchmarking studies from both international organisations and individual countries. The user will become the real focus of attention when governments realise that consumer choice in the e-government marketplace will be crucial for the necessary economies of scale and thus defining for the direction of further e-government progress. When things are up and running, e-government ecologies will become central. We end this chapter with a second quote of Edwin Lau [4], project leader of the OECD e-government project, on his vision of a future e-government. It is a vision in which the echoes of Nardi and O'Day can clearly be heard:

"E-government should be value-driven and not technology-driven. The

promised benefits of e-governments do not take place simply by

digitising information and placing it online. Instead, the challenge is to understand how the use of new ICT tools can be used to leverage a transformation in the culture and structure of government in order to provide better services to citizens. This entails determining the appropriate level of technology and service that meets the needs and the citizen preferences of a particular country; it does not mean importing wholesale systems and solutions regardless of whether citizens and businesses truly stand to benefit. Governments are beginning to understand better that real value can be obtained through the use of ICT, but that the need for basic assessments of benefits and costs, risks and opportunities remains".

References

1.   Zuurmond, A., *New Urban Management: SAP and the Role of Financial Management.* 2001, Nijmegen: Itafit.
2.   Nardi, B.A. and V.L. O'Day, *Information Ecologies: Using Technology with Heart.* 1999, Cambridge (MA): The MIT Press.
3.   Davenport, T.H., *Information Ecology: Mastering the information and knowledge environment.* 1997, Oxford: Oxford University Press.
4.   Lau, E., *Challenges for E-Government Developments.* 2003, Paper presented at the fifth Global Forum on Reinventing Government: Mexico City.
5.   Janssen, D., et al., *De praktijk van e-government in zeven landen van de OECD.* 2003, Leuven: Katholieke Universiteit Leuven.
6.   Janssen, D., et al., *Internationale trends inzake e-government.* 2003, Leuven: Katholieke Universiteit Leuven.
7.   Dolowitz, D. and D. Marsh, *Who Learns What From Whom: A Review of the Policy Transfer Literature.* Political Studies, 1996. **44**(2): p. 343-357.
8.   Rose, R., *Lesson Drawing in Public Policy. A Guide to Learning across Time and Space.* 1993, New Jersey: Chatham House Publishers.
9.   Bennett, C., *What is Policy Convergence and What Causes It?* British Journal of Political Science, 1991. **1**(1): p. 215-233.
10.   Bellamy, C. and J. Taylor, *Governing in the Information Age.* 1998, Buckingham: Open University Press.
11.   Pollitt, C.P., *Clarifying Convergence. Striking Similarities and Durable Differences in Public Management Reform.* Public Management Review, 2001. **4**(1): p. 471-492.

The Information Ecology of E-Government
V.J.J.M. Bekkers and V.M.F. Homburg (Eds.)
IOS Press, 2005

E-Government, Changing Jurisdictions and Boundary Management

Victor BEKKERS
Erasmus University Rotterdam, Faculty of Social Sciences,
Public Administration Group, PO Box 1738, 3000 DR Rotterdam, The Netherlands

Abstract. In the literature on public organisations in general and e-government in particular, little attention is given to whether information and communication technology (ICT), especially the use of network technology, actually changes the nature of organisational boundaries. This chapter analyses changing boundaries (and with that, changing jurisdictions), provides several scenarios regarding the changing nature of organisational boundaries.

1. Introduction

Information and communication technology plays an important role in rethinking the position and role of governments. In many western countries, e-government is synonymous with the modernisation of public administration. The modernisation potential of modern ICT, especially network technology such as the internet, lies in the use of ICT to support and/or redesign the relations that government organisations have with important stakeholders in their environment, such as citizens, companies, societal organisations and other government organisations. In these relations, the exchange of information and knowledge as well as communication plays an important role. E-government is seen as a capacity to transform public administration through the use of ICT, or indeed is used to describe a new form of government built around ICT [1]. In many writings on e-government, the blurring of boundaries is seen as a blessing (for an overview [1, 2]). Organisational, geographical and functional barriers can be overcome. 'Presence availability' is no longer a prerequisite for the deliverance of public services. The blurring of boundaries through the use of ICT adds to an improvement of the quality of services, the accessibility and transparency of government and an improvement in the efficiency of government operations.

In the literature on public organisations in general and e-government in particular, little attention is given to whether information and communication technology (ICT), especially the use of network technology, actually changes the nature of organisational boundaries. Posing this question is important because the blurring of organisation boundaries in public administration could have profound implications for the assumptions and doctrines that underlie the organisation and functioning of the government. There are three reasons why the boundary management of e-government projects in public administration is an issue that cannot be neglected.

First, changing organisational boundaries affects several organisational domains: the structure of the organisation, its processes, its culture(s) and the power relations within the organisation. Second, e-government can have a profound impact on the exchange and communication relations with relevant stakeholders in the environment of an organisation: the nature of existing relations could alter while new relations could be added. Third, the boundary management of e-government has important normative implications that are reflected in the notion of jurisdiction. This notion plays a significant role in the Weberian theory of bureaucracy and in political theory.

Studying changing organisational boundaries through the use of ICT is also interesting from the notion of the 'information ecology of e-government', which is put forward in this book. E-government projects should not be seen as sheer information management projects in which ICT is seen as a set of tools to achieve a better government. In Davenport's [3] idea of the 'information ecology', it is important to take into account the internal and external environment in which e-government initiatives are initiated. So, it is important to look at the interplay between the characteristics of ICT and the information architecture on the one hand and the business processes, the culture and staff, the organisational politics and the strategy of the organisation on the other hand in order to understand the efficacy of the use of ICT. Moreover, this interplay becomes more complex and dynamic when we add some characteristics that reflect the interactions with the business and technological environment. This interplay becomes even more complex if we look at the normative and institutional implications of the changing nature and direction of organisational boundaries. Hence, it is important to take the normative and institutional environment of e-government practices into account.

In this contribution, I have developed a conceptual framework that helps me investigate whether the nature of organisational boundaries is changing and in which direction boundaries are shifting as a result of e-government. The idea of organisational boundaries is a fuzzy concept, and it becomes even fuzzier if we accept that our understanding of organisations is multi-interpretable [4]. In Section Two, I define organisational boundaries from a legal and rational perspective. From this point of view, boundaries have a normative nature, but this is just one way of defining boundaries. In Section Three, I present other theoretical perspectives that define the boundaries of organisations in a different way. All of these definitions have one striking resemblance. They refer to the changeover between critical uncertainty and ambiguity of the outside world and uncertainty that can be controlled and managed in the organisation itself (Section Four). At the same time, I conclude that organisations become more (inter) dependent from each other, which very often leads to an increase in the exchange of information. ICT facilitates these exchange processes. In Section Five a number of characteristics of ICT are sketched, which can influence the definition of organisational boundaries and jurisdictions. In Section Six, I sketch some scenarios that show us how the boundaries of (semi-) public organisations are changing through e-government. The scenarios are constructed on empirical research that was conducted in the Dutch public sector [5]. In Section Seven, I demonstrate how e-government initiatives lead to a re-definition of organisational boundaries and jurisdictions in public administration. An information ecological perspective on e-government and on e-government boundary management can help us to understand the complex nature of these changes.

2. Organisational Jurisdictions and Legal Boundaries

In the Weberian theory of bureaucracy, the principal of official jurisdictional areas, which are generally ordered by rules, i.e. by laws or administrative regulations, plays an important role [2]. This implies that a) regular activities that are required for the purposes of the bureaucratically governed structure are assigned as official duties, b) the authority to give commands required for the discharge of these duties is distributed in stable way and is strictly delimited by rules and c) only persons who qualify under general rules are employed [2]. Weber delineation of jurisdiction supplies the kernel from which normative, theoretical and empirical concepts have been developed; ideas regarding the division of labour, hierarchy and functional and territorial differentiation of tasks, responsibilities and competences [2]. More generally, public administration can be seen as a collection of organisational jurisdictions and competences. Between these government organisations, but also between public and private organisations, information is exchanged in order to fulfil their tasks and to accomplish their policy goals. Jurisdictions are embedded in an network of information exchange and communication patterns and relations. Very often ICT is used to facilitate these exchange and communication relations.

I describe an organisational jurisdiction as the exclusive authority of an actor as a unified entity to determine rights and obligations of citizens in a task domain with (a certain degree of) discretion for which this actor is legally and politically accountable [5]. The board of the mayor and aldermen in a municipality (a unified entity) and the executing local social service agency has the exclusive authority to give citizens who live within the territory of the municipality social benefits under specific conditions. Citizens have certain legal rights and obligations to receive them while a municipality has also legal rights and obligations to render them. A municipality has the right, within a framework, to develop and implement its own social aids programme. The board of layman is politically accountable for this programme and the decisions based on it, to the council of the municipality.

Two ideas lay behind this notion of organisational jurisdiction. The first idea is that government should be seen as a rational organisation. After all, government bureaucracies should be seen as the expression of functional rationality as Weber once described it. The second idea is that government organisations should function according to some principles of the *'Rechtstaat'*.

2.1 The Rational Model of Organisation

The rational approach to organisation stresses that an organisation is a set of means and people to achieve a number of specific goals in an efficient and effective way [6]. These goals can only be accomplished if these means and people are rationally ordered. The emphasis lies on the structure of the organisation, which resembles the image of a machine and a pyramid. Mintzberg defines the organisation structure as the sum total of the ways in which labour is divided into distinct tasks and then its coordination is achieved among these tasks [7].

How are the boundaries of organisation conceived in the rational model? The goal of the organisation is decisive; a goal that is further operationalised and translated in sub-goals and corresponding tasks and competencies. This aspect is especially important for government organisations, because their tasks and competencies are laid down in all kinds of laws and regulations that define the organisational jurisdiction of a government organisation. If these tasks and competencies are changing, or become entangled with those of other organisations, boundaries and jurisdictions are changing.

Formalisation is another relevant factor in determining the boundaries of government organisations. Formalisation tries to make the individual behaviour predictable by reducing uncertainty, variety and subjectivity. The boundaries of an organisation become visible in situations where individual behaviour within the organisation has become uncertain and capricious. Uncertainty can be reduced by the further rationalisation of the organisation and by using new and more sophisticated ways of formalising, standardising and controlling organisational behaviour [6].

Rationality should also be mentioned. Simon [8] questioned the rationality of organisational decision making by introducing the concept of bounded rationality. Organisational boundaries refer to the limited cognitive capacity of individuals to make rational decisions. They are informational boundaries, determined by the limited information-processing (cognitive) capacity of an organisation that can be enlarged by using ICT.

2.2   The Legal Model of the Organisation

Government organisations are embedded in the 'Rechtstaat'. What are the principles that lay behind this idea and how do they influence the functioning of government organisations and the definition of jurisdictions? Typical for the 'Rechtstaat' is that government action which influences and very often restricts the behaviour of citizens should be based on the law. It is the law that allocates the competencies, tasks and responsibilities among government organisations and it is the law that defines the extent and the contents of these competencies, tasks and responsibilities.

We can discern a number of characteristics that are related to the attribution of legal competencies. First, there is the content of the legal task and competence. Second, there is the territorial and/or functional domain of the competency. Third, there is the degree of discretion a government organisation has in fulfilling its tasks. Does the law describe in detail how a task should be executed, what is the degree of formalisation, and to what extent the organisation is free in the execution of this task?

The degree of formalisation of the content of a task and the territorial and/or functional domain define to some extent the legal boundaries of government organisations. They become even more important if we look at another characteristic of the 'Rechtstaat', in which well-defined tasks and competencies are seen as a guarantee for preventing unwanted concentration of power in the hands of one government organisation. Doctrines such as the 'trias politica', the division of powers and 'checks and balances' are important principles that define the normative boundaries of government organisations and the patterns of accountability that accompany them.

Another relevant characteristic of the 'Rechtstaat' is the notion of the constitutional rights of citizens. They are seen as a safeguard against the abuse of power of government organisations such as the right of privacy. These rights also define the jurisdiction of government organisations. The last characteristic of the 'Rechtstaat' is the fact that citizens can appeal to an independent judge or court [9].

In this section, I have described the factors that influence the definition of organisational boundaries and jurisdictions. These boundaries have a normative nature. They refer to ideas of the 'Rechtstaat' and they refer to the specific goals that a government organisations should realise and that are laid down in a policy programme or in the law. However, the meaning of organisational boundaries cannot only be understood from a rational and legal. Other perspectives should also be taken into consideration.

3.   Other Organisational Models and Other Organisational Boundaries

If one tries to investigate whether organisational boundaries are changing through ICT, one has to broaden his scope. An organisation can be conceptualised in many ways, and this also influences the definition of these boundaries [4, 10]. Paying attention to these other boundaries is important, because there is interaction between the legal and rational boundaries of the organisation and other organisational boundaries. Legal boundaries are important, but they are not the only relevant ones.

3.1   The Cultural Model of Organisation

An organisation is a community in which people work and live. One of the characteristics of a community is that it has a culture, which can be described in terms of 'taken for granted assumptions', values and norms, rituals, heroes, legends and communication patterns [11]. Norms, values, rites, rituals, heroes, myths, legends etc. reduce uncertainty and create safety and stability. They give meaning to the life of the members of the organisation. Organisational boundaries symbolise the distinction between the well-known and sheltered world inside –(inclusion) and the relatively unknown world outside the organisation –(exclusion) [12, 13]. "A boundary line stands rather as a symbol or as a spatial embodiment of the criteria of inclusion-exclusion with respect to a system. It is a summary way of referring phenomenally to what we have included in or left out of a system" [12: 66]. Coding systems make people aware that he/she is leaving or entering the organisation. Certain symbols (e.g. the uniform of the porter, insignia such as badges), specific languages or grammar (e.g. the way a stranger is approached at the reception or by the telephone operator), rituals (such as procedures for checking in and out) are manifestations of organisational boundaries ands organisational jurisdictions [13]. These manifestations play an important role in the communication of people in the organisation and between organisations [14]. As Willke puts it: "Intersubjectiv geteilter Sinn grenzt systemspezifisch ab, was als sinnvoll und was als sinnlos zu gelten hat" [15: 30]. Boundaries are not only (re-)defined in the communication between people, but they also influence the meaningfulness of communication between people.

3.2   The Political Model of Organisation

An organisation is seen as an arena in the political perspective. This arena consists of a conglomerate of parties with conflicting, but also with mutual interests. Parties try to protect their interests by using power. They develop strategies and tactics to mobilise and employ different power resources, such as formal authority, financial funds, knowledge and expertise, information, relations, image etc. However, these resources are not always concentrated in the hands of just one party. They are distributed among several parties, which leads to all kinds of patterns of (inter)dependency and exchange. This creates uncertainty and controlling uncertainty opens the door to the employment of power [4, 16, 17].

The idea of controlling uncertainty and dependency as important power resources is important for establishing an insight in the nature of organisational boundaries. In the literature, attention is paid to those people or units that are called 'gatekeepers'. They are situated on the boundaries of the organisation and they fulfil or occupy 'boundary spanning functions or positions' [18]. Due to the differentiation and specialisation of tasks, there are, within an organisation, numerous sub-environments and corresponding gatekeepers and boundary spanning activities.

Characteristic for gatekeepers is that they open or close channels of communication, thereby filtering, summarising, analysing information and thus shaping knowledge with a view of the world that favours their interests [4]. They not only control information and knowledge, but they also control the distribution of it and thus employ power by influencing the perceptions and attitudes of those parties who are dependent on it [19].

According to Crozier and Friedberg [16] the (re-)definition of organisational boundaries is an ongoing political game which involves parties within and outside the organisation.

3.3   The Open System's Model of Organisation

In the system's approach, the organisation is seen as a set of loosely coupled, but interrelated elements or subsystems that are aimed at the achievement of certain goals. But, the ultimate goal is the organisation's survival within a specific environment. Organisations are seen as natural and open systems that are connected to an environment through all kinds of input and output processes. An organisation draws its resources from the environment (input), and transforms these resources (the throughput) into goods or services (output). An organisation is capable of surviving if it is able to attract those inputs necessary to survive and to produce those outputs that can be disposed of [6].

The introduction of an environment means that somewhere there is a changeover between the system and the environment. However, this changeover is not clear. Boundaries refer to the transactions i.e. interactions between a system and the environment. Transactions with the environment imply discontinuity and are therefore a source of uncertainty. On the one hand, these transactions are a threat to the stability of the system; on the other hand many of these transactions are vital for the survival of the system [13].

The idea of the 'organisational domain' could bring some relief in order to operationalise the empty concept of 'the environment'. The domain of the organisation consists of the claims it makes on products or services provided and populations served. The claims immediately relate it to a number of other organisations, such as suppliers, customers, competitors and regulatory groups such as governments that affect its behaviour and outcomes [20]. Organisational boundaries refer to the degree of consensus among the parties within an organisational domain about the correctness of their claims [21]. "Domain consensus defines a set of expectations both for the members of an organisation and for the others with whom they interact about what the organisation will and will not do" [20: 29]. The result of this consensus is that it stabilises the exchange relations between organisations. Zucker et al [22] see the production of trust - as a result of bargaining and communication in order to reduce uncertainty - as a necessary condition for establishing domain consensus. An organisational jurisdiction can be seen as the expression of domain consensus and trust with respect to the ways an public organisation exercises its legal competencies. They influence the legitimacy of a government organisation.

3.4   The Open's Systems Model of Organisation Extended: Interorganisational Relations

The definition of organisational boundaries is not only influenced by the legal domain of an organisation or its jurisdiction, but the exchange relations between organisation also play an important role [17, 20, 21, 23-27]. Government organisations are embedded in a network of information exchange relations that constitute a policy sector. The number and contents of exchange relations also influence the definition of organisational boundaries.

The fact that organisations are (inter)dependent has important implications for their autonomy. Pfeffer and Salancik [17] elaborate this idea. An organisation is only capable of surviving if it can reduce its dependency on resources that are vital or critical for its functioning and existence. However, the problem is that the access, distribution and availability of these resources are controlled by other organisations. The resulting dependency creates uncertainty. Organisations are not fully in control of themselves. There is some external control and power over them. Therefore Pfeffer and Salancik conclude that the boundary is "where the discretion of the organisation to control an activity is less than the discretion of another organisation or individual to control that activity" [17: 32]. In other words, "the organisation ends where its discretion ends and another's begins" [17: 32]. Discretion refers to capacity to control external resources. However, determining exactly where the discretion of an organisation ends and another's begins, is rather ambiguous.

Organisations develop several strategies to reduce external uncertainty and dependence. By re-defining their external relations they are capable of creating or enacting their own environment. The boundaries of the organisation shift, for instance through mergers, interlocking directorates, joint ventures and other strategic alliances. They also shift, if an organisation can determine the assumptions and premises of the decisions of other (dependent) organisations [17].

In the exchange model of organisations [21, 23-25] interdependency is related to the need for coordination and concerted action. Much attention is given to processes of communication, negotiation, competition and exchange. These processes move between two needs: the necessity to cooperate on the one hand and the desire to maintain the organisation's autonomy i.e. to secure the organisational boundaries on the other hand. Negotiation and communication processes are important in creating a balance between these two needs and in establishing a degree of consensus about the nature of the perceived dependency and the conditions under which exchange of resources could take place.

In studies about interorganisational relations, attention is not only given to the definition of these relations, but also to their structure. Several dimensions can be discerned [26-28]. First, interorganisational relations can be standardised and formalised, for instance in a contract or public regulation. For instance, is an exchange relation mandatory, and are specific procedures developed to exchange resources like information? Second, the intensity of the relationship tells us something about the degree of (inter)dependency. Intensity refers to the amount of resources exchanged as well as the frequency of exchange: it is this ad hoc or permanent? Another dimension is the degree of reciprocity. Is there symmetric or asymmetric dependency? Does the exchange of resources lead to a situation in which both parties can benefit? And, is there consensus about the nature of, and the conditions under which an exchange can take place? For instance, organisational boundaries become more important if an organisation has the obligation to exchange certain resources, like information or money, which affects the organisational autonomy. As these exchange relations become more standardised and intensified, the organisation becomes more entangled and its boundaries become more permeable. This is very often the case in public policy networks and in situations in which certain activities are outsourced or subcontracted.

These relations can become institutionalised and all kinds of stable patterns and forms of exchange and negotiation can emerge. Warren [24] has paid special attention to these forms of cooperation. The more exchange relations become permanent and institutionalised, the higher the degree of interdependency, the more the boundaries of organisations are being put under pressure.

4. About the Nature of Organisational Boundaries

The previous observations show that *the* organisation as such does not exist. Every model defines the boundaries of an organisation in a different way. An organisation is simultaneously rational and legally oriented, culturally embedded, subjected to a struggle for power, and engaged in all kinds of interactions with groups in the environment. Our notion of organisational boundaries is therefore relative.

However, a closer inspection reveals that these models do have something in common. Organisational boundaries refer to the management of critical uncertainty and ambiguity, but every model highlights other aspects about the nature and causes of uncertainty and ambiguity; critical, because this kind of uncertainty is vital for the stability and smooth functioning of the organisation.

The notion that *the* organisational boundaries do not exist also has important methodological implications. Some authors [10, 12, 17] observe that organisational boundaries are an analytical construct. "Organisational boundaries may be viewed as constructs invented by analysts who will draw them at different points, depending upon their theoretical interests" [10]. But these constructs refer to empirical manifestations, so what are they? Haas and Drabeck [10] and Pfeffer and Salancik [17] focus their attention on the interactions of actors (groups, individuals, units). Typical for these interactions is that they are accompanied by uncertainty, which could have different (e.g. cultural and political) meanings for the actors involved. The boundaries of an organisation are defined in the interactions between members and groups within the organisation and between members and groups outside the organisation.

However, there is another relevant observation. Boundaries differ according to the position of the actor involved. The boundaries a minister defines as meaningful differ from those of the director of a policy unit or the department's accountant. Organisational boundaries are also a normative construction [10, 15]. The actor's position or role defines the things which he sees as crucial to the discretion of the organisation and which can or should be influenced. In the case of a government organisation the normative nature of boundaries becomes even more important, because they are formulated in the law and they are embedded in the *'Rechtstaat'*.

5.   Interorganisational Information Processing

Relations and transactions between organisations often involve the exchange of information. ICT can facilitate these exchange processes. If we want to understand what impact these technologies have on the functioning of organisations and the changing nature of organisational boundaries, attention should be given to the characteristics of ICT [29, 30]. However, the characteristics of ICT and their translation into specific ICT applications should not be seen as neutral forces. They are linked to certain policy goals that an organisation would like to accomplish and the position and interests an organisation tries to protect within a policy sector or policy network.

Characteristics of ICT

Twenty years ago, information technology was primarily a technology used for calculation purposes and to undertake massive, standardised transactions. Automation was the key word. During the last ten years, we see that information technology has also become communication technology. The development of network technologies (EDI, Inter- and intranet), the coupling of data bases, telematics, groupware and all kinds of search systems have stressed the importance of other characteristics besides calculation.

First, there is the communication potential. The necessity of presence availability, in terms of sharing the same time, place and location is not an essential condition for effective communication anymore.

Second, network technologies offer new possibilities for establishing all kinds of links between people and organisations. They become 'wired' and the quality and quantity of their interactions increases. These linkages become even more meaningful if we look at the increased digital integration or interconnectivity between speech, images and sounds and the corresponding infrastructures and technologies [31].

Third, ICT enhances the transparency and access of organisations. The surrounding walls are falling down. For instance, the information systems of libraries, laboratories and government agencies can be consulted through the Internet, while intranets and groupware devices also make it possible to share organisation-wide information resources. Also, computers systems and databases are being coupled by using network technology and data is being matched. It becomes easier to detect relevant trends and development in policy fields, policy target groups, but also the outcomes of policy organisations can be made more visible. Fourth, transparency opens the door for more sophisticated ways of control and surveillance. Monitoring systems are deployed in order to watch the results of those policy units that implement certain policy programmes. But also the coupling of databases and the use of 'data mining' techniques and data profiles enable government organisations to reconstruct, follow and control the behaviour of (groups of) citizens, for instance in order to detect fraud of abuse of social security services. Fourth, there is virtual reality. In and by network technology new, virtual realities are shaped that stand apart from the real world in which people live, work, learn, shop and produce. It is the world of the virtual communities, cyber corporations and electronic markets. Everything that occurs in the real world also happens in cyberspace, but do boundaries exist in cyberspace if everything is connected?

These characteristics in combination with the interests which are at stake and goals an organisations wants to realise, influences the definition of organisational boundaries. Information processing, communication and interaction are being facilitated through these new technologies. The wiring of organisations means that those organisations that participate in a network lose some of their autonomy. For instance, they become more transparent, thereby enhancing the possibility of external or interorganisational control, which redefines the boundaries of the organisation. For instance, how permeable should a municipality be if it implements a policy programme that formulated by the Department of Social Affairs? Moreover the establishment of a network creates new interdependencies between organisations that can often be seen as the expression of trust or power. But also, working and planning processes between separate organisations can better integrated. This integration becomes more crucial if there are on-line and real-time connections.

Characteristics of Interorganisational Information Processing

These characteristics of ICT are not the only ones to affect organisational boundaries. Other factors, which are related to the broader concept of interorganisational information processing, should also be considered. First, there is the direction of information processing. Is this one-way processing, for instance a government agency which is obliged by mandate to give information to another agency or ministry? Or, do separate organisations share the same information systems and databases? Another factor is the intensity of interorganisational information processing. Do organisations exchange data permanently or on an ad hoc basis? For instance, the structural exchange of data could stimulate organisations to develop a common infrastructure and common data definitions. Another factor relates to the way data is transferred and processed. Is this for instance in a batch-mode or on-line and in real time? Is the data exchanged according to a format, or is the data unstructured? There is also the nature of the information to be processed? Does it concern technical and operational information which relates to the working processes within two or more organisations (e.g. name and address information), or does it concern allocative information (e.g. budgeting, planning and control information), or does it regard strategic information (e.g. market information). Or is it privacy sensitive information? The latter refers to the techniques of interorganisational information processing. The exchange of information through structured communication networks like the 'old' EDI has other implications for the blurring of organisational boundaries than open communication networks like the Internet.

6.   E-Government and the Re-Definition of Organisational Boundaries

Research on if and how the boundaries of organisations in the public sector change through e-government initiatives has led to the inductive development of a number of scenarios, which are based on studying and comparing large number of e-government projects in the Netherlands [5]. In general two types of scenarios are discerned. The first number of scenarios elaborates on the observation that boundaries move in several directions through the use of ICT. The second type of scenarios shows that the nature of organisational boundaries is changing and that they are being re-defined.

6.1   Scenarios about the Changing Direction of Organisational Boundaries

Scenario I: The colonisation of the environment by the focal organisation

In this scenario a government organisation tries to reduce uncertainty about the speed, quantity and quality of the data that should be delivered by other organisations. An organisation tries to formalise and discipline the exchange of data by extending its discretion. ICT is used as a way of colonising the environment, especially the data exchange relations with certain groups. Very often formats and protocols are developed, which other organisations are obliged to use when they exchange data. EDI and EDI-like technology especially favours this kind of colonisation strategy. Moreover, developing formats and using EDI offers all kinds of efficiency advantages that will ultimately lead to a further rationalisation of the internal information processing processes.

For instance, when a garage inspects a used car for safety -every car that is older than three years should be inspected every year - it is obliged to use a certain format to electronically exchange the relevant data with the Vehicle License Agency. Another example is the so-called SAGITTA-network of the Customs Administration. Companies that are active in the import of goods are obliged to pay taxes. An EDI-network that connects the Customs Administration and a large number of firms enables these firms to handle their taxes electronically. The result is that the boundaries of the Vehicle License Agency and the Customs Administration are extended. They control the exchange of information by the garages and the import companies by introducing a data-architecture which standardises the contents of data and data exchange and a communication-infrastructure which enable them to actually exchange the necessary information.

A number of factors favours this colonisation scenario. First, there is the powerful position of the organisations in question. Very often these organisations have a well-established position and reputation as a data administrator and registrar, like the Vehicle License Agency, the Tax and Customs Administration, the Land Registry and the Student Loans Agency. Their power is built on the fact that other organisations and individuals are legally obliged to exchange certain data and they have gained knowledge and experience in handling large amounts of data. Second, the most important characteristics of ICT that account for this scenario are the capability to facilitate massive transactions and to exercise control. Third, in this scenario we see that a specific type of ICT is used. EDI and data formats are used to extend the boundaries of the organisations in question. Also the kind of data that is exchanged favours this scenario: it is rather stable, operational, quantitative and well-structured, standardized data. The information relations are stable and have a rather intensive exchange character.

Looking at the models of organisation I have described in Section Two, we see that this scenario can be understood from the rational-legal and systems and the institutional approach of organisation. The rational approach stresses the importance of formalisation as a way of reducing uncertainty and enhancing the rationality of the internal information processing processes. The open systems and institutional model stresses the importance of dependency, due to legal obligations to deliver certain data.

Scenario II: The penetration of the focal organisation by the environment

In this scenario we see the opposite. An organisation can be penetrated by the environment thereby using ICT and confronting the focal organisation with new and unknown forms of uncertainty. The boundaries become electronically permeable. If an organisation lingers about whether its employees should have access to the Internet, the main question to be considered is very often do we lose control? And what do these new forms of electronic communication mean for the traditional procedures for handling messages that an organisation has developed to communicate with the outside world? What is the status of an e-mail message? Can a citizen appeal to these messages if he/she has a legal dispute with the agency in question?

If every employee has new forms of access, then he/she becomes a gatekeeper. This could be a threat to the more traditional gatekeepers. Their monopoly is being challenged. In a number of Dutch ministries, the question of whether a unit can have its own World-Wide Web page has been raised. Does this threaten the unity of the department? Or, is this a prerogative of the corporate communications and public relations unit? Moreover, if an individual unit opens its own page, what kind of information should be made accessible to outsiders?

The penetration of the organisation by the environment is not only perceived as a threat. For instance, Dutch university libraries conceive the possibilities that the Internet offers in terms of access as an opportunity. Here we observe that the goals i.e. tasks of libraries, for instance enabling people to learn and a low threshold, is connected to certain values of the virtual culture of the Internet: free information and universal access. In this example the permeability of organisational boundaries can be seen from a cultural perspective. Also, it would be interesting to see if the position and status of those civil servants who participate in discussion groups - which are sometimes initiated by agencies to discuss policy proposals - changes. Is there is a tension between the horizontal culture(s) of the Internet and the hierarchical culture of the agency they belong to? An experiment in the Dutch province of Brabant shows that an active civil servant who participated in such a discussion group, was asked by his fellow-participants if he spoke as a representative of the regional government. However, he did not have the position to do so, nor was he able - because of the speed of the discussion - to consult his colleagues and/or superiors. In the end he was only capable of participating as a person without a formal title. We can observe a process of 'exclusion' out of the existing organisation and a process of 'inclusion' in a new organisation, the discussion platform.

The 'unstructured' world of the Internet and the World Wide Web especially creates new sources of uncertainty that are sometimes seen as opportunity or as a threat. If we look at relevant characteristics of ICT we see that communication and transparency are important characteristics that account for the penetration of organisations. If we look at the information relations and patterns that occur, then we see that unstructured data is exchanged. Very often organisations try to protect themselves to these new forms of uncertainty, by trying to establish all kinds of procedures to protect the stability of the organisation and certain gatekeeper positions, which can be understood from the rational-legal and political model of the organisation. Process of 'inclusion and exclusion' can be understood form the cultural model of the organisation.

Scenario III: The integration of organisations

In this scenario the information between organisations is shared and exchanged in such a way, that organisations integrate or couple their information processing, planning and other working processes in order to further reduce uncertainty. This enhances the rationality of the organisations involved. Very often this integration takes place between organisations that are a member of the same value-chain. The electronic coupling of the links in the chain created new interdependencies between them. Sharing data in an electronic way means the further rationalising of added value.

In the health sector, we see that all kinds of electronic linkages are established between pharmacies, family doctors, hospitals, medical laboratories and nursing homes. In several cities and regions in the Netherlands we see that local doctors and pharmacies in a region have developed a common database to gain better insight in prescriptions. This system enables the pharmacists and doctors to see what kind of medication the patient had previously from another doctor or pharmacist. Enhancing the transparency of the patient and its medication leads to a better and more professional service delivery. At the same time in the city of Eindhoven, the Catharina Hospital has started electronic communication between regional and hospital doctors. When a physician in a hospital has released a patient the necessary letter of release, containing vital medical information, is sent electronically to the family doctor. This has the advantage that the family doctor has a better and much quicker insight in the medical history of the patient and the hospital's treatment. Also laboratory results, like blood test results, are given electronically. Moreover, the planning processes between hospitals and nursing homes are being coupled in certain regions. When a patient is released from hospital but he still needs professional medical care, which only a nursing home can give him, one major question is: which nursing home has the capability to nurse this patient? The coupling of capacity planning processes between hospitals and nursing homes has resulted in the total capacity in a region becoming more transparent, thereby improving the coordination between demand and supply of nursing capacity.

In social security, we see another kind of integration. The fight against abuse and fraud has led to an increasing awareness about the nature and number of interdependencies between a numerous public organisations with different but complementary tasks within this policy sector. This has led to the establishment of common information architecture and the development of a number of playing rules for exchanging data. The so-called RINIS concept tries to achieve procedural integration, thereby recognising the autonomy and the ownership of certain data of the in RINIS participating organisations.

The observations raised in this scenario can for instance be understood from the perspective of interorganisational relations, in which exchange and interdependency are the key concepts. To what extent do organisations share the same data? Can they alter the data? What does it mean for their autonomy? And in the example of the disclosure of the doctor's and pharmacist's prescriptions, how does it affect the professional behaviour of doctors in terms intercollegial monitoring, which has also important cultural and political implications. At the same time the rational model of organisations can give some important insights why and to what extent organisational boundaries in this scenario are shifting. Developing interorganisational information systems and infrastructures can increase the rationality of the internal information processing and decisionmaking processes.

Looking at these and other examples we see that transparency and communication are the most important characteristics of ICT, which lead to more permeable organisational boundaries. Moreover, more transparency opens the door to more external control.

However, control is a characteristic of ICT that always plays a role in shaping interorganisational relations.

The data that is exchanged has a rather stable and standardised character because it relates very often to operational data. The information relations are also rather stable and formalised, which also influences the kind of ICT. EDI systems and common data infrastructures, like regional medical systems, are favoured. We also see that formats and protocols are developed to facilitate a smoother exchange of data.

6.2   Scenarios Regarding the Changing Nature of Organisational Boundaries

As mentioned before, organisational boundaries can change in several directions. However, this is just one set of expectations. Another set deals with the changing nature of these boundaries.

Scenario I: The blurring of organisational boundaries

When organisations are electronically penetrated by the environment, or if organisations share information and integrate their operational and planning processes, we often see that boundaries begin to blur.

Boundary blurring can be understood from a cultural and a political model. If people from other organisations can look into certain information systems, this influences notions like awareness and interdependency. It influences how these people at the other end of the 'line' are conceived, for instance in terms of 'Big Brother'. Does it lead to a surveillance culture? In the Dutch city of Rotterdam members of the district attorney's office have limited authorisation to look at a select number of data in the operational systems of the regional police, which at a later stadium will be transferred to them on paper (the so-called record of evidence). The advantage is that the district attorney can subpoena a suspect more quickly. At the same time he can easily monitor the behaviour of the attending police officer. This example also underlines the scenario of the colonisation of the environment: the attorney's office can monitor the throughput of the police. Moreover it redefines the boundaries between the executive power (the police) and the judiciary (district attorney's office). It challenges constitutional principles like the division of power and the idea of checks and balances.

Another example is the Dutch BVE network. This is an Internet and World Wide Web application. Using the Internet, a web has been spun over a large number of schools for educational training and adult education. Students are given access to the courses and educational material of other schools. Learning at a distance has become a real option. We also see that a web has been spun over the university libraries in the Netherlands, and in other countries. The electronic linkages between the libraries and the schools have created a new organisation, crossing the traditional and physical boundaries of these schools and libraries by making them obsolete. The notion of a classroom is, for instance, fundamentally challenged. What we see here is that transparency, communication and virtual reality are important characteristics of ICT. Especially Internet technology fundamentally challenges the idea of organisational boundaries.

Scenario II: The fixation of organisational boundaries

Organisations are afraid of external uncertainty that is mobilised by ICT. They try to protect their own autonomy by establishing firewalls or buffers. Boundaries are reinforced by using ICT applications. The development of the so-called intranet is an example of this scenario. An intranet is a company-wide network that very often operates like the Internet, but has none or a limited amount of access to the outside world. Intra-nets aim at using the advantages of the Internet, in terms of e-mail or accessibility of company-wide databases but, on the other hand, it tries to protect its users from 'bad' influences from outside. Do these outside connections seduce users to surf all day on the Internet and prevent them from doing their work? How far can an outsider enter the organisation and use organisation-owned information? Does he need special authorisation procedures or code words? Are there special gatekeepers within the organisation who have privileged access to the Internet?

An example of a interorganisational intranet which connects separate public and private organisations and at the same time tries to protect its boundaries (this is sometimes called an extranet) is MIS, the Environmental Information Service System of the North Holland region. To some extent informational resources are shared between local and regional governments and private corporations, but citizens, who might also be interested in this information, are not given access to this Web page. So certain groups are included and other are excluded as a way of protecting organisational boundaries.

The RINIS concept also shows us another way of preserving the informational autonomy of the participating organisations. A number of these organisations control certain registers. The data of these registers are recognized by the other RINIS organisations as authentic data bases. So the Tax and Customs Administration has the monopoly on the income information, the GBA system has the monopoly on name, address, place of living, date of birth information and the Vehicle and License Agency has the only authentic data on vehicles. Another way of protecting organisational boundaries is the automatic referal index of the RINIS system. If one organisation asks certain data of another organisation, this question is dealt with by using a referral index. Certain questions are automatically transferred. Other questions get a special treatment if they do not meet the specifications of the protocols. This index functions as an automatic gatekeeper.

The examples show how insights from for instance the rational-legal, the political and the institutional model organisations can be used to see how organisational boundaries are being reinforced.

Scenario III: Controlled transparency

Two or more organisations can agree to exchange information to a certain degree. In this scenario the previous two scenarios are combined. The degree to which organisations become transparent to each other is fixed within certain limits. Within a well-defined framework they become mutually transparent. However, if an organisation wants to cross the framework's boundaries, bells go off. This means that only a limited number of data can be exchanged and used, or strict authorisation has to be given to look into or use a database.

The case of the Student Loans Agency shows us that students are only able to a certain, well-defined and well-protected level to cross the boundaries of the agency. However, they are able to check and alter this limited number of standardised data (e.g. changing the period and number of return-payments), by using the smart cart technology that is distributed by the Student Loans Agency in combination with the communication terminals that are distributed among the universities. They are also able to ask questions which will be answered in 24 hours. The Student Loans Agency shows that an organisation can colonise its environment by re-designing the relations with the student and at the same time become more transparent for its clients. The boundaries of the Agency have become more permeable, but on the conditions set by the agency. This also influences the internal structure of the Agency. They are now establishing 'front offices'. These offices consist of multi-disciplinary teams which can handle almost all the questions raised within one or two days. The controlled penetration of the outside world, which is made possible by ICT, leads to new ideas and values regarding client-friendliness within the Agency. Moreover these 'front offices' become important 'gatekeepers' because they have the monopoly of the communications with the outside world. The effectiveness and legitimacy of the Agency depends very much on these interactions.

So, to some degree organisation boundaries become permeable, begin to blur, but a there is a border which cannot be crossed. All kinds of procedures and firewalls are developed and introduced to protect the informational heart of the organisation. Very often privacy considerations or considerations of a strategic nature mark the informational domain that is not accessible for others. Moreover, one can protect this heart if an organisation or a coalition of organisations can determine the selection and use of ICT. Boundary changes can be understood from the interorganisational model of organisations (focusing on the external control of organisations), the rational-legal (focusing on the internal structure and the organisation's procedures) and the cultural model (referring to changing values and norms in the approach of clients).

7. The Management of Organisational Boundaries and Changing Organisational Jurisdictions

7.1 Organisational Boundaries and Jurisdictions on the Move

The redefinition of information exchange relations between government organisations and their environments - suppliers and clients - by using ICT implies that uncertainty can be reduced but at the same time that new forms of uncertainty are being introduced; this influences the stability and the autonomy of the organisation. Network technology opens 'literally' new horizons. Boundaries are going to change. They are on the move. We have seen that environments are being colonised, that organisations are being penetrated by the outside world, and that organisations integrate. Organisational boundaries begin to blur, fully or to some extent, or they are protected by new walls. Therefore, the management of organisational boundaries is an important strategic issue in the discussion about the nature of e-government because e-government initiatives influence the definition of organisational jurisdictions. Some jurisdictions become more powerful and dominant while other shrink or integrate. This raises the question of whether the original description and allocation of certain tasks and competencies still matches with these changing organisational boundaries and jurisdictions and the corresponding changes in the distribution of power among them. Checks and balances are challenged while perhaps new checks and balances are created which do not correspond with well-established principles of the legal system. In this section, I show how these changing boundaries influence some elements in the definition of organisational jurisdiction.

7.2 Exclusive Authority of an Actor as a Unified Entity

The sharing of information and knowledge between government organisations implies that organisational boundaries (partially) begin to blur. This can influence the exclusiveness of a certain authority. We can see this in the creation of integrated 'front offices' that try to deliver public services to citizens as a 'whole person'. However, there is a gap between the authority of these front offices and the authority of the 'back offices' that feed these front offices with information. These back offices have well-defined organisational jurisdictions. They have exclusive competencies, but in the 'front office' these competencies are shared and integrated. This also influences how these front offices and back offices are held accountable for their actions and decisions. I elaborate on this point later.

Other examples are the websites of certain units within a government agency and the e-mail facilities for civil servants. As already mentioned, the fact that these units are able to develop their own web sites is often seen as a threat for the unity of an organisation. What is the status of the information of these units? Who is politically responsible for them? Should there be some degree of central coordination? What is the status of an e-mail message if a civil servant participates in a discussion platform on the Internet, or if he answers to questions of citizens? E-mail is often seen as a 'slippery' way of communicating which enables civil servants to place themselves outside the control of the organisation.

7.3   Legal and Political Accountability

The changing of he boundaries of government organisations and the entanglement of informational domains can lead to difficulties in exercising political and public control. I can illustrate this problem by referring to the establishment of civic service centres or one-stop shops within a municipality. There can be a tension between the responsibility for the integrated front office and the responsibility for the separate back office organisations. Who can be held responsible if the front office organisation takes decisions towards its clients, if this information is unjust and incomplete and it is not quite clear if this is the results of faults in the databases of the back offices? When informational domains become entangled, it is quite difficult to find out where something has going wrong; certainly if the original data has been adapted. And if information is shared, where does the right of ownership lie? Who is responsible if new data is being created on the basis of the data given by the back offices? Who is responsible for the creation of new, virtual databases?

Accountability is enhanced if there are 'checks and balances' between organisations in order to prevent abuse of informational power. From the perspective of improving customer friendliness or attacking fraud, and achieving better insight in developments in a policy sector or target group, the integration of information systems and the sharing of information can be defended. The blurring of organisational boundaries is then a necessary consequence. However, this raises some questions that not only relate to the privacy aspect, but also to the distribution and concentration of informational power. The extension (i.e. colonisation) and integration of informational domains of government organisations has not been an issue that has raised a lot of public and political attention. It is a process that has passed very silently. It is an issue that is being discussed and dominated by civil servants and the bureaucracy. The notion of 'checks and balances' as a principle in (re)designing information relations in order to neutralise concentration of informational power does not play an important role in political and public discussions. Interorganisational information systems and data sharing have been primarily seen as an instrument to enhance the rationality of policy formulation, implementation and monitoring [29, 32].

However, in several political theories the existence of organisational boundaries play an important role as a way of creating 'checks and balances' in order to protect an undesired degree of power in the hand of one or a limited number of people and organisations. That it is possible to develop a common information architecture between organisations, which respects the autonomy and the 'checks and balances' between them, is shown by the RINIS concept. In RINIS there is the agreement that the ownership of certain data is protected. If an organisation wants to use certain data which is gathered and owned by other organisations, it does not collect the data themselves, but it asks (by an automated reference index) if it may use this data. The tax administration has the monopoly on income information while the municipalities have the monopoly on the correct data with respect to name, address, place and time of birth etc. However, in the construction of RINIS, no attention has been paid to introducing ' checks and balances' in the relationship between the informational power of the participating organisations and the citizen.

7.4 Determining Rights and Obligations of Citizens in a Task Domain

The fact that organisational boundaries become blurred, or that boundaries are enlarged and environments are colonised through ICT changes the position of the citizen vis à vis government and its informational rights and obligations. For instance, the coupling of databases means that more and more information is being gathered about a citizen, while he has never given his permission to combine these data and use the information created. He has only given his permission to use data for certain specific goals. The informational autonomy of citizens to determine how data is being used is challenged. Moreover, we see that through ICT a citizen is electronically linked with public administration. He becomes more a more a part of public administration. He is not seen as an autonomous individual, but as an information-providing agent. The handling of data by this agent is controlled and monitored in order to reduce uncertainty and increase the efficiency of internal processes. From a more democratic and legal perspective, one can argue that the boundaries between a government organisation and the citizen can be seen as a safeguard against abuse of power, as way of creating 'checks and balances'. These walls are broken down when a citizen is included in the organisation of public administration.

A Certain Degree of Discretion

The electronic integration of organisations (e.g. the example of RINIS) and the electronic colonisation of organisations also influence the discretion of organisations and citizens (e.g. the example of the Vehicle License Agency). Both scenarios point in the direction of Zuurmonds [33] infocracy. Typical of infocracy is the increased standardisation of data definitions and exchange relations, and corresponding procedures and routines. The organisation or coalition of organisations can develop and impose a common data architecture that can influence the degree of discretion of other organisations. If these organisations or even citizens want to exchange information they have to comply with the data definitions etc. of the data architecture. Developing and imposing a data architecture means that an organisation of coalition of organisations can influence the decision-making premises of the gathering and use of information by other organisations and citizens [34]. According to Pfeffer and Salancik [17] organisational boundaries are going to move if one is capable of altering and influencing these decision-making premises.

However, the degree of discretion can also change in another way. The line of reasoning above implies that the discretion of organisations and citizens is being limited. ICT, especially network technology like the Internet, can also increase the discretion of the participants in the network. If a member of organisation participates in a discussion group or platform on the Internet, he becomes part of virtual community. The formal background of the participant becomes less important and his discretion enlarges to act according his own wishes as the example of the civil servant of the Dutch province of Brabant who participated in a discussion group illustrates.

Multi-Dimensional Organisational Jurisdictions and the Management of Boundaries

Organisational boundaries are an important indication for organisational jurisdiction. E-government can alter both of them. However, it is important to note that organisational jurisdiction should not be limited to a narrow legal definition. The competencies of an organisation also affect the cultural and political contents of an organisation. It gives meaning to people and it enables certain people to exercise power within an organisation. Moreover, organisational jurisdictions also influence the exchange relations with other organisations. Some competencies can only be exercised if other organisations provide vital information. I can illustrate this with an example. In this Student Loans Agency, the call centre and help desk has been transformed to a professional front office. Within the near future, more than 75% of the communication with students will be handled electronically. This has important consequences for the culture and the management of the front office in contrast to the traditional administrative back offices. Certain values that play an important role in the front office can differ and clash with those in the back office when both offices are situated in the same organisation. The front office is necessarily more open for influences from the environment than the back office because they have a closer relationship with the students. Moreover the front office is team-oriented, client-oriented, technology-driven and has a problem-solving orientation, while the back office has a more bureaucratic and functional orientation. In the end, the division between front office and back office can lead to a shift in power between them.

This example shows that the management of boundaries takes places in several organisational spheres or domains. Redesigning external relationships leads to changing organisational boundaries, but these changes also have important consequences for organisational culture and politics. This means that processes of boundary management take place in several organisational spheres or domains that can conflict. Hence, it is important to analyse and assess e-government initiatives from a information ecological perspective: looking at the complex interplay of factors which relate to the internal, external and institutional environment of a government organisation and the technology which is selected, used and implemented.

References

1.   OECD, *The e-Government Imperative*. 2003, Paris: OECD.
2.   Fountain, J., *Building the Virtual State*. 2001, Washington DC: The Brookings Institute.
3.   Davenport, T.H., *Information Ecology: Mastering the information and knowledge environment*. 1997, Oxford: Oxford University Press.
4.   Morgan, G., *Images of Organizations*. 1986, Thousand Oaks: SAGE.
5.   Bekkers, V.J.J.M., *Grenzeloze overheid. Over informatisering en grensveranderingen in het openbaar bestuur*. 1998, Alphen aan den Rijn: Samsom.
6.   Scott, W.R., *Organisations*. 1992, Newbury Park / London / New Delhi: Prentice-Hall.
7.   Mintzberg, H., *Structure in Fives: Designing Effective Organizations*. 1983, Englewood Cliffs: Prentice Hall.
8.   Simon, H.A., *Administrative Behavior*. 1956, New York: The Free Press.
9.   Burkens, M.C.B., *Beginselen van de democratische rechtsstaat*. 1997, Deventer: W E J Tjeenk Willink.
10.   Haas, J.E. and T.E. Drabek, *Complex Organisations*. 1973, New York / London: MacMillan.
11.   Frissen, P.H.A., *Bureaucratische cultuur en informatisering*. 1989, Den Haag: SDU.
12.   Easton, D., *A Framework for Political Analysis*. 1965, Englewood Cliffs: Prentice Hall.
13.   Katz, D. and R.L. Kahn, *The Social Psychology of Organisation*. 1966, New York / London: Wiley.

14. Weick, K.E., *The Social Psychology of Organising.* 1969, Reading: Addison-Wesley.
15. Willke, H., *Systemtheorie.* 1992, Frankfurt / New York: Fischer.
16. Crozier, M. and E. Friedberg, *Actors and Systems.* 1980, Chicago: Chicago University Press.
17. Pfeffer, J. and G.R. Salancik, *The external control of organizations.* 1978, New York: Harper & Row.
18. Adams, J.S., *Interorganisational Processes and Organisation Boundary Activities,* in *Research in Organisational Behavior,* B.J. Staw and G.R. Salancik, Editors. 1980, JAI Press: Greenwich. p. 321-355.
19. Pfeffer, J., *Power in Organisations.* 1981, Cambridge: Ballinger.
20. Thompson, J.D., *Organisations in Action.* 1967, New York: McGraw Hill.
21. Levine, S. and P.E. White, *Exchange as a Conceptual Framework for the Study of Interorganisational Relationships.* Administrative Science Quarterly, 1961. **5**: p. 583-601.
22. Zucker, L.G., et al. *Collaboration Structure and Information Dilemmas in Biotechnology: Organisational Boundaries as Trust Production.* 1995. Cambridge: National Bureau of Economic Research.
23. Evan, W.M., *The Organisation-Set: Towards a Theory of Interorganisational Relations,* in *Approaches to Organisational Design,* J. Thompson, Editor. 1966, Pittsburg University Press: Pittsburg.
24. Warren, R.L., *The Interorganisational Field as a Focus for Investigation.* Administrative Science Quarterly, 1967. **12**: p. 396-419.
25. Benson, J.K., *The Interorganizational Network as a Political Economy.* Administrative Science Quarterly, 1975. **20**: p. 229-249.
26. Aldrich, H., *Organisations and Environments.* 1979, Englewood Cliff: Prentice Hall.
27. Van de Ven, A.H., W. G, and Liston, *Coordination Patterns within an Interorganisational Network.* Human Relations, 1979. **32**(1): p. 19-36.
28. Marret, C.B., *On the Specification of Interorganisational Dimensions.* Sociology and Social Research, 1971. **56**: p. 83-99.
29. Bekkers, V.J.J.M., *Nieuwe vormen van sturing en informatisering.* 1993, Delft: Eburon.
30. Frissen, P.H.A., *De virtuele staat.* 1996, Schoonhoven: Academic Press.
31. de Kerckhove, D., *Gekoppelde intelligentie (Linked Intelligence).* 1996, Ede: SMO.
32. van de Donk, W., *De arena in schema.* 1997, Lelystad: Koninklijke Vermande.
33. Zuurmond, A., *De infocratie.* 1994, Den Haag: Phaedrus.
34. Zuurmond, A., *From Bureaucracy to Infocracy: Are Democratic Institutions Lagging Behind?,* in *Administration in an Information Age. A Handbook,* I.T.M. Snellen and W.B.J.H. van de Donk, Editors. 1998, IOS Press: Amsterdam.

The Information Ecology of E-Government
V.J.J.M. Bekkers and V.M.F. Homburg (Eds.)
IOS Press, 2005

E-Government and the Emergence of Virtual Organisations in the Public Sector: An Exploration of the Interplay Between ICT and Socio-Organisational Networks

Victor BEKKERS

Erasmus University Rotterdam, Faculty of Social Sciences,
Public Administration Group, PO Box 1738, 3000 DR Rotterdam, The Netherlands

Abstract. Electronic government has been an important driver for the emergence of virtual organisations in the public sector. In this chapter, a typology of virtual organizations is conceptualised and examples of various types of virtual organisations are described. The typology shows that virtual organisations are the result of a complex interplay between and co-evolution of factors that relate to several environments: the technological environment, the institutional and the socio-organisational environment.

1. Introduction

The massive introduction and use of information and communication network technology in public administration has led to the establishment of a complex variety of new, virtual organisation forms within and outside the public sector. Electronic government has been an important driver for the emergence of virtual organisations in the public sector. However, our knowledge about these new emerging forms of virtual organisation has been limited, especially if we look at the public sector [1]. Although numerous studies have appeared in the last ten years in which several cases have been described and compared, systematic research into the world of virtual organisations is limited. Scholars who have a background in Business Administration and Information Science have dominated the studies, and they are more oriented to the private than the public sector.

In this article, I would like to grasp and understand the variety and complexity of virtual organisations in the public sector that emerge in the slipstream of numerous e-government initiatives. The development of an explorative typology of virtual organisations can help us reduce this variety. Moreover, it can help us identify possible factors and relations between them that account for the similarities and differences between the identified types of virtual organisations. Relevant factors are related to specific characteristics of the ICT network that is used, the socio-organisational network in which the virtual organisation has emerged, and several types of e-government services. By looking at the interplay of these factors, I will conceptualise the relationship between e-government and virtual organisations from an information ecology point of view which is dominant in this book: the idea that the effects of the use of ICT in organisations can be understand from the co-evolution of factors that relate to aspects of the technological, political, institutional and internal and external organisational environment, in which ICT is introduced [2, 3].

In Section Two, I describe e-government as a relevant phenomenon in public administration, which shows us how public administration is changing under influence of modern ICT. Virtual organisations are the manifestation of this change, but what does the notion of virtual organisation imply? In Section Three, I discuss some of the literature. In Section Four I discuss the research strategy that has been followed in order to develop a typology of virtual organisations, which is described in Section Five. In Section Six, I compare the specific types of virtual organisation and relate them to specific e-government services, specific characteristics of ICT networks and the socio-organisational network in which the virtual organisation has emerged, and formulate some conclusions.

2. The Concept of E-Government

ICT is often seen as a set of tools that can help reinvent government in such a way that existing institutional arrangements, in which the transactions and other interactions between government and its stakeholders are embedded, can be restructured and new arrangements can form [4, 5]. These new arrangements are often introduced under a flag of electronic government or e-government.

E-government is a policy and managerial concept with minimal theoretical foundation but supported by a large amount of empirical research focused on the effects of ICT on the functioning of public administration [4, 6-8]. Due to this nebulous variety of practices, the concept of e-government is ill defined and based on pragmatic experiences and visions.

E-government can be described as the use of modern ICT, at this moment especially internet and web technology, by a public organisation to support or redefine the existing and/or future (information, communication and transaction) relations with 'stakeholders' in the internal and external environment in order to create added value [9, 10]. Relevant stakeholders are citizens, companies, societal organisations, other government organisations and civil servants [11, 12]. Added value can be found in increasing the access to government, facilitating the quality of service delivery, stimulating internal efficiency, supporting public and political accountability, and increasing the political participation of citizens.

E-government is often described in relation to the kind of services to be provided [4, 9, 11]. Information services are focused on the disclosure of government information, for instance the possibility of downloading brochures, policy reports, regulations and other official documents. Contact services refer to the possibility of contacting public administration, i.e. to inquire about the application of certain rules and programmes or to make a complaint. Transaction services refer to the electronic intake and further handling of certain requests and applications of personal rights, benefits and obligations, such as digital tax assessments, the render of permits, licenses and subsidies. Participation services not only address the possibility of electronic voting, but they also include electronic forums and virtual communities that provide citizens a channel for becoming involved in the formulation and evaluation of policy programmes, like the reconstruction of a neighbourhood. The last type is data transfer services that refer to the exchange and sharing of (basic and standard) information between government agencies and between government and private organisations.

The development of these services implies ICT-driven intra-organisational and interorganisational changes and arrangements, which can be described as the virtualisation of public administration [4, 13]. Fountain [4] describes this process as the rapid transfer, sharing and integration of information and communication processes and flows across organisational boundaries. The emergence of the virtual organisations in public administration is the result.

3. The Concept of Virtual Organisation

There is a variety of definitions in the literature on virtual organisations; a variety that does not stimulate systematic research into this new organisational phenomenon. In literature, virtual organisations are described by pointing out the following characteristics:

- *The virtual organisation as a network organisation.* In this approach the emphasis is on the location-independent and temporary collaboration between separate organisations that is based on the notion of interdependency. Information and communication technology (ICT) supports the collaboration between these organisations by facilitating the exchange, distribution and sharing of information, knowledge, know how and other scarce and vital resources [6, 14-18].
- *The virtual organisation as fact and fiction.* Virtuality points at the notion of "something appears to exist when in actuality it does not" [19: 15]. Picot et al. call it in German '*Als-ob-Organization*' [17]. The virtual organisation describes a situation where people or facilities that are not a part of an organisation are linked to it as though they were. In this approach the emphasis is on the contrast between the people and resources, which, in some situations, are apparently a part of the organisation, while in other situations they are not.
- *The virtual organisation as an organisation in cyberspace.* Cyberspace specifically denotes the real and imaged space in which individuals meet in electronically mediated and simulated space [20]. The emphasis is on the establishment of an 'information space' that is created through the connection of computers and computer networks. The creation of this space facilitates the sharing of information and knowledge, as well as electronic communication [21, 22]. This connection results in the creation of a space of flows, which is compressed in time ('timeless time'). Castells [23] describes virtual organisations as the spaces of flows, which are the material organisation of time-sharing social practices that work through flows (of information, capital, images, sounds, symbols and interactions between organisations and people).
- *The virtual organisation as the organisation of memory.* Central here is the notion of the dynamic allocation of information processing capacity within a network of connected computers and computer networks. Time-sharing, made possible by the connection of computers and networks, enables the parallel disclosure and use of information and knowledge within a network. The interconnection of information processing capacities enables organisations to develop a common memory, across organisational boundaries [24, 25].

When we look at the literature on virtual organisations, we see that the attention is primarily focused on the virtual organisation as a network organisation, pointing out the changing nature of organisational boundaries. Network technologies facilitate processes of inclusion and exclusion of people and resources [15]. Hence, typologies of virtual organisation forms are often focused on the description of specific patterns of network relations [26]. For instance, Campbell [27] has distinguished the following types of virtual organisations: internal networks, stable networks, dynamic networks and web enterprises. However, the question can be posed of whether the network metaphor is distinctive enough to describe a virtual organisation because virtual organisations too closely resemble the idea of a network organisation. One reason reflects the idea that electronic networks and network organisations are in essence the same; or that a virtual organisation mirrors the electronic network which is seen as the basis for the development of a virtual organisation [28]. Other typologies are based on the combination of information architecture and e-business models [29]. Information architecture models, e-business models and models of virtual organisations are seen as three sides of the same triangle. For instance, the hub-model of the virtual organisation is an information-architecture model that facilitates logistical integration between the functions of separate organisation [26]; an approach that implies that models of virtual organisation are based on information planning models. In all of these typologies, a deterministic relationship is suggested between the structure of a virtual organisation and the structure of electronic network and/or the information-architecture model. However, one can doubt if this is a promising perspective.

4. Research Strategy

In order to understand the variety and complexity of virtual organisation in public administration, several steps have been made, but it is important to bear in mind that the results of this research project are based on an explorative design, which will be used for further theoretical and empirical research.

First, it is necessary to develop a view on virtual organisations. I define a virtual organisation as an informational space that facilitates the sharing of information and knowledge, as well as electronic communication in order to support collective action. In doing this I chose an instrumental and functional definition of virtual organisations. Virtual organisations can be seen as an instrument or a platform that enables people, groups, organisational units, or organisations to develop patterns of collective or concerted action [30]. In this view, an organisation can be seen as a set of coordination mechanisms. Hence, a virtual organisation can be seen as a platform that coordinates flows and processes of information and communication in order to create collective action among a group of actors. What kinds of informational spaces have been developed to support e-government services that in most cases cross-organisational boundaries? How can we describe these spaces? An understanding of the nature of coordination offers us the possibility of grasping a number of vital characteristics of the virtual organisation (as a coordination mechanism). Coordination can be described as a process of exchanging and processing information and/or a process of communication in order to achieve collective action [30, 31]. Sometimes this collective action is predetermined by a given and common goal, and sometimes this common goal has yet to be developed. At least two dimensions are important: first, it is important to understand the degree to which the exchange of information and communication are formalised by the introduction of a hierarchy or by the development of (standardised) rules, routines and procedures, which sometimes can be automated; and second, it is important to look at those actors who are actually involved in the exchange of information and communication and thus play a role in the coordination activities. This dimension refers to the degree of inclusion or exclusion. On the basis of these two dimensions, a study has been conducted on e-government initiatives in the Netherlands (Figure 2).

The second step was to look at the relationship between technology and the form and functioning of virtual organisations. As mentioned earlier, it is important not to step into a trap by looking at virtual organisation from a deterministic perspective, either by focusing too much on the characteristics of the ICT network or infrastructure or the information architecture. Hence, attention should be given to the interplay between the characteristics of the socio-organisational and ICT-network [32, 33] Moreover, it is important to bare in mind that the characteristics of an already existing virtual organisation will also influence the functioning and the socio-organisational network of actors, which uses the virtual organisation and the possibilities that the ICT network offers. The complex interplay between technology and (virtual) can be seen as a process of co-evolution of social, political, institutional and technological factors [3, 33, 34].

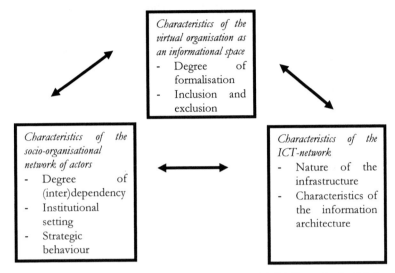

Figure 2: The Interaction between Socio-Organisational and ICT Networks in Relation to the Emergence of Virtual Organisations as an Informational Space

What characteristics of the socio-organisational network in which a virtual organisation is located potentially influence the shaping of the virtual organisation as coordination mechanism? First, there is the degree of dependency or interdependency between actors with respect to the access and use of vital resources, like information and knowledge. Special attention should be given to the existence of a hierarchical centre that is able to determine the relations between the actors in the virtual organisation [14, 15, 17]. Another factor is the institutional embedding of the virtual organisation. The relations and dependencies among actors in a virtual organisation are also influenced by the specific institutional setting in which they operate, like the relationship with the policy, laws and regulations, grown practices, the history of a policy field, the political sensitivity of a policy sector, the fragmented structure of a policy field, or the degree of professionalism within a policy field [35]. Both factors influence also the strategic behaviour of the actors who are involved in the shaping of a virtual organisation (e.g. [33, 36]). What interests and domains are at stake and how do actors try to protect their influence? How is the game played? Was there a clear win-win situation, or was one actor able to impose its will? Thus, the politics of collective behaviour is another issue to be addressed.

Looking at the relevant characteristics of the ICT-network, attention should be paid to the nature of the ICT infrastructure and dominant technology applications. For instance, EDI technology has different characteristics than Internet technology. EDI-like technology is heavily formalised because it works with standardised data exchange formats. This kind of technology offers more possibilities for standardisation, formalisation, fixed boundaries and even centralisation of the coordination in the virtual organisation. The specific qualities of the Internet, which are based on open communication standards, facilitate coordination processes, which are based on mutual adjustment through electronic communication. Also, the information architecture model that is used could be relevant. An information architecture determines what kind information should be exchanged and how it should be exchanged. A referral index can be seen as an architectural design that helps organisations automatically exchange information because the information that is available to an organisation and how it can be retrieved is precisely determined.

The third step was the study of e-government initiatives in the Netherlands and the virtual organisation-like patterns that emerged around them. In particular, I have looked how informational spaces have been created, how these spaces are formalised and who has been participating in these spaces. On the basis of this study, I developed a typology of virtual organisation that is presented in the next section. Several 'Ideal Types' of virtual organisations will be sketched. The next step is to relate this description of the shape and functioning of these 'Ideal Types' of virtual organisation to the interplay of the characteristics of ICT network and socio-organisational network. What are the relevant factors and relations between them? In Section Six, I present a preliminary explanation.

A last remark concerns the generalisation of the research findings if we relate them to the Dutch examples that are used. The emphasis is on the development of a theoretical and analytical framework to understand the variety of virtual organisations in public administration and not on 'statistical' and empirical generalisation. Further research should determine if country specific characteristics (as institutional characteristics of the socio-organisational network in which a virtual organisation emerges) influence the shape and functioning of the virtual organisation. The same line of reasoning can be used for a comparison with virtual organisation in the private sector. It is also possible to use the typology of virtual organisations in the private sector, but this was not the starting point of this research. Further research should elaborate this kind of generalisation.

5. A Typology of Virtual Organisations

On the basis of a study of numerous e-government initiatives in the Netherlands and a description of the information spaces that were created, I have been able to develop a typology of virtual organisations. This typology is based on two dimensions: the degree of formalisation and the openness of the inclusion and exclusion process of virtual organisation as an information space (Figure 3).

Degree of Formalisation

	High		Low
Closed	Federal organisation Concentric organisation		Platform organisation
Inclusion and Exclusion			
Open	Portal organisation		Web organisation

Figure 3: A Typology of Virtual Organisations

The following elements play a role in the description of each type. The specific type of virtual organisation is described and illustrated with an example. I demonstrate the nature of the formalisation of the information exchange and communication processes and determine if there is a closed or open and free participation of actors. A brief description is also given of the ICT infrastructure and architecture that is used. Moreover, I try to give a brief description of the socio-organisational network in which this type of virtual organisation has emerged. Each type in the typology will be illustrated with an example.

Moreover, I have tried to visualise how the coordination takes places in each of described organisational types.

The Federal Virtual Organisation *But he doesn't describe it!*

The Zealand Harbour Information System (ZHIS) is an example of a virtual organisation (Figure 4) in the Dutch ports of Vlissingen and Terneuzen. The ZHIS is a highly formalised electronic EDI network that facilitates the exchange of information and coordination between a variety of public and private organisations with different tasks and responsibilities in order improve their quality of services. Before its introduction, organisations like the Port Authority, the Coast Guard, the Customs Office, the Pilot Service, transport companies, import and export agencies and stevedores, who handle aspects of the arrival, the (un)loading and departure of ships in the harbour, had to contend with several communication and coordination problems. The logistical planning and transparency of the harbour was inefficient because every organisation used different arrival and departure times. Tasks and work processes could not be integrated. The new system has enabled better planning and handling of logistical and administrative tasks, routines and procedures, which in the case of the public organisations are based on the execution and enforcement of public rules and regulations.

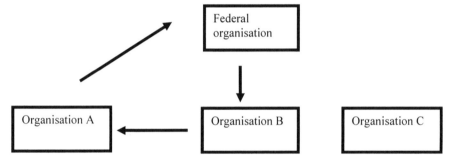

Figure 4: The Federative Virtual Organisation

The ZHIS is a federative virtual organisation. The autonomy and variety of the participating organisations (the 'States') is respected. They are responsible for the content and exploitation of their own information systems and related working processes, but these organisations recognise the interdependencies among them. They acknowledge that they can improve the efficiency and efficacy of their task performance if they share information. Through the introduction of a third party, called ZHIS Central as the federate level, a shared information space is created. This third party operates as an 'information broker' (as the dominant information architecture model) which coordinates the information exchange between the participating organisation. Questions are sent to the 'information broker', who will direct the question to the organisations that are able to answer the specific question. The information broker –ZHIS Central- can be seen as a super-ordinate organisation with a specific task: creating a shared information space within the ports of Vlissingen and Terneuzen.

In the realisation of the ZHIS, the Port Authority has played an important role. It took the initiative and presented a business case to the other actors who made clear what the content of the 'win-win' was and how this could be achieved. The ownership of the ZHIS is in the hands of all the parties involved

The Virtual Concentric Organisation

The virtual organisation (Figure 5) as a concentric organisation can be described as an information space that is created by the coupling of databases. Concentric circles of users can be identified around these databases that are located within and outside the organisation. Network technology facilitates real-time and online accessibility. These circles of user groups can process and share the information in the databases at the same time parallel to each another [37]. The information architecture tries to explore the benefits of database technology. The processing of the information is highly regulated and restricted to specific users and user groups.

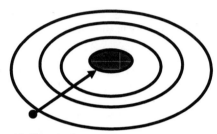

Figure 5: The Virtual Concentric Organisation

In the Dutch public sector, the Student Loans Administration is a concentric organisation. An informational heart is created through the coupling of databases that is accessible for front and back office employees as well as students who want to look at and alter (to a limited degree) their own data. The students form the outermost circle of users. The retrieval and altering of information in the databases is highly formalised and secured, and access to the database is limited to specific user groups that use the intranet or the Internet.

Another example is the Dutch Vehicle License Registration Agency, which also plays a role in the safety inspection of cars. Local and private garages carry out this inspection of cars older than 3 years. These garages have access to the specific inspection register. The actual inspection process is formalised and controlled by the information format, which they exchange with the Vehicle License Registration Agency. The agency primarily uses an information architecture that enables them to monitor the discretion of the local garages from a central point, while exchange of information takes place through the network of a third party – the network of the association of garages.

Both examples show that through the intervention of a dominant actor, who plays an important role in the execution and monitoring of public rules and regulations, an informational space is created that enables this central actor to control the information processing behaviour of groups within and outside the focal organisation.

The Virtual Platform Organisation

In the platform organisation, a digital platform is created that can be seen as a space for sharing of information and knowledge as well as a virtual meeting place for communication and interaction (Figure 6).

COPS is an example of a virtual platform organisation based on extranet technology. A closed information and communication domain has been created that enables civil servants, located in a variety of organisations with criminal investigation authority with specific tracking and tracing tasks (police, tax administration, animal protection etc.), to share information and to communicate with one another about their profession and professional development. For instance, within a secured area of COPS, the platform was used for writing a policy report on how to improve the efficacy of detective work and methods of the criminal investigation departments. Another example is the platform of experts who discussed the proposals that were made during the Convention of Europe. The Internet gave them access to the platform, for which one has to apply and for which guests have been invited to give their opinion.

The communication and information exchange processes within the platform are not highly formalised. There is open, unstructured communication, while the access to the platform is regulated. One has to be a member of a certain group to participate in the platform.

Figure 6: The Virtual Platform Organisation

The participation in the platform and is based on interdependency. Participants recognise that the sharing and exchange of information, knowledge and ideas could improve their own understanding. Moreover, it facilitates a process of mutual adjustment and shared understanding that can stimulate collective action. Most platforms can be found in formulation and evaluation phase of the policy process.

The Portal Organisation

In the portal organisation an information space is also created. Information and other sources of knowledge are brought together as well as links that lead to other information sources. The architecture model is based on the principle of linking; content management systems and models also play an import role (Figure 7).

In the Netherlands, www.overheid.nl (www.government.nl) functions as the gateway to Dutch public administration, which tries to enhance the transparency and access of public administration. Using several target group oriented entrances - like citizens, politicians and civil servants – information can be acquired about the central, local and regional government agencies. It is also possible, using 'deep linkages', to connect to web-enabled information resources that are administered by those agencies and that are located in their back offices. Sometimes portal organisations are also used for transactions purposes such as applying for permits, subsidies and assessing taxes. In the Netherlands, local virtual counters, focused on themes like 'living and building', 'care and welfare' and 'business', are created which are based on the portal concept.

The interactions that take place within the portal organisation are mostly structured and formalised, such as the number and content of resources, the number and kind of links, the organisation of the search functions and, for instance, the electronic form which could be used to order products of to ask for certain services. The access to the portal as information space is in most case free. The establishment of these e-government portals is mostly based on the notion of interdependency. The notion of integrated, electronic public service delivery, which is at the heart of many e-government programmes in the Netherlands and in other countries, is an important driver for organisations to share information in a portal.

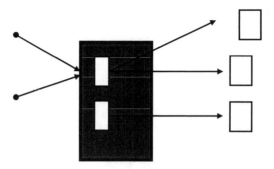

Figure 7: The Portal Organisation

The Virtual Web Organisation

The last type of virtual organisation is the web organisation (Figure 8). News and discussion groups on the Internet as well as virtual communities are illustrations of the web organisation. Schalken [38] has described in detail such a group, a group of biker enthusiasts. For bikers, this open discussion group is a source of information and a platform for communication about serious, policy-oriented issues – like security or changing legislation – and leisure and fun issues – like Harley Davidsons. Input from these discussions is often used by certain interest groups to influence the policymaking process. Moreover, parallel with an official electronic discussion forum, alternative and open discussion groups with lively debates about policy proposals have been started up [38].

Figure 8: The Virtual Web Organisation

Discussion groups can be seen as loosely coupled interactions and relations between discussants who created a shared information space. The Internet can be see as an infrastructure that enables people to organise themselves as a group, to explore the issues that appeal to common interests. Self-organisation and goal searching, which takes places through communication and interaction, are two important characteristics of the web organisation. Frissen [13] has used the metaphor of a rhizome to describe the form and functioning of this type of virtual organisation. The rhizome is a root system where fibres grow even faster, in all directions, then they die. When somebody is disappointed in a discussion or wants to explore a related issue, he will leave or he will start his own discussion, which will attract other new members. The result is a myriad of interrelated and isolated discussion and sub discussion groups.

6.   Conclusion

We can derive the following from the comparison of the several types of virtual organisations (Table 6). First, I have related the organisational types to e-government services that were discerned in section two, the dominant coordination mechanism, the degree of formalisation and the process of in and exclusion.

Table 6: Virtual Organisation Types Related to E-Government Services and Coordination Type

Virtual organisation	Federal	Concentric	Platform	Portal	Web
Dominant e-government service	Data transfer services, sometimes extended with transaction services	Data transfer services, sometimes extended with transaction services	Contact and participation services	Information and contact services, sometimes transaction	Contact and participation services
Dominant coordination mechanism	Exchange and disclosure of information in relation to a well defined goal	Processing and disclosure of information in relation to a well defined goal	Sharing of information and knowledge and communication in relation to an emergent goal	Exchange an disclosure of information; sometimes transaction in relation to a broader theme or target group	Sharing of information and knowledge and communication in relation to an emergent goal
Degree of formalisation	Formalisation and standardisation of process and content	Formalisation and standardisation of process and content	Formalisation of access, not of the exchange and communication process	Formalisation of the linking and searching process, as well as the delivery formats of content	No formalisation
Inclusion and exclusion of parties	Regulation of inclusion and exclusion; restricted number	Regulation of inclusion and exclusion; restricted number	Regulation of inclusion and exclusion	Open process	Open process

It is interesting to see that, apparently, there is a relationship between the rather heavily-regulated and restricted federal and concentric types of virtual organisations and predominantly data transfer (and to some extent transaction) services. The sensitivity of the exchange processes is a possible explanation. Very often additional demands are put forward because the integrity of the data is at stake, especially when agencies act upon these data in relation to the distribution of rights and obligations. Another reason is that federal and concentric organisations challenge the information domains of separate organisations [6]. They affect the autonomy of these organisations and the regulation of information relations is used to protect this autonomy.

In Table 7, I have related the types of virtual organisation to a number of characteristics of the socio-organisational network

Table 7: Relationships Between Types of Virtual Organisation and Characteristics of the Socio-Organisational Network

Virtual organisation\ socio-organisational network	Federal	Concentric	Platform	Portal	Web
Degree of dependency	Interdependency	Dependency	Interdependency	Interdependency	Horizontal relation
Existence of a (hierarchical centre)	Centre	Centre	Centre	Centre	No centre
Institutional embeddedness in the policy process	Implementation of policy programmes Execution and enforcement of rules Strong embeddedness	Implementation of policy programs Execution and enforcement of rules Strong embeddedness	Policy development and evaluation Strong embeddedness	The whole policy process, but with an emphasis on policy implementation and service delivery- Strong embeddedness	Policy development and evaluation No embeddedness
Strategic behaviour	Win-win	Imposing	Win-win	Win-win	Win-win

This table shows us that the platform and web organisations are often related to the development and evaluation of public policies, in which discussion and thus communication plays an important role. In the federative, platform and portal organisation, interdependency seems to be an important force to find a win-win situations that legitimises the establishment of a common information space that partially integrates different information domains. The concentric organisation creates an informational space that goes beyond its own organisational boundaries – redefining the process of inclusion because it has the power to do so. In the web organisation, the sharing of information, knowledge and communication takes place on a voluntary basis. Successful sharing and meaningful communication is based on the creation of shared understanding about policy issues.

Table 8: Relationships Between Types of Virtual Organisation and Characteristics of the ICT Network

Virtual organisation\ ICT-network	Federal	Concentric	Platform	Portal	Web
Nature ICT-network	Closed and formalised (mostly EDI-like)	Closed and formalised (intra- and extranet)	Closed (extranet) and open (internet)	Open (internet)	Open (internet)
Dominant information architecture model	Information broker/referral index model	Database model	Platform	Linking and content management models	No model

Attention should also be paid to the relationship between the type of virtual organisation and characteristics of the ICT network (Table 8). The need to formalise relationships in a socio-organisational network is sometimes reflected in a highly formalised network (like EDI) and in the information architecture that is used. This can be observed in the concentric and federal organisation. One reason for this mutual formalisation is that it concerns information exchange and processing activities that relate to the implementation of policy programmes and the execution and enforcement of rules on which legal rights and obligations are based. Using rather formalised information architecture models can also be seen as an expression for protecting a further loss of the autonomy of the information domains that are at stake. This can be observed in the concentric, the federal and portal organisation.

Another remark concerns the function and stability of the typology. This typology should be seen as a heuristic instrument that can help us improve our theoretical and empirical understanding of virtual organisations in public administration - which have not been systematically investigated up to now. It is a description that inventories characteristics and relationships among them. Further research should investigate whether the relationships that have been described actually exist.

Moreover, the typology offers us the possibility for seeking transition patterns and push and pull factors that can account for the hybrid characteristic of many virtual organisations [31]. Under what conditions does a web organisation develop itself into a platform organisation and vice versa? Such a transition process can interpreted as a process of (de-) institutionalisation of changing perceptions of (inter)dependency that leads to a changing process of inclusion and exclusion.

However, over emphasising the characteristics of a specific type can also be a risk. There is always a tension between the descriptive clarity of the typology and the ambiguity of reality in which all kinds of combinations of virtual organisation types occur.

The combinations of possible correlations between characteristics of the technology used, characteristics of e-government services and characteristics of the socio-organisational network (an its institutional embeddedness) in order to understand the emergence of virtual organisations, show us how fruitful an information ecology approach to e-government could be. It shows us that virtual organisations cannot be understood from an instrumental and functional perspective. It warns us that e-government should not be seen as the sheer use of ICT in order to describe and build new forms of government around ICT as the OECD recently suggests [39]. The emergence of new forms of government is the result of a complex co-evolution of factors that relate to several environments: the technological environment, the institutional and the socio-organisational environment [2, 3]. This process of co-evolution is per definition a contingent one, which explains the variety of virtual organisations that occur.

References

1. Bekkers, V.J.J.M., *Voorbij de virtuele organisatie? Over de bestuurskundige betekenis van virtuele variëteit, contingentie en parallel organiseren.* 2001, Den Haag: Elsevier Bedrijfsinformatie.
2. Davenport, T.H., *Information Ecology: Mastering the information and knowledge environment.* 1997, Oxford: Oxford University Press.
3. Nardi, B.A. and V.L. O'Day, *Information Ecologies: Using Technology with Heart.* 1999, Cambridge (MA): The MIT Press.
4. Fountain, J., *Building the Virtual State.* 2001, Washington DC: The Brookings Institute.
5. Heeks, R., *Reinventing Government in the Information Age: International Practice in IT-Enabled Public Sector Reform.* 2001, London: Routledge.
6. Bellamy, C. and J. Taylor, *Governing in the Information Age.* 1998, Buckingham: Open University Press.
7. Snellen, I.T.M. and W.B.H.J. van de Donk, *Public Administration in an Information Age. A handbook.* 1998, Amsterdam: IOS Press.
8. Danziger, J.N. and K. Viborg Andersen, *Impacts of information technology on public administration: An analysis of empirical research from the golden age of transformation.* International Journal of Public Administration, 2002. **25**(5): p. 591-627.

9.   Bekkers, V.J.J.M., *De strategische positionering van e-government*, in *Klantgericht werken bij de overheid*, H.P.M. van Duivenboden and A.M.B. Lips, Editors. 2001, Lemma: Utrecht. p. 49-66.

10.   Moon, M.J., *The evolution of e-government among municipalities: Rhetoric or reality?* Public Administration Review, 2002. **62**(4): p. 424-433.

11.   Gartner, *Western Europe Government Sector: IT Solution Opportunities*. 2000: Gartner Group.

12.   Chadwick, A. and C. May, *Interaction between states and citizens in the age of the Internet: 'e-government' in the United States, Britain and the European Union*. Governance, 2003. **16**(2): p. 271-300.

13.   Frissen, P.H.A., *Politics, Governance and Technology. A Postmodern Narrative on the Virtual State*. 1999, Cheltenham, UK: Edward Elgar.

14.   Rockart, J. and J. Short, *The Networked Organization and the Management of Interdependencies*, in *The Corporation of 1990s*, M.S. Scott Morton, Editor. 1991, Oxford University Press: Oxford. p. 189-219.

15.   Davidow, W. and M. Malone, *The Virtual Corporation*. 1992, New York: Harper.

16.   Byrne, W., *The Virtual Corporation*, in *Newsweek*. 1993. p. 98-103.

17.   Picot, A., R. Reichwald, and R. Wigand, *Die grenzenloze Unternehmunng*. 1995, Wiesbaden: Gabler.

18.   Sieber, P., *Internet-Unterstützung virtueller Unternehmungen*, in *Gestaltung von Organisationsgrenzen*, G. Schreijögg and J. Sydow, Editors. 1997, De Gruyter: Berlin.

19.   Martin, J., *Cybercorp*. 1996, New York: Amacon.

20.   Holmes, D., *Introduction*, in *Identity and Community in Cyberspace*, D. Holmes, Editor. 1997, SAGE: London. p. 1-25.

21.   O'Hara, M. and R. Johansen, *Global Work: Bridging Distance, Time and Culture*. 1994, San Francisco: Jossey-Bass.

22.   Barnatt, C., *Office Space, Cyberspace and Virtual Organization*. Journal of General Management, 1995. **20**(4): p. 78-91.

23.   Castells, M., *The Information Age. Economy, Society and Culture*. 1996, London: Blackwell.

24.   Mowshowitz, A., *Virtual Feudalism: A Vision of Political Organization in the Information Age*. Informatization in the Public Sector, 1992. **2**(3): p. 213-232.

25.   Mowshowitz, A., *Virtual Organization: A Vision of Management in the Information Age*. The Information Society, 1994. **10**: p. 267-288.

26.   Mintzberg, H., *Organigraphics. Drawing How Companies Really Work*. Organigraphics. Drawing How Companies Really Work, 1999. **Sept-Oct 1999**: p. 87-94.

27.   Campbell, A., *Knowledge Management in the Web Enterprise*, in *Virtual Working: Social and Organizational Dynamics*, P. Jackson, Editor. 1999, Routledge: London.

28.   McLoughlin, I. and P. Jackson, *Organizational Learning and the Virtual Organization*, in *irtual Working: Social and Organizational Dynamics*, P. Jackson, Editor. 1999, Routledge: London. p. 178-192.

29.   Tapscott, D., D. Ticoll, and A. Lowry, *Digital Capitalism*. 2000, London / Nashville: Brealey Publishing.

30.   Thompson, J.D., *Organisations in Action*. 1967, New York: McGraw Hill.

31.   Mintzberg, H., *Structure in Fives: Designing Effective Organizations*. 1983, Englewood Cliffs: Prentice Hall.

32.   Orlikowski, W.J. and D. Robey, *Information Technology and the Structuring of Organization*. Information System Research, 1991. **2**(2): p. 143-171.

33.   McLoughlin, I., *Creative Technological Change*. 1999, London: Routledge.

34.   Pinch, T.J., W.E. Bijker, and J.E. Hughes, *The Social Construction of Technological Systems: New Directions in the Sociology and History of Technology*. 1987, Cambridge: MIT Press.

35.   DiMaggio, P.J. and W.W. Powell, *The New Institutionalism in Organizational Analysis*. 1991, Chicago: Chicago University Press.

36.   Crozier, M. and E. Friedberg, *Actors and Systems*. 1980, Chicago: Chicago University Press.

37.   Zuboff, S., *In the age of the smart machine: the future of work and power*. 1988, New York: Basic Books.

38.   Schalken, K., *Motorfietsen op het digitale verkeersplein*. Bestuurskunde, 1999. **5**: p. 210-218.

39.   OECD, *The e-Government Imperative*. 2003, Paris: OECD.

The Back Office of E-Government: Managing Information Domains as Political Economies

Victor BEKKERS and Vincent HOMBURG
Erasmus University Rotterdam, Faculty of Social Sciences,
Public Administration Group, PO Box 1738, 3000 DR Rotterdam, The Netherlands

Abstract. Integration of back-offices is often stressed as critical success factor for e-government initiatives. However, at the same time, back-office integration is oftena surprisingly slow, cumbersome and sensitive process. This chapter provides an explanation why integration is so sensitive and cumbersome, and provides recommendations for a process management approach towards integrating back-offices.

1. Introduction

In the literature on e-government, the focus is often on the organisation of the website as one of the faces of the front office and on the interactions which take place in the front office between government and citizens and between government and companies. However, when these interactions become more intense, because contact and transaction services are provided, back office operations, and more specifically back office streamlining, should also be taken care of. The shaping of the relationships and interactions between the front office and the back office on the one hand and among back offices on the other hand create all kinds of interoperability problems which are crucial to the success and failure of many e-government services [1]. In a sense, back-office operations are the backbone of e-government, and they may require information exchange and knowledge sharing between various units, departments or organisations. In other words, back-office operations can be regarded as a Government-To-Government (G2G) interaction and the services that are to be delivered are primarily data-transfer services. The result is that organisational boundaries will fade and give way to innovative organisational design (see also the chapter on changing organisational boundaries). In this way, cooperation between administrative agencies will span wide: over distances, across organisational boundaries and even across hierarchical echelons [2, 3].

However, the realisation of more interactive e-government services shows that the practice of e-government may not be as attractive as some of its benevolent proponents might claim. The relationships between back offices can be regarded as networks of organisations in which goals do not necessarily overlap and interests may collide. In these intra- and interorganisational networks, information itself is the primary medium of value and exchange and the relatively uncontrolled sharing of such a powerful resource threatens information monopolies, provides those organisations which receive information with significant power gains and may even threaten the reason of existence of some of the organisations involved in the process of information sharing [4-8]. Consequently, existing dependencies in organisational networks might be affected and it can be expected that the exchange of information in back-offices will invoke a complex mixture of cooperation and conflict. This notion, which has been empirically tested, has important implications for our understanding of e-government and for the approach of e-government we propose in this book. In our understanding of e-government as an information ecology, it is important to look at the embeddedness of technological interventions in a network of actors, which all try influence the shape and content of e-government from their dominant interests, positions, frames of reference and (political) values. From an information ecological point of view, the studying of back office integration is especially interesting because it offers the possibility for understanding how the integration of not only technology but also of separate information domains is influenced by information politics and by the specific institutional context in which each information domain is embedded and the power and interests that are related to these domains.

In this chapter we describe the integration problems between front office and back office on the one hand and among back offices as managing information domains, seen from the perspective of a political economy [8] on the other hand. What do the nature and dynamics of interorganisational domains mean for the development and implementation of e-government services and systems, and what methods and strategies are used to design and implement these services and systems? In addressing this question we focus on the interorganisational relations that are mobilised through the integration of various back office systems [9, 10]. Furthermore, we analyse existing e-government initiatives using a political economy view on information exchange, and draw some lessons in relation to the management and governance of these initiatives [2, 8, 11, 12].

In Section Two, we address the forms of back office interoperability and the types of integration and co-ordination problems that occur. Section Three describes how students of business administration and information systems normally address these issues. We reframe these thinking models by using another perspective in which the control over the gathering, exchange and access of information and information relations is seen as a powerful resource that should be protected and can be used to serve certain interests and positions. Dealing with information and information relations as political economies can be seen as a major governance challenge because of the confusing mixture of conflict and cooperation. In Section Four we turn to the Dutch setting of e-government. In the elaboration of e-government in the Netherlands (but also in other countries), the establishment of so-called authentic registrations play an important role since information is gathered and stored in one place but is used by several front and back offices at other places. We present a number of lessons derived from a comparative case study of the development and implementation of five of these registrations in the Netherlands that demonstrate how the integration of information domains has been managed. In Section Six we address the added value of an information ecology approach to the study of back office integration that tries to facilitate e-government and show how fruitful it can be to introduce process management as a complementary approach to project management.

2. The Interoperability of Front and Back Offices

In setting the stage, it is important to look at the interoperability and integration challenges that e-government faces. Several re-engineering models can be described, which focus on the relations between front and back office and between back offices [13]. In the traditional structure of government, a citizen is confronted with many offices, which all carry out specific functions in relation to a government services or products, like the distributions of permits, licenses or subsidies. A citizens, who want to starts a company has to shop at several government agencies, giving them the necessary information in order to get a number of approvals from, for instance, the Chamber of Commerce or the Tax and Customs

Administration. In the practice of public administration, several ways can be distinguished to improve the delivery of the quality of services.

The first way is re-engineering the process of service delivery by the introduction of a front office, in which several agencies work together. Citizens and business are given access to government services through one entry-point, regardless of their purpose, rather than through a multitude of information, contact and transaction points which reflect the functional fragmentation of government. If a person wants to start a company, he can go to this one-stop shop and all of the necessary information will be provided as well as the intake of all necessary information that this person has to provide. The front office distributes the information among the several back offices that actually handle the specific request. Sometimes this front office can be a physical one-stop shop, but it can also be a portal. In the latter case, a virtual front office is established on top of the existing back offices and very often this virtual front office represents an additional information, communication and transaction channel.

As the front office logic become more dominant, in terms of more intensive and demand-oriented customer services, the pressure on the back offices increases. Interoperability problems become more clear and they become an important incentive to develop and redesign internal structures, processes, routines and procedures which can actually meet the needs of the citizen as a 'whole person'. It will be necessary to re-organise these back offices - or even to integrate them - so that they can work together in a more efficient way. From this perspective we can observe a process of centralisation and integration of back offices that used a large number of front offices. Sometimes they use the front offices and communication and transaction channels of other organisations, sometimes they have their own front offices. An example is the Dutch organisation of housing subsidies, in which a centralised back office has a number of different intake points that are physically located at other organisations, like local government and housing companies. Also a housing subsidy portal has been established which is accessible through the Internet.

The centralisation of back offices is not the only possibility for improving interoperability. When back offices are part of a common business process in which these back offices operate as sequential links in a chain, one step could be the improvement of the exchange of information. Work-flow management and supply-chain management can provided interesting insights about the informational needs of the interfaces between two connecting parts in chain. The family allowance in Ireland is an example of integrated interorganisational work-flow management that improves the interaction between several back offices. Moreover, one can also use an intermediary service or an information broker. 'Clearing house' constructions could be used to improve the exchange of information between several back offices through the introduction of a neutral intermediary organisation or intermediary server, which is sometimes called the 'mid office'. In the Netherlands, RINIS is an example of a clearing house which supports the exchange of income and social security information between a number of public and semi-public organisations, like the Tax and Customs Administration and the Student Loans Agency. The success of RINIS is based on the idea that only the exchange procedures has been standardised, while the content of the information which is exchanged will not be subject of harmonisation and standardisation. The existing information domains are respected, enabling agencies to use their legacy technologies and data. Another example is the 'Kruispuntbank van de Sociale Zekerheid' in Belgium, which also operates as an information broker between a large number of agencies that are involved in the execution of social security legislation and the service delivery processes which follow from the execution of these rules. In handling environmental permits in Finland, an intermediary service has also been introduced.

Another possibility reaches even further. The distinction between front office and back offices in informational terms is blurred when front and back offices use the same database or system of coupled databases. The relevant data could be collected at one administrative point or in relation with one administrative procedure and could be used and re-used by several other agencies. Authentic registrations could play an important role in this kind of re-engineering e-government service. In another chapter on the emergence of virtual organisations in relation to e-government, this development has been described as the emergence of the concentric virtual organisation. Around a database of a number of coupled databases, concentric circles of organisational units and agencies can be discerned which use the same information in order to provide specific services.

This kind of back integration also offers interesting possibilities for developing pro-active service delivery. In Scandinavian countries the citizens income tax is based on existing systems that send pre-prepared tax forms by post or even the internet. Moreover, it can provide more sophisticated ways of self-service because citizens can have direct access to certain information and ask for specific services on the basis of this information.

3. Major Barriers

The following problems are the major barriers that have to be dealt with in order to re-design and integrate e-government front and back office operations [1, 14].

3.1 Coordination Problems

The idea that services can be accessed at one point implies that back offices should cooperate and integrate their working procedures and routines. However, the practice of e-government shows that several coordination problems occur:

- Coordination problems at the administrative level because several agencies with specific tasks and competences have to work together, but sometimes these tasks and competences can overlap or conflict. Moreover, it is not always clear what the jurisdiction of the front office is, which back office (s) is (are) responsible for the operations in the front office, and what the jurisdictions of the involved back offices are;
- Coordination problems at the level of the case to be handled. Sometimes it is quite clear how a specific case should be handled, but in other case it is not obvious which back office should deal with the case, or it is not evident if the front office has the competence to deal with the specific questions raised by a case. Integral case management is not always present;
- Coordination problems between specific information, communication and transaction channels, because each channel has its own procedures, routines and information systems. Sometimes there are coordination problems between the call centre, the virtual front office and the physical front office, because they do not share the same (updated) information, for instance, if a citizen uses several channels at different times in dealing with one question or case.

3.2 The Plurality of the Network of Back Offices

Not only conflicting jurisdictions, but also the number and plurality of back offices that are involved in e-government services, can be a major barrier. That is why it is important to understand the complexity and the degree of differentiation of the intra and/or interorganisational network of back offices which are involved in specific e-government services as well as the nature of the (inter)dependencies of the business processes between them.

3.3   The Two Sides of ICT

On the one hand, ICT is a force that facilitates change and the redesign of procedures and organisation of public service; on the other hand, ICT is very often a major source of resistance. For instance, back offices have their own (legacy) systems, have heavily invested in these systems and in the specific knowledge and experience which are necessary for the operation of these systems, and have developed all kinds of working and information processing procedures and routines in relation to these systems. The integration of these systems is more than technological integration; it is also integrating existing practices which can lead to obstruction.

3.4   Limits of Information Gathering

Service provision, especially as it is related to approaching citizens as 'whole person', depends on the gathering, processing and combining several kinds of data and using several kinds of data systems. In some cases a specific back office is not able or, due to legal obligations, forbidden to gather additional information or to combine information which comes from other back offices, i.e. using data mining and data coupling methods and techniques. These limits may prohibit the development of new kind of electronic services, especially pro-actives services.

Interoperability problems can also refer to semantic interoperability problems. Back offices have to agree on the ontology of the services that they together provide in the front office. They have to develop common identifiers for the specific target groups and the kind of needs of these groups. Moreover, they have to develop common data definitions. For instance in the Netherlands, the income of a citizen has been defined in almost 200 different ways due to the large variety of laws and regulations in which income has been defined.

3.5   The Culture of Interoperability

The last barrier refers to the fact that each back office has its own culture, its own frame of reference and its own practices and 'rules' that guide the behaviour and choice of the people in the back office. Moreover, there is a cultural tension between those who work in the front office and those who work in the back office. One reason is that individuals in front offices experience the actual needs of citizens and companies on a daily basis, while these needs and problems are de-humanised and abstract problems for people in the back office. The nature of human resources, in terms of practical knowledge, experience and education (human capital) may also differ and could lead to integration problems because integration challenges how individuals are accustomed to doing certain things.

In this chapter we have looked at possible relations between front and back office and among back offices, and we have analysed the major barriers that obstruct the cooperation and integration of these offices. The next question is, how to obtain a better understanding of the impact of these barriers in relation to the need for cooperation in order to realise a seamless government?

4.   Interoperability and the Political Economy of Information Exchange

A large number of the barriers that have just been described relate to the integration of information domains in a network of back offices. Each back office can be seen as a specific and unique information domain, and the major challenge for e-government is to establish new information exchange and communication relations between them, to improve or even redesign these existing relations between them. An information domain can be described as a sphere of influence, ownership and control over information – its specification, format, exploitation and interpretation [10]. An information domain can be said to exist where significant control over access has been established, so that information is withheld or surrendered on terms, or in a form, negotiated by dominant actors. Thus, the existence of an information domain is signalled by a) a break in flows of information, b) compartmentalisation of information resources, c) idiosyncrasy of information specifications and d) the hegemony of specific discourses that shape information and influence in its creation and interpretation [10]. The result is that information domains determine, reflect and reinforce the structure and distribution of critical sets of information resources in government. E-government challenges the distribution of these critical sets, and thus the information domains that are addressed by e-government services as a result of the need to standardise, formalise and integrate these domains. The introduction of e-government often implies that established information domains are being challenged because the boundaries between them begin to blur and break down, or even because new domains emerge in the slipstream of these services. Often a battle of back offices is the result, and this further results in a very complex mixture of conflict and cooperation that emerges when organisations start exchanging information across traditional organisation boundaries [7, 8, 15]. This implies that we should leave behind a strictly instrumental and technological point of view. Instead we should be aware of information politicking.

4.1   Information Politicking

Information politicking is not specific to e-government, but the integration of back offices will be a major incentive for this kind of strategic and tactical behaviour in which back offices try to protect their interests and positions of power. Several examples of information politicking have been described in the literature, and they are situated in the public as well as the private sector (e.g. [6, 7, 16]).

A private sector illustration is the TransLease information system, an electronic commerce system owned by Cap Gemini and used by a thousand British repair agents working for seven vehicle leasing and contract hire companies [17]. TransLease uses standardised data formats throughout the network (which also enshrine the 'rules of trade') as the backbone of the system in order to simplify the processing of auditing invoices. In practice, that actual use of the system proved to be far below expectations. An evaluation showed that the TransLease system did not provide the envisaged mutual benefits to its participants: "[a] dominant theme for repair agent complaints was their perception of an 'unfair' balance of power, which meant they felt that lease companies would tie them into a system that would reinforce and amplify existing power structures" [17: 10].

A public sector illustration is the Criminal Justice System in the United Kingdom [10]. The UK has heavily decentralised and compartmentalised criminal justice agencies, including for instance, the police, the probation service and the magistrates courts. Early work on automated support centred on an elaborate dataflow model that showed the benefits of a new information system. It was soon clear, though, that the costs and benefits were unevenly divided among the parties involved, and that the specific cultures and professional norms of the various agencies were not reflected in operational methods and information management priorities. Therefore, a more piecemeal, incremental approach was chosen, in which various professional groups (lawyers, police officers, probation officers and prison officers) were allowed idiosyncratic discourses embedded in distinctive data definitions and standards, yet these distinctive domains were very selectively connected using EDI interfaces and e-mail links.

Beynon-Davies [18] describes an attempt to develop a generalised model of healthcare data to be used for information exchange in the British National Health Service (NHS). Despite substantial efforts, the data model was severely resisted and has never actually been implemented. Although the development of the data model was originally portrayed as a neutral and technocratic exercise, the participating organisations very actively opposed the data model because it raised unforeseen, partly unintended and very fundamental questions about accountability within the network of cooperating organisations. Markus [4] refers to these kinds of situations as attempts to 'ferret out how the knaves are doing in the trenches'.

The TransLease, CJS and the NHS cases are examples of situations in which the exchange of information using information systems that cross organisational boundaries resulted in politicking, hoarding of information, sabotaging interorganisational information systems, et cetera. These phenomena have also been observed in specific e-government initiatives where information exchange in back offices resulted in data wars [1, 19]. How can we understood, or even manage this information politicking? In general three approaches can be discerned [8, 11].

4.2   A Project Management View on Information Exchange

In the world of system development and management consulting, the management of (standardizing) information exchange has often been seen as a challenge in terms of a project management approach. Typical for project management is that a temporary endeavour is undertaken in order to create some sort of system architecture (including a standardised data format), terms of use and information handling procedures as the backbones of the information exchange. Goals are fixed and formalised, and implementation is carried out in a step-by-step manner. The step-by-step manner is a way to identify results to be accomplished throughout the period of time the project lasts, and thus a way to reduce risks. Furthermore, a project management approach implies a rather centralised management approach. It is the project manager or a supervisory group that tries to implement the project in time and according to the goals. Strong leadership is important.

More recently, in recommendations made by the OECD [1] while studying e-government initiatives in several countries, a strong plea for an intensive project management approach in combination with strong leadership has been made in order to improve the cooperation between back offices.

Intuitively, however, in developing interorganisational information systems, it should be clear that a wide variety of interests has to be dealt with -- and this is not an easy task using typical project management techniques. We discern two approaches from the literature that deal with the variety of interests and the plurality of actors that are involved in the development, implementation and use of interorganisational ICT projects.

4.3   A Political View on Information Exchange

Core to the TransLease and CJS illustrations is the notion of a delicate balance between 'resource dependence' of organisations in networks and the nourishment of organisations' informational autonomy [8]. According to resource dependence theory (e.g. [20]), organisations in networks may be willing to set up and use information systems that cross organisational boundaries in order to gain access to information controlled by other organisations, but they may be unwilling to comply with arrangements that may not be designed to suit them (i.e., information handling procedures, terms of use and data models). In fact, in information partnerships, according to resource dependence theory, every organisations strives to optimise its self-interest by (1) minimising their dependence on other organisations and (2) maximising the dependence of other organisations on them. Consequently, standardisation (for example, of data definitions) is an especially sensitive subject since it touches upon culturally or professionally accepted procedures that may not be given up easily. Bellamy illustrates this by stating that attempts to exchange information across organisational boundaries "(...) not only reflect the structure of information domains, but in so doing reflect, legitimate and re-produce the discourses of powerful groups, validate their ways of steering and thinking, and give tangible force for to their influence on organisational life" [10: 299].

According to resource dependence theory, information exchange, and especially standardisation, may result in shifts in power balances between organisations. These shifts may even ultimately result in organisations losing their reasons to exist. So it is not surprising that organisations are very cautious in (unconditionally) exchanging information across organisational boundaries. It is unlikely that information exchange in back offices is an exception to this general observation.

4.4   An Economic View on Information Exchange

Although resource dependency theory provides an explanation for the organisation-political struggle surrounding the development and use of information systems that cross organisational boundaries, decision makers or actors in general are usually less realistically depicted as aberrant managers or deviant technologists, focusing on political aspects, unconditionally nurturing organisational autonomy and ignoring effectiveness and efficiency. The politicking in relation to interorganisational information systems, however, is capable of being understood in other ways, among other things in ways that also include aspects of efficiency. In order to show how a more sophisticated understanding could throw more light on the topics under investigation here, we discuss a body of knowledge complementary to resource dependence theory: (information) property rights theory.

Property rights theory provides an analysis of behaviour of individuals with respect to assets (including information assets), or behaviour of organisations in G2G networks with respect to information assets [21, 22]. Crucial is the assumption of bounded rationality; in this context, bounded rationality refers to the impossibility of formalising all kinds of behaviour in contracts that encompass all future contingencies. If we regard information systems as information assets, it is possible to analyse behaviour with respect to these kinds of information systems with property rights theory.

In property rights theory, the notion of 'ownership' is emphasised. Full ownership of information systems, for example, involves the right to use an information system, to modify it with quality-enhancing or cost-saving features, and to appropriate the benefits of these adaptations. Using a neoclassical line of reasoning, it can be shown that an asset owner has intensive incentives to perform well.

Because of bounded rationality, there will always be an 'incompleteness' of contracts, implying that there will always be residual property rights not covered in a contract. The institution that allocates these residual rights of is ownership, and hence, the owner is 'residual claimant' [21]. This situation occurs in a network of organisations when one organisation fully owns a central database while other organisations use it (that is, look in the database and/or enter information into the database) and contribute in the costs of the system through an agreed-upon lease contract. Such a separation of ownership and actual use has important consequences for behaviour with respect to information assets, which can be characterised by the phrase 'rental cars are driven less carefully than cars driven by their owners' [21].

For the specific situation described previously, it is relevant that the grand designs of information systems that cross organisational boundaries confronts participating organisations' with an attenuation of property rights, and hence, their incentives to perform well are partly mitigated. This mitigation of incentives results in subtle intangible costs of low effort that will eventually appear as distorted, missing, or unusable data. The line of reasoning can be summarised as follows: the more the sense of 'ownership' is diminished, the less intense incentives will be. Consequently, the level of investments in the interorganisational information system will typically be lower, which in turn affects the functionality, profitability, and eventually the viability of information sharing.

4.5   Synthesis: The Political Economy of Information Exchange

After reviewing both resource dependence theory and information property rights theory, some light is shed on the specific phenomena in the TransLease, NHS and CJS cases, and probably on issues of project management in developing interorganisational information systems in general. The standardisation of data definitions and data standards that is pursued in order to exchange information across organisational boundaries may be geared to the requirements of some organisations participating in an organisational network, but not necessarily to the requirements of all organisations. In terms of resource dependence theory, standardisation may intensify existing dependencies and enshrine these dependencies in the technology. In terms of information property rights theory, standardisation of data definitions and data standards can be conceived as a mitigation of property rights with respect to the information system. Consequently, participants are less inclined to invest in the system and to enhance the information system with cost-saving or quality-enhancing features, and eventually such a diminishment of incentives results in less profitable, less functional and even less viable interorganisational information systems. A typical symptom of lack of incentives is poor data quality, resulting from under-investment in human and technical capital.

Both theoretical streams may be used to question the typical project management approach (which is, as has been stated above, readily defensible from a more or less naïve policy development and/or ICT system development point of view). Both resource dependence theory as well as information property rights theory indicate that typical project management techniques, sub-optimal incentives and organisations striving to optimise their information autonomy result in obstruction of decision making and even in data wars. Typical solutions, however, are provided neither resource dependence theory nor in property rights theory.

The integration of back offices implies that one has to recognise the plurality of interests and domains that are at stake and the loss of autonomy that accompanies this integration process. How do back offices deal with these possible threats? In the next section, a number of lessons will be described. They show us under which conditions it is possible to organise cooperation and collective action that leads to the integration of separate information domains.

5.   Authentic Registrations and Back Office Integration: Some Lessons Learned

In the development of e-government in the Netherlands, some attention has been given to the role of authentic registration in the integration of back offices. Very basic information has been stored in these registrations, such as the name and address of citizens. In the practice of many local and central agencies, this kind of data is not only used very often, but each agency gathers this kind of information itself, according to its own definitions and wishes. The result is that a citizen or a company, when confronted with those agencies involved in the handling of a request – for instance a license or subsidy- has to produce the same information several times with only slight differences. The main principle of authentic registrations is that data that have been gathered once at the source can be used again and again by other organisations for different purposes. For instance, the Dutch Municipal Register of Citizens' Residential Data (the so-called GBA system, which is called *Gemeentelijke Basis Administratie* in Dutch) is an authentic registration in which name, address, date of birth, gender, nationality, et cetera of residents in the Netherlands are recorded. When the father or mother registers the name etc. of the newly born child, residential information will automatically be sent to other, public and private, organisations. One of these agencies is the Social Security Bank (Sociale Verzekeringsbank). On the basis of the GBA –information, this agency automatically grants the parents of a new born child a specific allowance. It will not trouble the parents with the necessary paper work. The regional vaccination agency will also get this information, and on the basis of this information parents will be periodically asked to come to the local health agency to vaccinate their children.

The exchange of this basic information not only stimulates pro-active forms of public service delivery, it also allows major efficiency improvements and process innovations. However, a necessary condition is that agencies which use this residential data accept that the data stored in the GBA system is authentic, that is reliable information and that they will not gather this same information again.

In Dutch administration, several authentic registrations can be distinguished. Sometimes their authenticity has been established in legalisation like the GBA, sometimes the users of these registrations have been convinced of the reliability of the information and of the advantages of sharing this information, that they perceive such a registration as an authentic registration [23]. In most cases, user conditions have been formalised in multilateral agreements, like an 'information statute' The ownership of authentic registrations has been attributed to specific organisations which will be responsible for (and have an interest in) ensuring the quality of data. These specific organisations can be regarded as 'information owners'. Inversely, the authentic registration can grant other organisations (designated) property rights by means of interchange agreements, but they are by definition 'residual claimants', implying that the right to allocate rights not explicitly covered by an interchange agreement resides with the information owner.

In this section we present a number of lessons learned that relate to which factors influence the shared development of the authentic registrations. It concerns the following registrations in Dutch public administration [23]:

-   The already mentioned Dutch Municipal Register of Citizens' Residential Data (GBA), which is a decentralised register where information is stored according to a well-defined format. The register is to be used and is partly administered by more than 500 municipalities (they own the register), while the data is exchanged with and used by more than 300 public and private organisations.
-   Dutch Vehicle Registration (NKR). The goal of the registration was to identify owners of licensed vehicles and vessels. Uses can be found in the fields of taxation, liability, criminal prosecution, traffic safety projects, and environmental policy. The Centre for Vehicle Technology and Information, which is a quasi-autonomous agency, owns the registration.
-   Emission Registration, which is register in which data is stored concerning levels of air, water, soil and noise pollution. Companies, local and regional governments, water

boards, agencies, public research institutions and ministries used this kind information for several purposes. The Ministry of Environmental Affairs owns the registration.
- Fiscal Income Registration. The Tax and Customs Administration owns the registration and the data is used by a large number of public and semi-public organisations like the Social Security Bank, the Students Loans Administrations, the social security departments of the municipalities and the Housing Subsidy Administration.
- Credit Loans Registry, which gathers data on the credit worthiness of citizens and compares information when citizens apply for (new) loans or mortgages. This is a private registration that was established by the financial world, but it has legal basis in public law and has important public effects. Not only private but also public organisations use the data. Moreover, public agencies have recently entrusted the organisation that administers the register with other public registers.

The central question in this cross case analysis has been to look at the development process of these registers and to identify those factors that could explain why these organisations were able to define a common practice of back office integration that has led to successful interorganisational information systems. Thereby, an inductive research approach has been used. In addition to studying documents, we also asked stakeholders to identify the factors that account for the success of these registrations.

5.1   It is the Content that Brings Together

Initially, when discussing the possibility of a common registration, it is important not to start with a discussion about competencies and jurisdictions of the organisations involved. Also a discussion about the distribution of costs and benefits among the possible owners and users of the register should be avoided. It was frequently stated that it is important to look at possible common goals or complementary interests. The content of the problem to be tackled has been the major incentive for organisations to explore the need for cooperation. Moreover, it is the nature of the problem that shows how the organisations involved have become interdependent on each another. The recognition of interdependency was the major motive for cooperation, which can be illustrated by the Income Registration.

The practice of Dutch administration was that agencies that had a role in the execution of income related rules and legislation checked if the provided income information was accurate after, for instance, a subsidy, an allowance or a remission of debts had already been given. However, checking this information at the beginning of the application process has several advantages. First, it could improve customer satisfaction because in a preliminary phase it is clear if additional information should be provided. Second, additional control procedures could be eliminated, cost efficiency could be realised and the execution process could be simplified. Third, fraud could also be detected more easily. However, these advantages could only be optimised if agencies involved were willing to share information from a common pool system. Because the information of the Income Registration of the Tax Administration was needed by all of those other agencies and the information was not corrupted, other agencies were willing to use the fiscal information of the Tax Administration.

The ability to recognise interdependency opens the door for defining 'win-win' situations. Win-win situations played an important role in the development and implementation of all of the registers studied. Credit loan companies have opposing interests because they are competitors, but they also have also a common interest: to check if people who apply for a loan are able to meet the interest and mortgage conditions and to detect them in an earlier stage before the loan has been granted. A corrupted credit system can damage the economy and the integrity of the financial system, which is a public as well as a private interest.

5.2   *The Continuous Recognition of Interdependency*

The development and implementation of a register is a process in which several rounds can be discerned and which also influences the recognition of interdependencies; rounds are played in closely and loosely linked arenas (later on, we refer to this notion). But also during the development process it is important to reconfirm earlier defined interdependencies and to identify new and emerging interdependencies. For instance, the GBA started with clear boundaries between those activities that should be done by the Dutch municipalities and those activities that should be done by the GBA project organisation at a central level. The project organisation should focus on an information exchange network between the municipalities and the other client organisations as well as on the definition of the data format, while the municipalities should focus on the implementation of the GBA application at the local level and the improvement of the quality of the local residential information. But a first test showed that the quality of data at the local source was rather poor and that the necessary knowledge and competencies that were needed to use the application was lacking. Still, both parties had a common interest: a prosperous implementation of the system, which was related to a legally fixed deadline. The municipalities accepted the help of the project organisation to improve the quality of the information and accepted the necessary education given by the project organisation. The consequences of the municipalities accepting the assistance of the project organisation led to an extension of the jurisdiction and influence of the central level. At the beginning of the debate about the necessity of the GBA system, the safeguarding of the balance of power between the local and central levels was a rather delicate issue, but the recognition of these new interdependencies led to a blurring of boundaries between the central and local levels and new patterns of cooperation emerged.

Thus, during the development and implementation process, new interdependencies should be recognised that could lead to a redefinition of established practices and rules. If organisations are unable or unwilling to understand the dynamics of this process of interdependency recognition, the development of a registration could be obstructed.

5.3   *Trust*

Again, no data or evidence

The ability to recognise interdependency has everything to do with trust or the lack of trust. Analytically, the nature of a problem can make these interdependencies transparent, but sometimes organisations and individuals are unable to see these interdependencies because their perception is blurred by negative experiences from the past in their relationship. A minimum of trust is therefore a necessary condition to create a shared understanding about the added value of a register that connects several back offices. The Emission Registration illustrates this. At the start of the registration, a discussion about the distribution of costs and benefits was avoided because this could harm the emerging trust between the organisations involved. There was a silent and informal agreement not to discuss the subject because each organisation was able to benefit from the new system. But the established trust of the relations between the organisations was put under a lot of pressure when certain parties tried to change the playing rules. A number of the involved agencies had become (semi-) privatised, like the Topographical Agency, and began to charge money for the delivery of specific information, which in turn stimulated other organisations to ask for money. This ultimately led to a break down in trust and commitment.

5.4 Managing Rationalities in Different Arenas

It is important to understand the development and implementation of a register from more than a one-dimensional perspective - which is sometimes dominant in an information systems point of view or a project management point of view. Establishing registrations implies the management of different rationalities that compete with each other. Each rationality stresses the importance of other critical factors that are not always complementary. At the very least, the following rationalities are important: the political, legal, organisational, economic and the (information) technological rationality. The development and implementation of an authentic register can be situated in a complex and dynamic system of push and pull factors that can be derived from these rationalities that can sometimes conflict and can sometimes re-enforce each other.

For instance, for the Centre for Vehicle Technology and Information (in Dutch: RDW), the implementation of the Vehicle Registration implied that the existing organisation and the existing procedures would be abolished. And the implementation of the Residential Information Register (GBA) challenged the existing culture of the municipalities. The GBA offered the possibility of improving the quality of public services. This was the organisational rationality that was dominant in those registers.

From a political perspective, it is important to look for political support. The success of the Residential Information Register and the Vehicle Register can be explained in part by the support that the responsible minister gave. Moreover, managing the delicate balance of power between the responsibilities of the central and local levels in the development of the GBA residential information system was very important during the development of this register. Another important political issue is the recognition that the control over the access and distribution of information and information relations is an important power resource and that changes could imply shifts in power. For instance, the fact that a large number of agencies uses the Fiscal Income Register of the Tax Administration has strengthened the already strong position of this agency. However, other agencies accepted this because the added value and the reliability of the register have compensated this loss of control. Otherwise, the same Tax Administration could not accept the fact that they would be dependent on the information provided by the Vehicle Register. At this moment, the Tax Administration still has its own vehicle registration information system.

Recognizing the multi-rationality of the establishment of authentic registers enables us - beforehand and through the eyes of the various perspectives - to identify possible risks. The Centre for Vehicle Technology and Information recognised at a very earlier stage that the implementation of a 'common pool' data system was more than managing the implementation of a database. The whole project was seen as organisation development project. So, they gave certain key people who knew the culture of the organisation and were respected by the other members of the organisation a place in the project organisation rather then selecting people based on their professional (ICT or in this case also legal) knowledge.

The complexity of the development of these registers that connects several back offices becomes even bigger if we add the notion of multiple arenas to the idea of multiple rationalities. Arenas are sometimes closely linked together; sometimes they are loosely coupled; arenas have some of the same players, but they also have different players; new players enter the arena while other players leave the arena.

Six arenas could be distinguished in the GBA case. The first arena addressed the legislation process on which the implementation of the system was based. The second arena was the development of the logical and functional model of the system. Some tension arose between these two arenas that were closely coupled , because of two conflicting rationalities: the frames of references of the lawyers did not always match with the frames of reference of the system developers. In the end, a solution was found in the development of the legal framework that took place in parallel with the development of the system itself. The third arena was the arena of the development of the exchange network. The fourth arena was the arena of the approximately 600 municipalities that would implement the system at the local level. The fifth arena was the arena of approximately 300 other organisations that would also be using the data that were collected by the municipalities. The sixth arena was the political arena, in which a discussion took place about the contents of the legislation and how central values should be protected, like safeguarding privacy and safeguarding the autonomy of the municipalities.

The interaction within a specific arena can be described in terms of games, played in several rounds; sometimes these games were played in more than one arena. For instance, in the local implementation arena and the arena that was focussed on the description of the functional data model, an important issue was how to protect the autonomy of the municipalities to choose their own software programmes and how to reduce the interventions of the GBA project organisation to a minimum during the local implementation of the GBA system. This question referred to a bigger issue: there were disputes with respect to whether there should be a centralised system or a decentralised system. When the decision was taken to implement a decentralised system, there were more or less constant quarrels over control and ownership issues with respect to several aspects of the system. As a result, the composition of project teams changed as individual members left these groups and others joined them. Eventually, in the process of waxing and waning, a solution was found by granting municipalities control and ownership over the data (municipalities were responsible for the acquisition, maintenance and dispersion of data), whereas central government was responsible for the system level (i.e. the development of a data model, on the basis of which eventually 15 system suppliers developed applications). During the pilot phase, there were serious doubts about the quality of the local residential data. If the data was corrupted and would be exchanged with other municipalities and other organisations, the whole system would be corrupted. How could this data be improved without strong central interventions? In dealing with this question, the old issue of the balance of power between the local and central levels returned to the agenda in several arenas.

5.5   Managing the Political Agenda

During the development and implementation of a registration, it is important to be aware of the changing political and societal agenda. Agenda management and management of the political environment is an important issue. The changing of the political agenda implies that it could be necessary to look for new arguments that could legitimise the necessity of the registration, which could imply that new stakeholders enter the arena and new coalitions emerge. For instance, at the start of the GBA project, privacy was an important issue, but during the development, the political agenda changed and the pursuit of fraud and the misuse of social security benefits became more important which has altered the view on the added value of the GBA.

5.6   The Allocation of Costs and Benefits

A major issue is the allocation of costs and benefits among the most important stakeholders. Who benefits from the registration and who will have to bear the costs? An important barrier for cooperation is an unjust distribution of costs and benefits, which leads to a concentration of the costs on one party while another party collects all the benefits. For stakeholders it is important for costs and benefits to be in balance. Moreover it is important to understand that this equilibrium can be distorted. In the Emission registration, as mentioned earlier, this balance was distorted through the privatisation of one agency, which led to the development of a system of prices that the so-called Topographical Agency wanted to use for the delivery of data for the registration while other agencies did not charge for the delivery of relevant data.

Another issue is to look for other ways of compensation than financial compensation. In doing so it is important to have a rather open mind in the definition of relevant costs and benefits. Not only monetary costs and benefits should be considered; it is important to include qualitative costs and benefits as well. In the GBA case there was originally a distortion between the costs and large investments that the municipalities had to make and the large benefits and rather small investments of the other organisations that would use the data, like the Tax and Customs Administration. The municipalities not only had to install new information systems but they also needed to invest in measures to improve the quality of data, in changing procedures and routines and in improving the necessary skills. However, during the process of implementation, municipalities had become aware of the fact that the GBA could be a major incentive to improve the quality and modernisation of public service delivery and the pursuit of fraud, which led to reassessment of costs and benefits.

5.7   Seeking Continuous Commitment

Due to changes in the political environments that requires new forms of legitimisation, the changing perceptions of costs and benefits and the changing interests that are at stake, it is important to look for continuous commitment. In the Vehicle Registration and GBA, the political commitment of the responsible minister was rather important. Moreover, it was important to develop an ingenious network of discussion and consultation groups. For instance, in the development of the so-called EVA system, which registers bank and insurance fraud and which is exploited by the Credit Registration, 27 representatives of relevant interest groups have been heard on a regular basis.

6.   Conclusion: Managing Political Economies in the Information Ecology

Back-office integration implies the integration of rather autonomous information domains. Cooperation is not a given because of the interest that are at stake and the loss of power and control that accompanies these integration and standardisation processes. That is why back-office integration can be understood as managing information domains as political economies, in which competition, negotiation, exchange of resources and the use of power are important features of the dynamics in these economies. We have also discussed some experiences with the development of registers in the Netherlands which show that back-office integration can work if we recognise a number of driving forces that go beyond the classical project management approach that is dominant in the information systems world. It is important to complement this project management approach with an approach that is called 'process management' [12]. In relation to back office integration, a process management approach can be described as facilitating a process in which actors created a shared understanding about the necessity of back-office integration, based the recognition of interdependency in several rounds and in several – closely and loosely linked - arenas. However, this shared understanding is not assumed, but should be developed in a process of negotiation and consensus building, in which actors try to define such a dynamic balance of (qualitative and quantitative) costs and benefits (in the short but also in the long run) so that a 'win-win' situation emerges.

Table 9 sketches the main characteristics and differences between a project management and process management approach of back-office integration.

Table 9: Project- and Process Management Characteristics (adapted from [12])

	Project Management	**Process Management**
Activities	Unique	Multiple
Goal(s)	Singular, under shared regime	Various, under shared regime
Orientation	Short term	Long term
Culture	Heterogeneous	Heterogeneous, ambiguous and dynamic
Organisation	Temporary project organisation	Interorganisational interactions to coordinate behaviour
Environment	Uncertainty with respect to performance, costs, schedule	Ambiguity with respect to performance, costs, schedule
Conventions and procedures	Affects existing conventions and procedures	Seeks new conventions and procedures

Our research shows that the use of process management techniques in the development of interorganisational information systems (and: in the integration of back offices) provides a promising perspective on the problem of integrating the back office of e-government initiatives. Central to the idea of process management of (interorganisational) ICT is that managing interorganisational ICT requires attention to processes of 'consensus building' and 'cooperative behaviour' rather than that of a step-by-step development of an ICT architecture. Since the process of 'consensus building' and 'establishing cooperative behaviour' is hard to achieve beforehand, process management's goal-seeking behaviour (within general constraints) is more appealing than project management's goal formalisation.

However, one has to be careful not to overemphasise the differences between project and process management approaches of back-office integration. Once consensus has been established about the goals and content of the system, it is possible to use a more project management-oriented approach, but at the same time (as the research in the previous sections illustrates) consensus will not last forever, which could imply that a process management approach would be necessary to define new consensus. Hence, process and project management approaches alternate.

This exposé about the political economy of back-office integration shows us how important it is to consider the network of actors, their interests, the resources they can mobilise, the strategies they employ, the information domains they control and the dependencies and interdependencies between them. The issue of back-office integration especially addresses the political dimension of the information ecology concept and show us how the technological environment and the political environment of e-government co-evolves, but not only from an organic perspective as Nardi and O'Day [24] suggest.

Interoperability issues between the front and back offices and among back offices can be made visible from an arena-perspective in which actors and domains meet each other and try to protect their own interests and frames of references. Struggle, competition and negotiation are thus vital elements in the information ecology of e-government. Moreover, this chapter show us that these arenas are local and functional arenas, closely related to the particular dimensions of a specific policy issue. The solutions that emerge are rather contingent outcomes of the closely and loosely coupled games between specific actors in several kinds of arenas. This chapter also shows that back-office integration can also be seen as managing different rationalities – political, technological, organisational, economic and legal - that go even further than the interaction between different subsystems that Davenport and Prusak [25] have discerned. Davenport describes the information ecology as the co-evolution between the technological, political and cultural subsystem of an organisation in which ICT has been introduced. In sum, we can conclude that studying back-office integration as one of the cornerstones of the realisation of e-government shows us the importance of an information-ecological approach, but it even shows that the content of the information-ecology concept as has been described by Nardi and O'Day [24] and Davenport and Prusak [25] is even too narrow because it pays too little attention to the political economy-aspect of the integration of information domains.

References

1. OECD, *The e-Government Imperative*. 2003, Paris: OECD.
2. Bekkers, V.J.J.M., *Voorbij de virtuele organisatie? Over de bestuurskundige betekenis van virtuele variëteit, contingentie en parallel organiseren*. 2001, Den Haag: Elsevier Bedrijfsinformatie.
3. Wimmer, M., R. Traunmueller, and K. Lenk. *Electronic Business Invading the Public Sector*. in *HICSS*. 2001. Hawaii: IEEE Press.
4. Markus, M.L., *Politics and MIS Implementation*. Communications of the ACM, 1983. 26(6): p. 430-440.
5. Davenport, T.H., R.G. Eccles, and L. Prusak, *Information Politics*. Sloan Management Review, 1992. 34(1): p. 53-65.
6. Knights, D. and F. Murray, *Politics and Pain in Managing Information Technology: A Case Study in Insurance*. Organization Studies, 1992. 13(2): p. 211-228.
7. Kumar, K. and H.G. van Dissel, *Sustainable collaboration: managing conflict and collaboration in interorganizational information systems*. MIS Quarterly, 1996. 20(3): p. 279-300.
8. Homburg, V.M.F., *The Political Economy of Information Management (A Theoretical and Empirical Study on the Development and Use of Interorganizational Information Systems),*. 1999, Groningen: SOM.
9. Bellamy, C. and J. Taylor, *Governing in the Information Age*. 1998, Buckingham: Open University Press.
10. Bellamy, C., *ICTs and Governance: Beyond Policy Networks? The Case of the Criminal Justice System*, in *Public Administration in an Information Age*, I.T.M. Snellen and W.B.J.H. van de Donk, Editors. 1998, IOS Press: Amsterdam. p. 293-306.
11. Homburg, V.M.F. and V.J.J.M. Bekkers. *The Back-Office of E-Government (Managing Information Domains as Political Economies)*. in *HICSS*. 2002. Waikoloa Village, Waikoloa, Hawaii: IEEE Press.
12. de Bruijn, J.A., E.F. ten Heuvelhof, and R.J. In 't Veld, *Procesmanagement, over procesontwerp en besluitvorming*. 1998, Schoonhoven: Academic Service.

13. Kubicek, H., *The Relationship Between Government and Citizens: Key Policy and Research Issues.*, in *Paper prepared for the IPTS/EU workshop on E-Government in the EU in 2010: Key policy and research challenges Workshop, IPTS Seville (Spain), 4-5 March 2004.* 2004: Bremen.
14. van Venrooij, A., *Nieuwe vormen van interorganisationele publieke dienstverlening.* 2002, Delft: Technical University of Delft.
15. Bekkers, V.J.J.M., *Wiring Public Organizations and Changing Organizational Juridisctions.*, in *Public Administration in an Information Age*, I.T.M. Snellen and W.B.H.J.v.d. Donk, Editors. 1998, IOS Press: Amsterdam. p. 57-77.
16. Cunningham, C. and C. Tynan, *Electronic Trading, Inter-organizational Systems and the Nature of Buyer-Seller Relationships: The Need for a Network Perspective.* Journal of Information Management, 1993. **13**(1): p. 3-28.
17. Allen, D., et al., *Trust, power and interorganizational information systems: the case of the electronic trading community TransLease.* Information systems journal, 2000. **10**(1): p. 21-40.
18. Beynon-Davies, P., *Information Management in the British National Health Service: The Pragmatics of Strategic Data Planning.* International Journal of Information Management, 1994. **14**(2): p. 84-94.
19. Teicher, J. and N. Dow, *E-Government in Australia, Promise and Progress.* The Information Polity, 2002. **7**: p. 231-246.
20. Pfeffer, J. and G.R. Salancik, *The external control of organizations.* 1978, New York: Harper & Row.
21. Van Alstyne, M., E. Brynjolfsson, and S. Madnick, *Why Not One Big Database? Principles for Data Ownership.* Decision Support Systems, 1995. **15**(4): p. 267-284.
22. Bakos, J.Y. and B. Nault, *Ownership and Investment in Electronic Networks.* Information System Research, 1997. **8**(4): p. 321-341.
23. Bekkers, V.J.J.M., *Schaken op meerdere borden - Over procesmanagement en de ontwikkeling van basisregistraties binnen de publieke sector.* Management & Informatie, 2002. **3**: p. 23-34.
24. Nardi, B.A. and V.L. O'Day, *Information Ecologies: Using Technology with Heart.* 1999, Cambridge (MA): The MIT Press.
25. Davenport, T.H., *Information Ecology: Mastering the information and knowledge environment.* 1997, Oxford: Oxford University Press.

The Information Ecology of E-Government
V.J.J.M. Bekkers and V.M.F. Homburg (Eds.)
IOS Press, 2005

Digital Visions – The Role of Politicians in Transition

Birgit JÆGER

Roskilde University, Department of Social Sciences,
Universitetsvej 1, PO Box 260, DK 4000 Roskilde, Denmark

Abstract. The concrete configuration of E-government institutionalises communications between the public sector and external actors. In an age when public sector regulation is increasingly based on networks including the participation of an array of various external actors, communication with these actors attains considerable political significance. The manner with which this communication becomes institutionalised is therefore important. At present, administrators are primarily determining the concrete design of e-government, resulting in a democratic deficit. This chapter focuses on how the actual role of the politician gets in the way of politicians' active participation in the design of e-government. The chapter thus describes the conceptions of the role of the politicians and conceptions of technology, respectively, and presents reflections concerning how the modification of these conceptions can help pave the way for the participation of politicians in decision-making processes regarding technology.

1. Introduction

This chapter stems from a larger research project entitled: "Roles in Transition – Politicians and administrators between hierarchy and network", in which I have examined the interaction between the development of governance, e-government and roles in the public administration. This study was grounded in earlier research on the use of ICT in public administration, where I had observed that the administrators dominate the development of e-government [1]. Accordingly, the politicians do not relate to the concrete decisions about the development and use of this technology. That the politicians do not regard this as being their responsibility could be explained in light of the circumstance that politicians do not perceive involvement in technical matters as being part of their role as politicians. To what degree does the conception of the role of politicians pose a barrier to their participation in the development of e-government? This chapter represents an attempt at providing analysis in response to this question.

I will begin by focusing on how politicians generally conceive of their role in connection with the development and utilisation of technology, which corresponds to their conception of technology. In the following section I will therefore focus on a very widespread conception of what technology is; the technology-politics relationship is subsequently discussed on this background.

The general and theoretical considerations pertaining to role conceptions among politicians and conceptions about technology will henceforth serve as the basis for an empirical analysis of how the politicians in a selected municipality regard their role in connection with the development of e-government.

2.   The Role of the Politician – the Relationship to Technology

Hesitancy among politicians towards becoming involved in the development of technology and determining the means by which it is utilised in administration can largely owe to their role conception, i.e. they do not perceive involvement in such concrete, technical tasks as being a part of their role. I will elaborate on this argument; first by accounting for how I employ the role concept, thereafter by analysing how the distribution of roles among politicians and administrators serves as a barrier for the involvement of politicians in decisions concerning technology.

2.1   The Role Concept

Roles are a fundamental element in all societies. We draw upon them as fixed reference points, making it possible to navigate amongst the social relations we all engage in. Without such roles, it would become necessary to define our counterparts and ourselves every time we met a new person. Roles exist in all aspects of social life; the individual person assumes a multitude of roles simultaneously, e.g. mother, wife, daughter, sister, neighbour, citizen, voter, colleague, automobile owner, user of services provided by a welfare society, user of technology, etc. Continue the list yourself! It is possible to hold all of these roles; all we must know is when we are expected to assume which role, and what the individual role entails. It is therefore impossible to conceive of a society entirely without roles.

The basis for this analysis is a constructivist perspective on the role concept[1]. This implies that I understand roles as being constructed by social actors engaging in ongoing interplay with others. The role concept therefore encompasses both the level of the actor, where the individual actor plays a role, and a collective level, where the role becomes institutionalised, thereby attaining a structural character. The individual social actor interprets the content of the role; however, it first becomes a role when other actors attribute the same content to it. Once this interpretation becomes institutionalised in the interaction between actors, the role has become constructed as a common reference point.

Upon its construction, the role comprises a structure for the actors who live with it. The role sets clear limits for the actions of the individual actor, while at the same time creating a specific room for manoeuvre for the actor. The role can therefore be experienced both as a resource, i.e. making certain actions possible, and as a limitation, i.e. if one wishes to do something that lies outside of the role. The role therefore serves as a structure resulting from interplay between social actors and which demarcates a specific framework for the actions of the individual actor; however, roles are also dynamic. Once a role has been constructed, its content does not necessarily remain constant for all eternity. Like all other socially created structures, roles can vary. This is not always that easy, however, as such change can be associated with significant expense for the individual in terms of challenging established structures.

The role concept stems from the theatre and is therefore often explained on the basis of a dramatic metaphor [2]. On the basis of this metaphor, the role can be understood as the position from which the individual actor can provide his contribution to the total play. The role places words in the mouth of the actor, but the individual actor also has opportunity to attribute his/her own interpretation to the role in terms of the way the words (and play) are to be toned and expressed.

Roles are often attributed internal and external dimensions. Remaining within the rhetoric of drama, one can say that the external dimension is the common manuscript. This

---

[1] For an examination of the theoretical development of the role concept, see Poulsen, forthcoming.

is where the common interpretation and institutionalisation of the role is expressed. The external dimension of the role encompasses the expectations, responsibilities, norms, values, etc. that the surroundings impose upon the 'holder' of a given role. The internal dimension of the role describes how the individual person adapts to – or interprets – the role. As in the world of theatre, a professional role in the public sector can also be expressed in countless different ways. People with different experiences, backgrounds, educations, etc. will interpret the same role in different ways; the role will therefore attain different expressions, dependent on the person assuming the role.

In this analysis I have distinguished between the construction and handling of roles. The construction of roles refers to the collective process involved in the interaction between social actors, i.e. where the role is constructed. In terms of handling, I set focus on the manner with which the individual actor fills out the role. Handling the role provides the individual actor with opportunity to make a contribution to the construction process. Remaining within the dramatic rhetoric, a capable actor can play the role in a manner providing it with new meaning; the character of the entire play thereby shifts. The same role can be handled quite differently; while some actors are capable of dealing with the complexity inherent in a role, others will struggle with it. Instead of discovering the manoeuvring room inherent in a role, the latter experience that the role leads to restrictive dilemmas.

2.2 The Role of the Politician

As already mentioned, focus in this chapter is on the role of the politician. The concrete requirements of the role of the politician have changed by virtue of the comprehensive development in the public sector that has occurred over recent decades. Reforms resulting from New Public Management, decentralisation, outsourcing, etc. have led to the development of the public sector from a hierarchical bureaucracy to an organisation based on networks with many participating actors. This entire development is often described in terms of the transformation of public sector regulation from government to governance.

Sørensen [3] describes the new requirements made of politicians under governance regulation as different means of exercising meta-regulation. Meta-regulation encompasses new regulatory forms aiming to regulate self-regulating networks. Meta-regulation places demands on politicians that starkly contrast with the traditional role requirements. The requirements made of politicians exercising meta-regulation concern the creation of framings to allow other actors to participate in the regulatory process, e.g. private companies carrying out publicly-commissioned services, civic groups in the local community, or organised interest organisations. The role of the politicians as meta-governors is then to specify the competence that various actors have to make decisions. In order to get this range of independent actors to work in the same direction, the politicians are also responsible for standing forth to offer political leadership capable of creating meaning via a common understanding of the general goals and the direction that the public sector is to develop in. The politicians must then also acknowledge that they are not alone in demarcating the framework for further development. They must therefore be prepared to engage in open debate with other competing groups of elites, allowing the emergence of democratic debate concerning the general objectives for societal regulation.

2.3 Distinction between Politics and Technology

While we can observe developments in the requirements made of the role of the politician, there is not talk of two separate, demarcated roles that the individual politician can freely choose between. Some of the fundamental conceptions concerning the politician role thus run contrary to the two sets of requirements. One of the aspects found in both sets of requirements is the conception that the role of the politician builds on a sharp distinction between politics and administration. Both sets of requirements build on the idea that the role of the politician is to represent the people that have elected them and lay out grand political visions for societal development. Conversely, the administrator's role is to serve the politicians by carrying out their visions in practice and generally administrating society on the basis of the politically defined framework. The means by which administrators implement and administer political decisions is regarded as a technical matter of administrative character. The administrators themselves can therefore choose the methods and instruments they consider to be most suitable and efficient in the given situation. According to this perception of the division of roles, it is clearly up to the administrators to determine whether it is appropriate to utilise a specific technology. Technological issues are therefore irrelevant to the politician role; in light of the clear distinction between the roles, it is almost taboo for politicians to involve themselves in the instruments and technologies the administrators choose to use.

The conception of this distribution of roles between politicians and administrators / practicians has lengthy historical roots. In ancient Greece, practical and technical questions were regarded as the domain of the slaves and therefore unworthy to become engage in if one sought the answers to the grand questions of life and politics. Plato thus describes [4] how the technological area can be potentially dangerous to become involved in, inasmuch as technical innovations can be a source of dangerous and detrimental changes to social life. He argues that true knowledge does not stem from the world of material things; rather, it originates from the exchange of ideas. He thus explains that the "real" table is not that which is fabricated by the carpenter, but rather the very idea about a table. He therefore places practical workers and craftsmen in the lowest of three social classes. It is impossible to maintain any form of power within this class and he therefore advises those with aspirations to rule to maintain the greatest distance possible from everyday practical and technical activities.

Aristotle goes one step further. In his description of the ideal society, the citizen (or the politician, as we would refer to him today) is a free and independent man participating in the political decisions played out in public life. This citizen raises himself above his own narrow interests and those of his family, instead attempting to serve common societal interests. In addition to defining the role of the citizen, Aristotle also specifies those excluded from this role. He points at servants and craftsmen, who were often slaves, as being excluded from citizenship. He argues that the physical wear and tear on practical instruments/technology forces them down into the necessity of the material world. They thereby lose the freedom of thought necessary to fulfil the role of the citizen. Consequently, Aristotle also argues against citizens acquiring knowledge regarding craftsmanship and technology. Technical matters in ancient Greece were therefore narrowly associated with slaves and servants; the ruling class was to avoid dealing with such matters. This very brief examination illustrates that the ancient Greeks had a sense of:
- technology and politics existing as two distinct domains;
- technology and practical work as being of low standing, unworthy of citizens;
- politics and philosophy as a matter for citizens and politicians.

While much has changed since ancient Greece, these thoughts continue to form the basis for our conceptions of roles and technology. We no longer regard craftsmanship and technology as being of low standing and that one lose one's freedom of thought by dealing with such matters; nevertheless, we maintain the distinction between technology and politics. Technology and other practical endeavours are still regarded as something politicians are not supposed to sully themselves with. As this conception has roots stemming back to ancient Greece, it is so fundamental that we do not even reflect over it or question it. It is therefore extremely difficult to shake this conception and alter practices arising from it.

Distinction between politics and technology becomes further fortified by the development of the role of the politician resulting from the transition to governance regulation. On the background of an empirical investigation in selected Danish municipalities, Sørensen [3] concludes that meta-regulation has led to the development of a role for politicians whereby they set objectives and frameworks. Determining objectives and frameworks is increasingly interpreted in terms of politicians deciding upon the political goals and the economic framings, while conversely they are to refrain from meddling with the institutional framings, e.g. the framework created by the utilisation of information technology. Management by Objectives is further interpreted as dictating that politicians ought not to become involved in individual cases. Questions pertaining to the development and utilisation of technology are perceived to be such concrete individual cases, which is yet another reason why such questions fall outside of the conception of the role of the politician.

All things considered, I am thus able to state that questions regarding the development and utilisation of technology have no place in the conception of the contemporary role of the politician. As already described in general terms in the beginning of this section, the perception of a role functions as a structural frame for the individual actor, i.e. while it might be possible to find examples of politicians who feel it is important to relate to the development of e-government, it can nevertheless be quite difficult for the individual actor to do so because of his/her role. I will later return to the opportunity of the individual actor to develop the role so as to include technological questions; however, we must first examine the political dimension in the development of technology.

3.   The Political Dimension in the Development of Technology

In addition to the circumstance that the conception of the role of the politician can act as a barrier for the participation of politicians in decisions regarding technology, conceptions about technology can also act as a barrier. The prevailing conception about technology is that technology is created as a neutral instrument to serve humankind in its pursuit of a better life. According to this conception, technology is not characterised by any political dimension; the technological development therefore has nothing to do with policy or politics. On the basis of this conception, technology is not a political issue, not something for politicians to become involve in.

I will challenge this conception in the following section. On the basis of constructivist technology theory, I will demonstrate how technological development is characterised by a considerable political dimension. I will subsequently place this understanding of technology in relation to the interpretation of the role of the politician and briefly conclude on the requirements that this understanding of the relationship between technology and politics places on politicians.

3.1   The Technology Concept

The aforementioned traditional conception of technology is based upon a technological deterministic approach to technology according to which technology is *the* driving force in societal development. This perception builds on an assumption that humankind will always strive for a better life; technology is regarded as a neutral instrument in this pursuit. The technological development is therefore considered to constitute the foundation for the development of humankind, i.e. the key to wealth and happiness [5]. Technology is developed by virtue of our exploitation of nature and utilisation of its laws. In that sense, technology has its origins in nature and is therefore attributed the same objective, value-neutral status that is attributed to nature itself. Attributing neutral and objective status to technology also serves to remove it from the political agenda.

By deconstructing a number of existing technologies, STS (Science and Technology Studies) researchers argue against this technological deterministic understanding [6-9]. Their counter-claim is that technology is created in a developmental process in which it enters into interplay with a number of different actors, e.g. researchers, technicians and designers, as well as advertisers, grassroots movements, and not least the users/consumers of technology. These actors often hold contrasting interpretations as to what technology ought to be used for, interpretations grounded in their contrasting needs, norms, political opinions and values. Controversies between contrasting interpretations of the significance of technology can therefore easily arise.

Technology is constructed via a process in which there is a power struggle between different groups of actors over whose interpretation of technology is to be dominant. Decisions regarding the concrete significance of technology are made within this construction process. These decisions can subsequently attain far-reaching political implications, as they can lead to unintended consequences, e.g. mad cow disease or IT projects that run off course. These controversies are eventually concluded, either by a powerful actor hegemonising his/her interpretation of the technology or via the emergence of consensus whereby the different actors arrive at a shared interpretation of the significance of technology. If the controversies are not concluded, no result comes of the process; no new technology is created. The closing of controversies entails a stabilisation of the technology by virtue of the construction of a network of relations between it and the various groups of actors in which the interpretation of its significance is stable.

My description of the network constructed around technology and the actors involved in this network builds on the approach to technology theory, often referred to as actor-network theory. French Professor Bruno Latour has been one of the driving forces behind this approach. I have earlier argued that the network concept can be employed both to describe the technological networks emerging in connection with the construction of technology as well as to describe policy networks emerging in the public sector in the network society [10]. My point is that when technology is employed to support policy networks, the two types of networks become engaged in such tight interplay that it is meaningless to attempt to analyse them separately. The networks become that which Castells refers to as information networks [11]. Nardi and O'Day [12] describe the relationships between technology and the actors using it as information ecologies. Without engaging in a comprehensive discussion of the network and information ecologies concepts, I will claim that the two concepts can be used parallel to one another. Both concepts attempt to capture the complicated correlation between technology and the various actors developing and using it, as well as the relations that emerge and develop over time. While the two concepts are therefore largely overlapping, I will nevertheless continue to use the network concept in the task at hand.

Actor-network theory operates with two different types of actors: human or social actors and non-human actors. The latter includes that which we normally understand as belonging to nature: forests, rivers, lakes, fields, animals, bacteria, mussels, the atmosphere and much more. It can, however, also include that which we normally understand as things and technology: tools, machines, doorstops, road bumps, safety belts, chips, etc.

It is important to immediately make clear that Latour has never argued that non-human actors possess consciousness. He has consistently argued that non-human actors can neither speak nor develop strategy; however, he employs empirical examples to demonstrate that non-human actors play a role in a given network inasmuch as they create conditions that force human actors to act in specific ways.

The human and non-human actors are engaged side-by-side in actor-network theory. Obviously, however, the non-human actors do not become involved in the network in the same way as human actors inasmuch as they cannot speak, possess consciousness nor plan strategy. Nevertheless, their lack of ability to express themselves does not prevent the non-human actors from playing a role in the network. One of the most important points in actor-network theory is thus that social and non-human actors are to be analysed from the same perspective. While their concrete actions are different, they are all engaged in a common network that eludes understanding and analysis if one neglects the one type of actor (and it is equally erroneous, regardless which actor is omitted).

Once the network has been stabilised and the technology has attained momentum [13], the character shifts. Henceforth it can be very difficult to modify, as alterations will require change in the network, which has otherwise been laboriously constructed and stabilised. One can then begin to talk about technology attaining a deterministic character. Once it has established momentum it will more or less begin to function as a structure, demarcating the framework for the actors who must use it.

The individual actor engages in an array of different technological networks. Dutch Professor Wiebe Bijker has developed the concept inclusion [6] to describe the extent to which the individual actor is associated to a given technological network. The concept describes how everyone is associated to numerous networks, as well as how the character of the association can vary. An actor that is fully included in the network thinks and acts on the basis of the consensus regarding the significance of technology developed in the network; the network structures the way the person acts. Conversely, the network will have a limited effect on a loosely included actor.

Bijker also uses the inclusion concept to describe situations in which entirely new ideas for the development of technology emerge. According to Bijker, this often occurs when an actor with a loose attachment to a network under construction transmits elements from another network, which she might have a closer relationship to. These types of situations often lead to radical innovations, resulting in the development of entirely new technologies [6].

The situation is entirely different if the network has been constructed completely. The opportunity to apply new interpretations and innovation is limited in this instance. New actors must adapt to the network if they wish to be included. Once the network has been constructed completely, new actors must relate to the foundation the network operates on. They must thus undergo a learning process to discover the values serving as the basis for the network, i.e. which routines and procedures it is based upon, how the non-human actors are engaged in the network, etc. The mutual relationships and learning processes emerging in the meeting between technology and the actors developing and using it are described in detail in [14].

Focusing on the political dimension of technology, I am primarily interested in the construction process; however, it is not always unproblematic to determine when the construction process has been concluded. In the case of information technology, certain elements are constructed completely, e.g. elements of hardware, just as there are standardised programs for a great number of different purposes. While these elements have been constructed completely, an aspect of construction remains when an organisation implements new programs; also despite being standard programs. The network must be constructed anew, which can entail changes for both social and non-human actors.

The new programs might require modification to be compatible with those programs the organisation is already using. It might be necessary to transfer data from an earlier used program, or special applications might require development for specific tasks. Social actors must also adapt to the new network. Work routines and organisation might require modification to be able to interface with the new program, or new actors with other qualifications must be added to the network. So while the ongoing digitalisation of municipal administration largely consists of the implementation of standard programs designed for use in all municipalities in Denmark, every municipality must nevertheless undergo a process in which a network consisting of both social and non-human actors is constructed. This is the process that the theory regarding the dissemination of technology [15] describes with the concept re-invention: a technology requires re-invention every time a new organisation implements it

In summary then, constructivist technology research has successfully developed a new theoretical understanding of the technology concept in recent decades. On the basis of a criticism of technological determinism, constructivist technology theory casts light on the degree to which technology represents a political field inasmuch as it is developed in mutual interplay with an array of different actors; it is therefore based on the political opinions, norms and values of these actors. The actors engaging in the construction process and the manner with which they stabilise the technological network thus have political consequences.

3.2   The Requirements of Technological Development for the Role of the Politician

The accounting of the constructivist approach to the study of technology has shown that the development of technology has intrinsic political dimensions; the concrete decisions regarding the design and utilisation of technology ought therefore be construed to be political decision-making processes. Perception of the role of the politician therefore requires revision inasmuch as political decisions ought to be made by politicians. Exclusively entrusting them to the administrators would result in a democratic deficit.

The theoretical description of the construction process also demonstrates that the significance of technology is determined in micro-processes otherwise often referred to as 'technical problems'. Such an understanding of technology and its development demands that politicians assume a stance on problems that they would otherwise regard as technical/individual cases and leave to the administration in keeping with their usual role conception.

The momentum concept emphasises that it matters when politicians become involved in the process. Once the construction of technology is complete, once the network is stabilised and has attained momentum, then the technology determined in the technological network comes to serve as a structural framework for the further utilisation of the technology. If this structural framework is not to be experienced later as a straightjacket, inhibiting the realisation of various political visions, it is crucial that politicians exercise influence over the development of the network before the technology has been constructed completely.

Considered as a whole, revision of the conception of technology also entails a need to revise the conception of the role of the politician in connection with the development and utilisation of technology in the public sector. If politicians are to gain influence on the development of e-government, exercising meta-regulation by demarcating general economic framings for the resources administration is allowed to use on the project will not suffice. They must become involved in the network processes through which technology is constructed. Furthermore, they must also engage in the process at an early stage to be able to impact the construction of the framework for the utilisation of the technology in question.

Becoming involved in the construction process requires participation in the technological networks under construction. They must adopt a stance on the functions e.g. e-government is to include, play a role in developing an interpretation of the significance of e-government and thereby contribute to the construction of the technological network. It is not enough for politicians to exercise meta-regulation by determining the framework for the development of the technology; they must perceive of technology as a dimension of the institutional framework for network regulation, just as they must conceive of technology as part of their work to create meaning and identity, as well as in their work with the construction and support of various policy networks. In the following section I will empirically investigate how politicians concretely engage in the development of e-government in a selected municipality.

4. The Development of E-Government

The empirical aspect of the investigation is comprised of a case study in a selected municipality. The municipality was chosen because it is a frontrunner municipality in many ways; they are further than most municipalities in terms of the development of e-government as well as network regulation, e.g. in the form of decentralisation, outsourcing, etc. Choosing this municipality as the basis for a case study ensured access to a public authority where role conceptions are presumably challenged by network regulation as well as e-government. The case study consisted of examination of various written (incl. electronic) sources describing the development in the municipality, as well as interviews with selected key figures among politicians and administrators. The analysis in this chapter primarily builds on two of these interviews.

In this section I will focus on how politicians have actually related to the development of e-government. I will particularly investigate the role of politicians in the early phase of development in which the network is not yet constructed and there is therefore abundant opportunity to interpret the technology and engage in interaction with other actors about the significance to be attributed to the technology. I will therefore begin by focusing on how the decision-making process surrounding e-government has unfolded, after which I will identify who had the ideas as to how e-government was to be fashioned.

4.1   The Decision-Making Process

When enquiring with the Mayor as to the responsibility for the development of e-government in the municipality, he responds that the Municipal Council naturally has the political responsibility for the general development, while the job of the administration is to put those decisions into practice. In the following quote he describes how the municipal council demarcates the general framework, and the administration attends to the practical details in carrying out the decisions.

"The Municipal Council has the political responsibility, but the management clearly has the administrative responsibility to make things work in practice … it's exactly the same as if you also interviewed the chairman of one of the big banks; I'm absolutely certain he would say the same thing: management is responsible for the necessary connections being available in all of the bank branches … the board doesn't get involved with how this is done in practice, but we are making the appropriations, as large banks like this require enormous appropriations – and this is a matter for the board, I'm sure. That's also the way it is around here. Fundamentally it's the Municipal Council – aside from the fact that in the bank most are elected by the general assembly – the citizens politically elect us, but in many instances we act like a board where we simply say that we will employ some people for this or that, ensuring the signals that we either confirm or give are carried out by the administration."

The quote displays the Mayor's very clear conception of the sharp distinction between his responsibility as politician and the responsibility of the Chief Executive for the administrative dimension. The politicians mark out the 'big picture' or issue political signals, and it is up to the administrative employees to ensure that the politicians' visions are carried out in practice. As the development and utilisation of technology are part of the practical implementation of visions, this conception dictates that technological matters are referred to the domain of the administration.

Examining the question about the distribution of roles more closely, however, it becomes apparent that the Chief Executive is also largely responsible for the formulation of the general framework. The mayor describes this process in the following manner:

"At a point in time one can say that we got a kind of general orientation from administration – which in our case means our Chief Executive, because he's incredibly sharp and very interested in everything related to computers – so he probably gave us a kind of general assessment of the technology. Probably in connection with him requesting an appropriation of some size or another ... that's a long time ago, but I would imagine he made a presentation to the Finance Committee, thereby also the Municipal Council, about how this technical stuff is available and that kind of thing."

The general framework for the development of e-government is thus formulated by the administration and confirmed, or approved, by the Finance Committee and thereby also the Municipal Council. This description of the decision-making process leaves a sense that there was no political debate about the basis for the decision; however, the Mayor does not regard this as necessary. He does not consider the decision regarding the digitalisation of the administration to be a political issue; the decisions about the individual aspects of the development have therefore never been on the agenda. He says:

"... but a lot of the things we are talking about here are simply things that are set in action because the service is there – it isn't particularly political that citizens can read about the cases they are involved in [on the municipal website - BJ]. To the contrary, it would be political if someone were to start saying that we don't want those kinds of systems in our municipality. So I can't really remember that there

was a time when there was a point on the agenda saying that now one should have

access to one's own tax accounts, that one should be able to look in all of this stuff

... I just don't think those kinds of things make for party politics.

... it has to do with kroner and øre (pounds and pence) in connection with an

appropriation; and these debates that come up in the Economics Committee and

Municipal Council are not of a particularly political nature, it isn't something that

parts the waters, so to speak ... No, it's not party politics. All parties agree

completely that new technology of any kind of benefit to the citizens should be

implemented."

It becomes apparent from these quotes that the politicians in this municipality subscribe to the traditional deterministic conception of technology described in the preceding section. Technology is fundamentally regarded as a positive, capable of creating growth and welfare for the good of the citizens; it is therefore not a matter for party politics whether or not technology is to be utilised. Of course it shall.

The Chief Executive has a corresponding image of how the decision-making process proceeds. He describes how the big picture surrounding the digitalisation of the administration was plotted out in the beginning of the 1990s in connection with the passage of the first IT strategy in the municipality. Subsequently the development has been concentrated around certain areas where the Finances Committee has set projects afloat by outlining frameworks for projects and providing grants. The political regulation of the project is accordingly entrusted to the committee with the relevant political responsibility, which establishes a steering-group to assume responsibility for the actual regulation of the project. The Chief Executive describes this in the following:

"When you ask in more general terms, 'What is all of this centred around?' then it is the

Finances Committee. When we were working on the strategy for school-IT, it was the

Committee for Children and Cultural Affairs who were in the centre. At a point in time

when we also had a comprehensive plan for the use of IT in relation to senior services –

also in relation to the individual resident – there it was also the committee responsible

for that area that drew up the strategy. That's the way things are distributed. We

decentralise a lot. The Finances Committee ... has the formal responsibility ... but says:

'just do it this way', on a very general level. Regarding school-IT, I think that it was

very general. Perhaps it was merely a tiny little statement, saying something about how

we have to have something more for the school kids – we need to get some computers

and get them on-line. There are a few points, and then they are appropriated a general

grant, which in this particular case was quite large, and then the Committee for Children and Cultural Affairs are told that it is up to them, so they are the ones who suddenly become responsible for the regulation, even though the Finances Committee has authority as far as IT is concerned."

While the Mayor does not regard deciding whether and how the administration is to be digitalised to be a matter of party politics, he nevertheless feels that it is somewhat political, i.e. policy on a more general level e.g. in terms of open administration. However, the politicians do not take a stance on the selection of the specific technical solution to create openness of which supplier is to provide the technology; this is entrusted to the administration. It shall merely support the general objectives of the politicians, including their goal regarding open administration. The politicians also play a role in deciding how the development of e-government is to proceed inasmuch as they demarcate the framework for the general development in the municipality. The Chief Executive says the following:

"That thing with the seniors also has to do with making some goals that don't have anything to do with technology, but have to do with the fact that one must be very precise when making agreements with the seniors about when one is to come and when was there, etc. That's what they were occupied by – it wasn't that they had any idea about the technology. It was more a matter of them saying that we had to make improvements, and then this enters into the picture ..."

The analysis of the actual development of e-government in the municipality thus shows that the politicians retain their responsibility for the general policy demarcating the outline for the development of e-government. The contours of this outline were formed through appropriations to specific IT projects formulated by administrators or through general goals concerning the development of various services the administration then finds an IT solution for. At the same time they maintain the distinction between policy and technology, i.e. they take care of the policy, the administration takes care of the technology; they therefore take no stance on the specific technical solutions, entrusting these to the administration.

4.2   Visions about E-Government

Another way of influencing the decision-making process concerning the digitalisation of administration is by establishing visions for how the e-government ought to be formed. The Chief Executive describes how the ideas for the further development occasionally have their origins in several different points, e.g. it is difficult to say precisely where the idea for the school IT project originated. There is a period when ideas are circulating among school leaders, school boards, administration and politicians; then suddenly someone addresses it as a matter of policy, i.e. now it is time to do something about the use of IT in the schools. He describes how the politicians are often better than the administrators at picking up on the signals from the other actors in the system. He says:

"You can call them ideas, needs or interests that emerge, like 'we have to do something about that!' In the case with the schools, I think that there was a period of a year or two where we weren't going to do anything. And then there were some people saying something out in the school boards – or perhaps said something to the Committee for Children and Cultural Affairs in a dialogue meeting or that kind of thing, 'Why don't we do something about that?' Suddenly things 'jump' – there's something that must be done. In this case it was very much a matter of politics being pushed to the forefront ... Yes, I think that the politicians have almost been dominant. At the same time, perhaps slightly lower in the system, at the level of the teachers and some of the school boards there were a few individuals had a lot to say – that might be where the politicians got it from. In that sense the politicians are sometimes better at picking up on signals. All of us probably hear it, but they might be better at putting things together, getting a sense of how there are a number of signals that we must react to. "

According to the Chief Executive, the politicians serve to bring the voice of the people into the political system; however, what about the politicians' own ideas about the development of e-government? As to whether he is the one with the ideas regarding what technology can be used for, the Mayor responds:

"No, but I'm right on top of things as soon as I hear about something. I have a seat in the shareholders' committee in KMD[2] where I occasionally get information I immediately have investigated in terms of how we work with it at home. And when I discover articles dealing with these kinds of electronics, I read them and investigate whether we are up to speed. In that way I feel my role in that area is to make sure that we don't fall behind. But I'm very privileged to have a Chief Executive – my closest adviser – who is incredibly keen with this kind of thing, keen on being among the leaders, also among his colleagues, in terms of utilising technology. He is the one who deserves the credit for our progress – certainly not me."

4.3   To Be or Not To Be an IT user

The Mayor, then, has no ideas himself as to how technology is to be used, but he listens to the ideas of others and ensures that his own municipality keeps up with the development in other municipalities. His own lack of ideas presumably relates to the fact that he does not actively use the technology himself.

Similar to many other politicians I have encountered in various studies, the Mayor in our case municipality does not use his computer much. It is difficult to determine whether this is owing to a generational dynamic or whether it is an expression of a traditional

[2] KMD is a former public owned, now privatized, software company.

conception of technology; however, when the pc was launched in the mid-1980s, it was widely regarded as a sophisticated typewriter. A typewriter is clearly an instrument for administrative employees as opposed to something a politician would use – i.e. there are people employed for that kind of thing! Whatever the reason, the Mayor does not use his computer terribly much. He describes this situation in the following:

> BJ: "In your dialogue with residents – does technology play a role, or is it more in the produce section in the grocery store and that kind of thing?"
>
> IP: "It's slowly becoming involved. It hasn't been too significant until now. It's probably a combination of a couple of things – as I say, our residents aren't really started with this yet, not on the political level. It's more like – people write a real letter to me and they receive a response; we almost always do so on paper, but occasionally also electronically. But it's also a matter of a lack of personal involvement on my part."
>
> BJ: "I was going to ask you about that."
>
> IP: "I'm pretty relaxed about it."
>
> BJ: "I can see that your computer is off".
>
> IP: "That isn't the latest model over there. I will also be honest with you and admit that email and that kind of thing are printed out for me, so I get it on paper".
>
> BJ: "Your secretary does it?"
>
> IP: "Yes, because otherwise I couldn't be certain that everything would be answered."
>
> BJ: "In other words, you don't really make use of the technology particularly much?"
>
> IP: "No, not very much."
>
> BJ: "The administration serves things to you on paper?"
>
> IP: "Yes, that's right. They also help me to respond: I stand there and formulate it and then there's someone who writes it all down."

The quote clearly indicates that the Mayor hardly uses his computer. His secretary prints out his emails, just as she also writes out the responses he dictates. The distribution of roles between the Mayor and his secretary has not changed since the days when the secretary was working on a typewriter. The Mayor cites two factors to account for this situation: first, it is not necessary for him to use a computer to communicate with municipal citizens, as they usually write conventional correspondence to him. The other factor is his lacking interest. Nevertheless he does manage limited employ of the technology as a part of his daily routine, with his secretary as intermediary.

While the Mayor can use IT through his secretary, he himself has not yet become an IT user. Becoming an IT user is also a role that one must acquire through a learning process in which one gains experience with the computer. In a study of use of IT among seniors, [16] has mapped the processes that make seniors IT users. The seniors describe being afraid of the computer in the beginning, but through the course of training in which they gain computer-experience, they acquire a new perception of the activity, the computer and themselves.

In the beginning, the use of a computer was on the edge of social acceptability; however, the seniors acquire a new perspective according to which it is good and positive to use IT. The experiences with the computer can be positive and negative. Johannson [16] describes how seniors' experiences with computers span the entire range of emotions, from happiness and pride felt the first time they send an email and receive response from their children or grandchildren, to anger and frustration when they encounter viruses on their machine, when the machine shuts down without reason or does other strange things they do not understand. All of these experiences impact seniors' perspectives hold towards the computer. It is also through these experiences that the seniors experience what they can use the computers for, and they get ideas as to how they can become part of their lives; from being something unknown and dangerous they can become an indispensable aspect of their everyday life.

The users also acquire a new perception of themselves en route; from regarding oneself as a non-IT user, to not only thinking of oneself as someone who can use IT but perhaps also being *good* at it. The new identity as IT user meant greater self-confidence for many seniors, as they no longer felt excluded from society, as was the case prior to using IT. Now they regard themselves as being capable of following the development in society. Becoming an IT user is an irreversible process. While one can step out of the user role and cease using IT, one can never return to the understanding of the world one had prior to becoming an IT user.

In some situations the altered self-perception also means that one experiences a newfound sense of difference in relation to those one previously identified with. According to one of the seniors in the study: "I have some old girlfriends – good friends – that just don't understand me. I have to hold a low profile with this stuff, because they don't have a PC" [16: 13]. Becoming an IT user is thus not a question about how many minutes or hours one sits in front of the PC each day, or which programs one is capable of working with; rather, it is a matter of how individuals defines themselves, i.e. whether one assumes the role as IT user or not.

The role as IT user is in keeping with the new role for seniors under development in recent years, i.e. the active senior [17]. This means that there are two different roles mutually supplementing one another; however, being an IT user is not so much in keeping with the role of the politician. Assuming the role of IT user will include a break with the conception of a distinction between the political and administrative domains. The Mayor must thus re-interpret the role of the politician in a slightly different manner to handle the role in a way so as to allow it to play together with the IT user role. It is therefore quite conceivable that the role of the politician can act as a barrier for the Mayor to assume the IT user role.

While the actual person serving as mayor at present could very well wish to assume the IT user role and get it to work together with the politician role, this could be difficult on account of the institutionalisation of the role of the politician; this is also expressed by the external dimension of the role. The surroundings do not necessarily expect the mayor to be an IT user. It is highly doubtful that his secretary has complained about having to print out the Mayor's emails, just as the IT suppliers do not send information to him or make an appointment to meet the Mayor – they approach the Chief Executive directly.

As the Mayor is not an IT user himself, he has not undergone a learning process to adopt the new technology [14]. He has had neither positive nor negative experiences with the computer; similarly, his self-perception in this area has not changed. In other words, he has not been included in the digital network regarding e-government. As it is this very learning process and concrete experiences with technology that inspire ideas regarding technology use – and thereby ideas as to how it can be interpreted – it is very difficult to imagine a non-IT user capable of developing visions concerning IT development and interpretation in the future within the public sector. It is therefore hardly surprising that the Mayor has not had ideas as to e.g. how the municipal website should be configured, just as his own lack of experience with the Internet must make it difficult for him to relate to enquiries about the municipal website. In other words, one cannot expect a non-IT using politician to assume responsibility to participate in the construction of the e-government. Of course, being an IT user does not guarantee one is capable of assuming responsibility to develop visions for e-government. The point is merely that "IT user status" is the first step in that direction.

Naturally the Mayor is not the only politician in the municipality in question. The study has also revealed that some of the other municipal politicians are IT users, some of whom actually have visions concerning the development of e-government. According to the Mayor, the younger members of the Municipal Council occasionally have ideas about the continued IT development. It is therefore tempting to assume that we are merely dealing with a matter of generational change; that it is a question of time before the non-IT using politicians have disappeared. This cannot be taken for granted, however. As the distinction between politics and technology serves as the basis for the conception of the role, there is talk of a structural barrier. The individual politician can well attempt to handle the role in a manner allowing them to overcome the limitations inherent to the role, thereby altering it, but this would require such significant effort on the part of the individual that most will likely choose to hold their technological visions close to their chest, leaving the development to the administration.

5.   Conclusion: Politician Influence on the Design of E-Government

The empirical investigation of the case municipality demonstrated that they are further than many other public authorities inasmuch as the politicians here are actually present when the general framework for developing the utilisation of IT in the municipal administration is laid out. The politicians are also responsible for the appropriations necessary for creating the economic framework for various IT projects. Furthermore, there are no striking examples in this municipality of regulatory deficiencies in which IT projects have derailed.

However, the conclusion of this investigation is that the involvement of the politicians is limited to the general, frame-setting level. They do not relate to the concrete development of e-government, just as most of them do not have any ideas as to how e-government ought to be arranged and utilised. In the last section I argued that the design of e-government has intrinsic political dimensions. The political dimensions manifest themselves e.g. in decisions concerning the specific design of how municipal communications are constructed and in the sorting of information made available to the public. For democratic reasons, these decision-making processes ought to be subject to political meta-regulation. The politicians ought therefore be closer to the forefront.

The manner with which municipalities and other public authorities are presently co-ordinating their utilisation of IT will determine the electronic infrastructure these authorities must use internally and with citizens, enterprises and other external actors for many years to come. If the politicians are to have influence on the decisions determining the future municipal electronic infrastructure, then they must participate in configuring the technology. They must also participate in the micro-processes in which the functions and significance of technology are determined. In other words, the politicians must become far more involved in the process of constructing the technological network surrounding the e-government. The politicians in the case municipality are not represented in the steering groups responsible for the daily management of the development projects or in the project groups developing the technology. Thus, they have no impact on the construction process, nor do they get involved in which IT suppliers and software companies the municipality collaborates with; they thereby refrain from relating to the various opportunities for development offered by the different IT suppliers.

As seen in the theoretical accounting of the technology concept above, opportunity to influence the development of the technology primarily lies in the construction process. It is therefore important that politicians immediately attain greater influence on the decision-making processes surrounding the development of the electronic infrastructure of the future. The construction of networks related to e-government is already well underway; for each decision made concerning the configuration of the technology, the network is further stabilised. The network regarding e-government has yet to be constructed completely, both in the case municipality and in connection with the general framework for e-government [10]. Therefore it remains possible to attain influence in terms of the significance attributed to e-government and the interpretation of it that is to become dominant; however, the politicians must engage in the process immediately, so that they do not first relate to the concrete design of the e-government after the network has been constructed completely and the opportunities to attain influence on its content are limited.

This is easier said than done, however. The examination of the case at hand has demonstrated that the age-old distinction between politics and technology continues to serve as the foundation for the conception of the role of the politician, thereby continuing to condition the distribution of roles between politicians and administrators. The widespread perception remains that politicians have the overriding responsibility and are to attend to the 'big lines', while the administrators are responsible for the practical execution of the political decisions and therefore also the choice of methods and technology. Nor does it appear as though this conception will change any time soon, as the new MBO aspect of the role of the politician supports this distinction between politics and technology.

Furthermore, the distribution of roles means that some politicians opt out of the IT user role, presumably because they do not wish to invest the time and resources required to undergo the learning process involved in adapting to a new technological network, thereby acquiring a new user role. The non-IT using politicians therefore lack the concrete experience with technology necessary to be able to envision the possibilities and limitations inherent to the technology. It then becomes difficult for them to establish visions for the further development and utilisation of IT in the public sector; however, while some politicians are IT users and actually possess some ideas and visions for the development of the e-government of the future, the politicians' visions do not dominate the concrete development. The administrators are clearly wearing the leader's jersey when it comes to the construction of the e-government.

On the basis of the traditional conceptions about technology and the distribution of roles between politicians and administrators, the conclusion to this chapter could very well be that politics and technology are two separate domains, which have absolutely nothing in common; it is therefore best that they are not mixed together. The answer to the question posed in the introduction of this chapter, on the basis of these conceptions, will therefore be that the role of the politicians constitutes a barrier making it impossible for them to participate in the development of e-government.

However, as shown by the examination of conceptions of roles and technology, the traditional conceptions have been challenged by the development of recent decades. The roles and the perception of technology are in transition; nevertheless, we remain distant from the point where the conceptions of roles no longer constitute a barrier to the participation of politicians in technological construction processes.

Nor will it be a mean feat to arrive at that point. Modifying a conception of roles and an age-old division of roles between politicians and administrators is an extremely difficult process requiring immense resources and much time; nonetheless, the first step on the path can be getting a glimpse of the fundamental conceptions regarding technology and roles that serve as the basis for the present practice. Once one first gets a glimpse of the conceptions, it also becomes possible to modify them, thereby altering the conditions for practice.

While the conception regarding the role of the politician is changing by virtue of the new requirements about exercising meta-regulation, the modification of the role conception has not yet led to politicians embracing the task to concretise e-government. Assuming this task requires that politicians revise their conceptions regarding technology and roles. They must therefore revise their ideas that:
- technology is apolitical;
- the division of roles between politicians and administrators builds on a separation of politics and technology;
- politicians are not to relate to the development and utilisation of technology

In the empirical study I concluded that the conception of a sharp distinction between politics and administration is alive and well. The changes I observed in the case municipality are not related to the actual distinction, but rather, where the limits between the two roles run. There is thus a clear tendency; the administrators in the case municipality violate the border between the two roles. I discovered several examples of administrators surrendering the position as neutral advisor, acknowledging instead that they play an active role in developing policy [17]. If the politicians are to participate in the construction of e-government in the future, it is their turn to shove against the boundary between politics and administration. Doing so requires acknowledging that the development of e-government involves political decisions requiring a political stance. They must surrender their position as those not required to deal with practical, technical questions and begin developing ideas and visions for how e-government can be utilised as an institutional framework for the regulation of self-regulating networks.

As it is so difficult to modify the existing roles and distribution of tasks between the roles, a helping hand can become necessary. It can come from researchers (as here) or from citizens. If citizens begin raising questions to the municipalities about why e.g. information cannot be found on the municipal website, or if private enterprises that have assumed the provision of municipal services begin making demands that they must have access to the municipal intranet, then they can shake the politicians' conception that they are not to deal with technological questions. Similarly, the electorate could hold politicians accountable for their IT policies at election meetings, or the members of the various parties could demand that IT policies be included in party programmes. Granted, such demands could contribute to agitating the role of the politician and shaking up the traditional conceptions concerning technology and roles.

References

1.   Jæger, B., *Digitale byer i København og Europa*, in *Informationsteknologi, organisation og forandring - den offenlige sektor under forvandling*, H.W. Nicolajsen, Editor. 1999, Jurist- og Økonomomforbundets Forlag: København. p. Kapitel 5, s. 89-110.

2. Goffman, E., *Vore rollespil i hverdagen*. 1956/92, København: Hans Reitzels Forlag.
3. Sørensen, E., *Politikerne og netværksdemokratiet. Fra suveræn politiker til meta-guvernør*. 2002, København: Jurist- og Økonomforbundets Forlag.
4. Winner, L., *Citizen Virtues in a Technological Order*, in *Technology and the Politics of Knowledge*, A. Hannay, Editor. 1995, Indianna University Press: Bloomington. p. 65-84.
5. Feenberg, *Teknikk og modernitet*. 1999, Oslo: Universitetsforlaget.
6. Bijker, W.E., *Of Bicycles, Bakelites, and Bulbs. Towards a Theory of sociotechnical Change*. 1995, Cambridge, Massachusetts: The MIT Press.
7. Smith, M.R. and L. Marx, eds. *Does Technology Drive History? The Dilemma of Technological Determinism*. 1994, The MIT Press: Cambridge, Mass.
8. Latour, B., *Science in Action. How to follow scientists and engineers through society*. 1987, Cambridge, Massachusetts: Harvard University Press.
9. MacKenzie, D. and J. Wajcman, eds. *The Social Shaping of Technology. How the refrigerator got its hum*. 1985, Open University Press: Philadelphia.
10. Jæger, B., *Kommuner på nettet. Roller i den digitale forvaltning*. 2003b, København: Jurist- og Økonomforbundets Forlag.
11. Castells, M., *Materials for an exploratory theory of the network society*. British Journal of Sociology, 2000. **No. 51**(No. 1 (January/March 2000)): p. 5-24.
12. Nardi, B.A. and V.L. O'Day, *Information Ecologies. Using Technology with Heart*. 1999, Cambridge: The MIT Press.
13. Hughes, T.P., *Technological Momentum*, in *Does Techology Drive History? The Dilemma of Technological Determinism*, L. Marx, Editor. 1994, The MIT Press: Cambridge. p. 101-113.
14. Williams, R., J. Stewart, and R. Slack, *Experimenting with Information and Communication Technologies: Social Learning in Technological Innovation -*. Under publicering: Edward Elgar.
15. Rogers, E.M. and J.-I. Kim, *Diffusion of Innovations in Public Organizations*, in *Innovation in the Public Sector*, A.I. Merritt, Editor. 1985, Sage.
16. Johansson, S., *Projekt Seniornet på Nordfyn - Fra ikke-brugere til brugere og ex-brugere i et socialt forsøg med IT*. 2002, Inst. for Samfundsvidenskab og Erhvervsøkonomi: Roskilde.
17. Jæger, B., *Det grå guld søger politisk indflydelse*, in *IT, magt og demokrati*, J. Hoff, Editor. Under publicering, Samfundslitteratur: København.

Niches for New Intermediaries: Toward an Evolutionary View of 'Digital Democracy'

Arthur EDWARDS

Erasmus University Rotterdam, Faculty of Social Sciences,
Public Administration Group, PO Box 1738, 3000 DR Rotterdam, The Netherlands

Abstract. In this chapter, disintermediation is analysed. One of the early claims
made about the effects of ICTs on democracy has been that ICTs would remove
intermediaries, thereby leading to an unbiased representation of citizens' demands.
In practice, numerous initiatives have been started, but empirical evidence for either
disintermediation or re-intermediation is scarce. However, it can be stated that the
new intermediaries that have emerged on the Internet offer various options for
democratic involvement to different democratic publics.

1. Introduction

One of the early claims made about the effects of ICTs on democracy has been that ICTs
would remove intermediaries, thereby leading to unbiased representation of citizens'
demands [1]. Because ICTs would enable the citizens to bypass intermediaries, such as
journalists, political parties and representatives, a direct democracy would be possible, in
the plebiscitary form of a 'push button' democracy or in the deliberative variant of a
'virtual agora', where people meet to conduct discussions. Empirical developments,
however, seem to indicate that the expectation that ICTs, in particular the Internet, favours
such a 'disintermediation' is ill-founded. Traditional intermediaries, such as interest groups
and political parties, gradually adopt and use new ICTs [2, 3]. Moreover, new
intermediaries emerge on the Internet, such as online news platforms, protest networks and
moderators [4, 5]. Instead of a disintermediation of democracy, we seem to be witnessing
the opposite, a re-intermediation that may lead to a reconfiguration of positions between
'old' and 'new' intermediaries in democracy in the long run. The aim of this chapter is to
contribute to an evolutionary account of the development of democracy under the influence
of new ICTs by focusing on the positions of intermediaries, in particular on the emergence
of new intermediaries in democratic processes.

In the literature on electronic markets, the future of intermediation is a much-discussed
issue. In the early literature it was suggested that since electronic transactions would result
in decreased costs for buyers and sellers, this would lead to the elimination of
intermediaries from electronic value chains. More recent analyses reveal a different picture.
If intermediaries provide value-adding functions, then, in circumstances where transaction
costs diminish, even small added values can be profitably added to value chains [6]. It
seems that while the actual dynamics of market restructuring will indeed lead to some
disintermediation, it will also provide new opportunities for intermediaries. In particular,
new intermediaries, including 'cybermediaries', enter the market with innovative business
models that may have transformative effects on the industry itself [7].

Finding and implementing these 'innovative models' for democratic practices is not an easy
task. Obviously, the Internet offers many more practices other than those that are effective

in meeting the citizens' needs and orientations. The performance of new democratic intermediaries on the Internet will be a process of trial-and-error, in which a limited number will be successful in finding a niche and survive. In order to explain this process, we need to address a number of issues for theoretical and empirical exploration. These include the opportunities available for new intermediaries within various democratic regimes, the strategies pursued by these new intermediaries, competition between old and new intermediaries, and the ways in which citizens develop their political roles and Internet practices. This chapter focuses on the first issue. The core of this chapter is a discussion of some new democratic intermediaries that have emerged on the Internet. These new intermediaries are viewed as new 'species' that may succeed in joining the 'community' of existing species of intermediaries within various democratic regimes. In order to assess their significance for democratic practices, the concept of 'information ecologies', as used by Nardi and O'Day [8] provides a useful starting-point. This concept can be further developed along the lines of social theory, combining elements of social constructivism and new institutionalism.

In the next section, I outline my basic theoretical framework. In Section 3, an overview of various democratic regimes will be given, and examples of new intermediaries in each of these regimes are presented. Section 4 focuses on competitive democracy and on the new information intermediaries that have emerged on the Internet in the last decade. One example that will be discussed in more detail, is a Dutch website aimed at introducing a practice of holding elected representatives accountable for their past performance. In Section 5, conclusions are presented.

2. The Basic Theoretical Framework

Nardi and O'Day [8] define an information ecology as 'a system of people, practices, values, and technologies in a particular local environment'. In the examples they discuss, such as a library and a hospital intensive care unit, people engage in recurrent patterns of action and interaction (practices) that envelop certain uses of technology. These processes take place within an institutional realm, in which certain roles and values guide the ways in which 'people and technology come together'. In their account of information ecologies, Nardi and O'Day acknowledge the interplay between human agency, technology, social processes and institutions. Other authors have suggested such an approach. In the context of technologically mediated democratic practices, Hoff [9], for instance, proposed a framework inspired by the 'social construction of technology' literature (e.g. [10]), but he adds an institutional dimension to it. Hoff refers to Giddens' structuration theory [11, 12]. Giddens' theory provides a way to embed the concept of information ecologies in social theory, and to align it with related approaches of technology. I follow Giddens' concept of a social system that can be defined as a set of situated activities of interrelated human agents, reproduced across time and space [12]. Social systems 'have' a structure, understood as social rules and resources. A central notion in the theory is 'the duality of structure', in which structure is seen as both 'objective' (and unacknowledged) conditions guiding social practices, and as socially constructed phenomena [12]. Institutional change can be the intended or unintended effect of the reproduction of structure in social practices. On the basis of these starting-points, I develop my basic model (Figure 9).

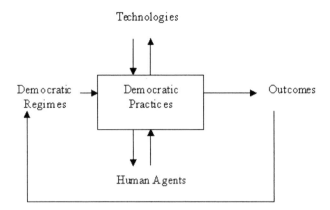

Figure 9: An institutional approach of information ecologies in democracy ('Systems of digitally mediated democratic practices')

For dealing with the more or less organised practices in democracy that are mediated by modern ICTs, I propose the concept of 'systems of digitally mediated democratic practices' (SDMDPs).[1] Since social systems can be identified at any level that is appropriate for specific research purposes and may vary in their degree of 'systemness', including groups, collectivities and organisations [11, 12], SDMDPs cover a wide range of phenomena in democracy. They can range from formal organisations that have appropriated the Internet to digital discussion platforms or e-mail networks. SDMDPs commonly have specific outcomes, as intended or negotiated by their members, such as the articulation of political demands, as in the case of online protest networks, or the provision of information by online news portals.

For understanding the interplay between technology and social practices one can draw upon the social construction of technology theory. According to this theory, different social groups that are involved in the development and actual use of the technology interpret a technological artefact in different ways. In a gradual process of social construction, these groups may reach consensus on the dominant meaning of the artefact [10]. Historical examples of the social construction of information and communication technologies by their users are the incorporation of the telephone, originally advertised as an aid to business, by women as an instrument for social intercourse, and the reinvention of the Minitel videotex technology in France, originally designed as an information tool for marketing purposes, into a communication tool for social interaction and discussions [13]. In Fountain's conceptualisation, these technologies underwent a process of 'enactment' by their users [14].[2]

The interplay between practices and human agents, as depicted in Figure 9, accounts for the learning capabilities of people. As agents in democratic processes, individuals or groups draw upon various interpretative schemes and values. Of particular importance are the frames and narratives of democracy, by which people conceptualise their political roles, civic duties and competences [15]. Further research into these conceptualisations, and the

---

[1] Hoff, Horrocks and Tops (2000) proposed the concept of 'technologically mediated innovations in political practices (TMIPPs). My concept of SDMDPs includes every democratic practice enhanced or enabled by ICTs, without the assumption that they are necessarily innovative.

[2] In the design of figure 1, I drew upon Fountain's framework as depicted in her figure 1.1 (Fountain, 1999: 11).

ways in which people appropriate the Internet in this, is needed to get a fuller account of the importance of democratic intermediaries on the Internet.[3]

SDMDPs bear the institutional properties of the democratic regime in which they function. I use the concept of a democratic regime to denote a configuration of institutional and organisational elements centred around a specific decision-making mechanism [16]. In the next section, I distinguish various democratic regimes that make up the democratic polity that is characteristic for modern network societies. Each regime includes specific legal frameworks, procedures, institutionalised values, norms and social rules that define appropriate political behaviour. SDMDPs reproduce the institutional properties of the regime in which they function. This may lead to an enhancement of the institutional 'status quo' but also to innovation. As Barley [17: 80] sets out in his structurationist account of the functioning of technology, the vagaries that occur in social interactions will commonly result in some 'slippage' between 'the institutional template and the exigencies of daily life'. The likelihood of slippage increases 'when a social system encounters exogenous shocks, such as the entrance of new members or the arrival of new technologies'. This suggests that in all processes of reproduction seeds may be laid for institutional innovation. In particular, ICTs exert a constant attraction on the practice of politics and public administration [18]. They elicit certain perceptions about opportunities to innovate democracy. Political actors, as well as initiators in civil society, may develop new 'business models' for providing political information, articulating demands and other political functions, that may have transformative effects on democracy.

Along these lines, the concept of SDMDPs provides an opportunity for developing the idea of coevolution of social and technical aspects of information ecologies [8: 52-53]. Giddens' structuration theory provides a framework within which various mechanisms of institutional change can be explicated.

3. Democratic Regimes

In modern network societies, a de-centring of collective decision-making has taken place to arenas, outside the realm of representative democracy. Politics has been 'relocated' to interorganisational networks spanning different levels of government [19]. From a normative point of view, this poses the problem of a 'democratic deficit'. As Rhodes [20] has argued, the traditional mechanisms of parliamentary control were not designed to cope with collective decision-making in fragmented policy systems. It is unclear whether the practice of governance has already yielded full-fledged substitutes or additions for democratic representation and accountability via parliaments. The following account of a democratic polity, in which various models of democracy coexist, can be seen as an anticipation of such a development. The idea of making connections between different democratic devices is, of course, not new. In his account of democracy, Dahl [21] included the indirect mechanisms of pluralistic interest intermediation and representative democracy, as well as deliberative devices. In recent discussions about democratic innovation, new institutional designs are searched for in which different models of democracy can work in ways that are mutually supportive [22, 23, see also 24]

I define democracy as 'responsive rule', i.e. in terms of the correspondence between acts of governance and the (equally weighted) felt interests of citizens with respect of those

---

[3] In this way, specific democratic publics can be distinguished. In a recent study, a group of Dutch social researchers (Motivaction, 2001) identified four 'styles of citizenship': the pragmatic-conformist style (42% of the population in the age between 15 and 80), the deferent-dependent style (22%), the critical-responsible style (20%), and the inactive-outsiders style (16%). In their description of these styles, the reseachers also included some general characterizations of media uses.

acts. This definition is borrowed from Saward [22]. As an outcomes-based definition, it does not indicate a specific mechanism for achieving responsiveness. This is the next step. Figure 10 depicts a democratic polity in the context of governance.[4] On the right, the vertical, multi-level dimension of governance is pictured, at the bottom the horizontal dimension of cooperation between (quasi-) public and private agencies. At the top, I place the representative bodies and elected executives. The three thick arrows on the left stand for the political activities of citizens, either individually or in civic organisations, such as political parties, referendum committees and interest groups.

I distinguish six democratic regimes, each providing a specific mechanism and appropriate institutions for achieving responsiveness. I place *deliberative democracy* in the centre of this figure, in the immediate environment of the interorganisational networks in which public policies are formulated and implemented. It includes all those arrangements in which citizens can discuss public issues, and exchange their views with politicians and officials representing the (semi-) public and private agencies that are involved in public policies. Examples are procedures of participatory governance, citizen juries and online policy exercises. *Pluralist democracy* constitutes the arena in which interest groups, social movements, and other citizens' initiatives articulate citizens' concerns and demands, and try to exert influence on political agenda-setting and decision-making. Pluralist democracy and deliberative democracy address the citizen as active participants or co-producers of public policies. In *competitive democracy* [26] political parties or individual candidates aggregate citizens' demands in political programs, and compete for electoral support for gaining positions in government. In contrast, *plebiscitary* (or 'direct') *democracy* provides the citizenry with opportunities to make their own political decisions on specific issues. Competitive democracy and plebiscitary democracy involve the citizen in his role as a voter. Lastly, *customer democracy* addresses citizens in their role of service users. It provides them, individually or in their client associations, with opportunities to give feedback on public service delivery. In *associative democracy,* service provision is devolved to self-governing associations functioning internally as representative or direct democracies [27, 28].

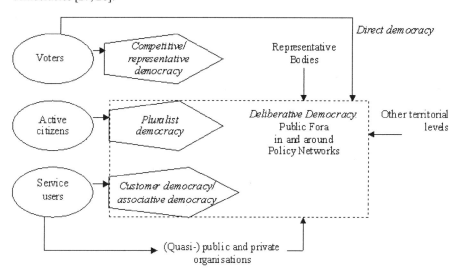

Figure 10: Democratic arrangements in the network society

---

[4] For a similar approach, but without the models of democracy, see Anttiroiko [25].

The picture given in Figure 10 can be elaborated into an ecological metaphor. The different democratic regimes can be seen as institutional 'regions' within a polity. In each region, a specific 'community' of 'species' of organisational forms function. For instance, the community of species within competitive democracy includes political parties, candidates and their campaign organisations, parliaments, and various types of new intermediaries for the voters (see Figure 11 in the next section). Within a species, various sub-species can be distinguished. The members of such species ('organisms') occupy a specific 'niche'. The niche of a new intermediary can be defined in terms of the specific functional role it tries to fullfill.[5] In a gradual process of adaptation, some species will succeed in their functional specialisation, occupy a niche and survive.

Because ICTs facilitate the development of horizontal arrangements between actors involved in policy processes, they will further the de-centring of political decision-making, but they may also facilitate new forms of representation and accountability, partly outside the traditional parliamentary institutions [29]. In this way, opportunities are created for new intermediaries in democratic processes. Digital technologies enter democracy in two ways. ICTs can be adopted within existing systems of democratic practices, such as traditional political parties, elections and parliaments, or in the form of new SDMDPs, such as online mobilization platforms or virtual political parties. As a result of these developments, one can speak of a digitally mediated democracy (or 'digital democracy') that comes into being.[6]

The digital discussion platforms that governments in many Western countries are experimenting with are one example of new SDMDPs in deliberative democracy. I view the moderators of these discussions as new democratic intermediaries [5]. Within pluralist democracy, various online platforms come into being that mobilise citizens in a range of campaigns directed at governments, intergovernmental organisations and multinational corporations. In competitive democracy, we witness, for instance, the emergence of new information intermediaries for the voters. Familiar examples are the digital voting-indicators (see next section, footnote 7). In the region of customer democracy, I can point to the websites of 'communities' of service users, like patients, elderly people or parents of school age children, engaging in the monitoring of public service delivery.

In some cases, a new SDMDP can be regarded as a democratic intermediary in itself, as in the case of online mobilisation platforms. In other cases, it can be fruitful to identify a specific actor within a new SDMDP as an intermediary, as in the case of the moderator in online discussion platforms. In the case of a 'cybermediary', such as the digital voting-indicator, the enveloping practices of using this device (together with other information resources), would be the relevant SDMDP.

4. New Intermediaries in Competitive Democracy

4.1 Information and Communication Relationships and Intermediaries

Figure 11 gives an overview of the intermediation between voters and political decision makers (the political executive).

[5] In ecological theory, a distinction is made between the 'habitat niche', which refers to the physical space occupied by the organism and the 'ecological niche', which refers to the role it plays within the community of organisms found in the habitat (Encyclopaedia Britannica, 1992). I adopt the term in its second meaning.
[6] As for the use of 'digital' instead of 'electronic' I refer to Hacker and Van Dijk (2000).

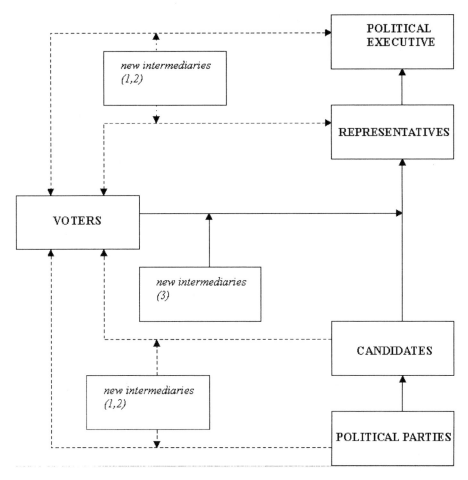

Figure 11: New intermediaries in competitive/representative democracy

The continuous lines represent the various selection processes in the political linkage chain [30]. The dotted lines represent the information and communication relationships between voters, political parties, candidates, representatives and the political executive. Broadcasting corporations and the written press are the traditional information intermediaries in these relationships. In addition to face-to-face meetings, the Internet enables political parties and other political actors to bypass these intermediaries and to communicate directly with the voters. However, in each of these relationships new intermediaries may provide added value. Focusing on the added value for the voters, thus taking the electorate as the principal, I distinguish between (1) new *information intermediaries* that provide the voters with information about political parties, candidates, representatives or the executive and (2) *preference intermediaries* that provide the voters with new options for expressing demands. Furthermore, I distinguish (3) *interaction intermediaries* that give the voters possibilities for coordinating their individual voting decisions (e.g. vote-swapping).[7]

---

[7] For example: www.tacticalvoter.net . Retrieved August 10, 2004 from the World Wide Web.

4.2   New Information Intermediaries for Voters

In the last decades, at least in Western countries, considerations regarding issues or policies have been gaining weight in voting decisions, probably due to rising education levels and media exposure [26].This would imply that voters have become more interested in information that enables them to relate their policy preferences to the stances of political parties and candidates. Studies of the cognitive aspects of electoral behaviour have revealed that voters use various information shortcuts to reduce their information costs (e.g. [31, 32]). These insights suggest that high expectations about the Internet's potential for increasing the voters' level of information may be ill-founded. Still, because of the Internet's possibilities of providing information from various sources, structuring it in efficient formats, and tailoring it to individual needs, the Internet has the potential of changing the cost structure of gathering information.

During the 1990s, a huge variety of online information resources has come into being. In addition to the websites of political parties, candidates and representatives, voters can gather information from the websites of the traditional media organisations and interest groups, as well as from a host of new online intermediaries, often initiated by existing civic organisations or (as in the United States) by organisations in the profit sector. An early example was the issue-grid in the United States, designed in 1996 by the Democracy Network (D-Net) that offered an overview of the points of view of candidates on a number of political issues [33]. Several websites became available in the U.S. with overviews of voting-records and performance ratings of incumbents and candidates. The website of the Project Vote Smart has emerged as one of the most well-known and comprehensive sources of this information.[8] At the 1998 parliamentary elections in the Netherlands, the first voting indicators for party choice became available on the Internet. The StemWijzer, developed by the Institute for Public and Politics (an independent institute for civic education), has become the most popular one, with 2 million voting recommendations in the parliamentary elections of 2002.[9] At the same occasion, a new species was launched, namely a website for evaluating the past performance of political parties in the Dutch parliament.

4.3   GeenWoorden.nl: An Emerging Practice of Evaluating Party Performance[10]

In the Netherlands, election campaigns have a predominantly prospective orientation. The political parties formulate their platforms and the campaigning politicians express their promises for the coming incumbency. There is no tradition of comparing the past performance of political parties in parliament, let alone of individual representatives. Institutional factors may account for this. In the Dutch multi-party system, in combination with proportional representation, elections do not result in clear-cut majorities. Governments are formed by coalitions. In this context, it is generally difficult to relate the performance of the government to specific contributions of the individual parties in the coalition. Moreover, the political leadership of the party exercises a strong control over the individual representatives. On most issues, the parliamentary voting relations between the government coalition and the opposition parties are fixed. This also means that the opposition parties' 'deeds' are difficult to assess in terms of their practical significance.

Six weeks before the parliamentary elections on 15 May 2002, the website GeenWoorden.nl was launched: an initiative of the Institute for Public and Politics (IPP)

---

[8] www.votesmart.org Retrieved August 10, 2004 from the World Wide Web.
[9] For information about voting indicators in some European countries: www.votingindicator.net Retrieved August 10, 2004 from the World Wide Web.
[10] The name of this website (in English 'NoWords') refers to the song of the football club Feyenoord "No words, but deeds".

and the Catholic Broadcasting Association (KRO). The project had two aims. The first aim was to provide the voters with information about the past performance of the political parties in parliament; the second aim was to promote a practice of holding politicians accountable for their deeds in office. A website was developed with four parts:
- Summaries of the 1998 election platforms of the parties represented in parliament on twelve themes;
- An overview of their deeds;
- Expert evaluations of the reported deeds;
- A discussion forum for the site visitors.

Two specific themes were chosen within the following policy areas:
- Multi-cultural society: in particular migration and integration policy;
- Education: in particular on issues of primary and secondary education;
- Transportation policy: public transport and the abatement of slow-moving traffic;
- Public health: waiting lists and shortages of staff;
- Moral issues: euthanasia and gene-technology;
- Democracy: involving the citizens in politics as voters and active participants.

The project staff of the two initiating organisations made summaries of the 1998 election platforms. The political parties were asked to indicate what they had done to fulfill their promises (in 200 words on each theme). Experts (staff from interest groups, academic experts and 'experience experts' from the field) were asked to evaluate the truth and effectiveness of the reported deeds (100 words on each theme). On the discussion forum site visitors could give their own comments on the information and provide additional reactions. Finally, the KRO broadcasted a number of programmes on radio and TV that took up the idea of the project. For instance, on a few TV programmes politicians were invited to undergo a kind of 'job evaluation interview'.

With its aim to promote a practice of holding politicians accountable, the website was intended as a democratic innovation. Figure 9 can serve as a guideline for a short description of how this project has functioned. First, I highlight the conduct of the various participants. I also discuss their use of the available technology. Then, I assess the project's contribution to democratic innovation and establish which factors might account for its success or failure.

The politicians had to suggest the material on which they would be evaluated. Apparently, they were not used to providing clear descriptions of their actions in parliament and of these actions' (potential) impact on the solution of social problems. For instance, parliamentary parties often presented 'motions' and 'proposals' as their actions, or even expressed, in some instances, additional promises, i.e. 'more words', as one member of the project team put it. Politicians, experts, and citizens, as well as the initiators themselves had to determine what should count as meaningful 'deeds' by politicians, as well as what should count as meaningful accounts of these deeds. The role assigned to the experts was to evaluate the reported deeds from different angles. In addition, they had to become accustomed to this idea. According to the project team, several interest groups initially mailed reports, in which formulations of the organisations' positions on the issues were more prominent than the factual evaluations they were expected to give. On the other hand, the 'experience experts' were sometimes too modest in their (initial) evaluations. In the radio and TV programmes, the idea of the project served as inspiration, but the information on the website was barely used by journalists for further research or comment. The website counted 60,000 visitors. The vast majority of people visited the website to acquire information, not to conduct discussions. Nevertheless, on some issues, in particular on the multicultural society, lively discussions ensued. In these discussions, politicians were almost absent. A politician gave a short reaction on only one occasion. There was almost no interaction between voters and incumbent politicians on the website.

For such an interaction to occur, a reinterpretation of the available technology should have been taken place. The discussion forum was explicitly presented as a facility for 'the public' to 'react'. The discussants expressed strong opinions, but they did not urge the politicians to answer to them. The fact that a reinterpretation of the facility as a space for communication between politicians and voters did not take place, can be attributed to reluctance on the politicians' side, as well as to a lack of interest on the side of the visiting citizens. Research on visitors of political websites has established that there is much more interest in information than in discussion with politicians [34]. Another factor might have been the absence of a moderator. An important feature of an information ecology, as Nardi and O'Day [8] use this notion, is the presence of 'mediators' as a 'keystone species', "people who build bridges across institutional boundaries and translate across disciplines" (p. 54). They continue:

> "Although the success of new tools may rely on the facilitation of mediators who can shape the tools to fit local circumstances, technology is too often designed and introduced without regard to the roles these people play".

Elsewhere, I have highlighted the roles of the moderator in government-initiated online discussions [5]. Moderators put substantial effort into enhancing the interactivity of the discussions. Moderators fulfill an important intermediary role ('across institutional boundaries'), especially in cases, where they stir politicians and other institutional actors to react to contributions of citizens. Moderators use various methods and devices for this.[11]

In the preparatory phase of the project, the project team actively dealt with the hesitation and lack of experience showed by politicians and experts. Initial contributions were critically commented upon and returned to the authors. With respect to the journalists, the project manager of the KRO, in her evaluation of the project, suggested that she could have played a more active role. An active use of the online information resources by the journalists, in combination with a moderated discussion forum for interaction between citizens, politicians and experts, could have contributed to the innovation that this project intended to be.

5. Conclusion

In the Dutch landscape of political information intermediaries the website GeenWoorden tried to occupy unchartered territory. It constituted a new 'business model' for providing the voters with retrospective political information, and holding politicians accountable for their past performance. By looking at this website as an 'information ecology' we can start with an assessment of how it has functioned. Participants from diverse institutional origins, politicians, experts, journalists, site visitors and the project team, had to work together to accomplish the two main goals of the project. They had to share the basic underlying values of the project, voter empowerment and political accountability, and to develop appropriate practices to make the website work. A simple website was designed with facilities for

---

[11] For instance, in a discussion organized by a Dutch Ministry in 1997, the moderator invited a politician to become the 'Politician of the month'. The moderator selected some contributions of participants and forwarded them to the politician to react. This enhanced the attractiveness of the site and stimulated the discussion, although several participants were not always satisfied about the way in which the politicians performed their job, i.e. giving non-committal answers (Edwards, 2002, p. 11).

information retrieval and a discussion forum for site visitors. As we have seen, politicians, experts and journalists were not familiar with the basic idea of the project. This can be attributed to the traditional roles these actors play in the settings in which they routinely do their daily work: parliamentary parties, interest groups and media-organisations. Regarding the technology two conclusions can be drawn. First, as an information facility, the website was perhaps too cumbersome for the users. For future occasions, the designers envisage a simpler format, in which, for instance, ratings or 'report marks' may be assigned to the political parties. Second, the discussion forum did not function as a platform for interaction between voters and politicians.

A lot can be learned from this project. From an evolutionary point of view, this experiment was not more than a first attempt. The website functioned for just six weeks, too short for having a lasting influence. Nevertheless, in view of the introduction of an improved model on future elections, it may have laid the seeds for institutional innovation. As for the concept of information ecology, my analysis of this incipient 'SDMDP', with participants from different institutional origins, underlined the importance of an institutional elaboration of the concept.

The website attracted 60,000 visitors, much less than the very popular voting indicator StemWijzer that provided 2 million voting recommendations in the 2002 election period. Clearly, the StemWijzer served a much wider public due to its simple format, its efficiency in use and because it was already more widely known. In order to assess the website's potential for voter empowerment, we have to know more about the way in which people appropriate such online facilities in their voting decisions. Possibly, different information intermediaries attract specific publics. It is, for example, conceivable that voting-indicators are particularly attractive to the large group of 'pragmatic-conformist' voters (see: note 3), for whom politics is not in the centre of their 'economy of attention', but still regard their role as a voter as a serious civic duty. A website that invites people to engage in a practice of holding politicians accountable, might be more selective and draw visitors from the smaller public of 'critical-responsible' citizens. In fact, these are the kind of patterns that are encouraged by network technologies, 'a world of demassified niches' [7: 103], in which intermediaries offer various options for democratic involvement to different democratic publics.

References

1. Bryan, C., R. Tsagarousianou, and D. Tambini, *Electronic Democracy and the Civic Networking Movement in Context*, in *Cyberdemocracy: Technology, Cities and Civic Networks*, R. Tsagarousinou, D. Tambini, and C. Bryan, Editors. 1998, Routledge: London.

2. Davis, R., *The Web of Politics: The Internet's Impact on the American Political System*. 1999, Oxford: Oxford University Press.

3. Gibson, R., P. Nixon, and S. Ward, *Net Gain? Political Parties and the Impact of New Information and Communication Technologies*. 2003, London: Routledge.

4. Van de Donk, W.B.H.J., et al., *Cyberprotest: New Media, Citizens and Social Movements*. 2004, London: Routledge.

5. Edwards, A., *The Moderator as an Emerging Intermediary. The Role of the Moderator in Internet Discussions about Public Issues.* Information Polity, 2002. 7: p. 3-20.

6. Kelly, K., *New Rules for the New Economy: 10 Ways the Network Economy is Changing Everything*. 1998, London: Fourth Estate.

7.   Giaglis, G.M., S. Klein, and R.M. O'Keefe, *The Role of Intermediaries in Electronic Marketplaces: Developing a Contingency Model.* Information Systems Journal, 2002. **12**: p. 231-246.
8.   Nardi, B.A. and V.L. O'Day, *Information Ecologies: Using Technology with Heart.* 1999, Cambridge (MA): The MIT Press.
9.   Hoff, J., I. Horrocks, and P.W. Tops, *Introduction: New Technology and the 'Crisis' of Democracy,* in *Democratic Governance and New Technology. Technologically Mediated Innovations in Political Practice in Western Europe,* J. Hoff, I. Horrocks, and P.W. Tops, Editors. 2000, Routledge: London.
10.   Bijker, W.E., *Of Bicycles, Bakelites and Bulbs: Towards a Theory of Sociotechnical Change.* 1995, Cambridge: MIT Press.
11.   Giddens, A., *New Rules of Sociological Method.* 1976, Cambridge: Polity Press.
12.   Giddens, A., *The Constitution of Society.* 1984, Cambridge: Polity Press.
13.   Feenberg, A., *Alternative Modernity: The Technical Turn in Philosophy and Social Theory.* 1995, Berkeley: University of California Press.
14.   Fountain, J., *Building the Virtual State.* 2001, Washington DC: The Brookings Institute.
15.   Dryzek, J.S. and J. Berejikian, *Reconstructive Democratic Theory.* American Political Science Review, 1993. **87**(1): p. 48-60.
16.   Eder, K., *Die Dynamik demokratischer Institutionenbildung. Strukturelle Voraussettzungwen deliberativer Demokratie in fortgeschrittenen Industriegesellschaften,* in *Politische Institutionen im Wandel,* B. Nedelman, Editor. 1995, Kölner Zeitschrift für Sociologie und Sozialpsychologie (Sonderheft 35). p. 327-345.
17.   Barley, S.R., *Technology as an Occasion for Structuring: Evidence from Observations of CT Scanners and the Social Order of Radiology Departments.* Administrative Science Quarterly, 1986. **31**: p. 78-108.
18.   Snellen, I.T.M., *ICT: A Revolutionizing Force in Public Administration?* Informatization in the Public Sector, 1994. **3**: p. 283-304.
19.   Bovens, M., et al., *De verplaatsing van de politiek. Een agenda voor democratische vernieuwing.* 1995, Amsterdam: Wiarda Beckman Stichting.
20.   Rhodes, R., *Understanding Governance.* 1997, Buckingham: Open University Press.
21.   Dahl, R.A., *Democracy and its critics.* 1989, New Haven, London: Yale University Press.
22.   Saward, M., *The Terms of Democracy.* 1998, Cambridge: Polity Press.
23.   Saward, M., *Democratic Connections: Political Equality, Deliberation and Direct Democracy.* Acta Politica, 2001(4): p. 361-379.
24.   Papadopoulos, Y., *Cooperative Forms of Governance: Problems of Democratic Accountability in Complex Environments.* European Journal of Political Research, 2003. **42**: p. 473-501.
25.   Anttiroiko, A.V., *Introduction to Democratic e-Governance,* in *eTransformation in Governance. New Directions in Government and Politics,* M. Mälkiä, A.V. Anttiroiko, and R. Savolainen, Editors. 2004, Idea Group: Hershey. p. 22-49.
26.   Miller, D., *The Competitive Model of Democracy,* in *Democratic Theory and Practice,* G. Duncan, Editor. 1983, Cambrifge University Press: Cambridge. p. 133-155.
27.   Hirst, P., *Associative Democracy.* 1994, Cambridge: Polity Press.
28.   Hirst, P., *Democracy and Governance,* in *Debating Governance,* J. Pierre, Editor. 2000, Oxford University Press: Oxford.

29. Frissen, P.H.A., *Representative Democracy and Information Society: A Postmodern Perspective.* Information Polity, 2002/2003. 7: p. 175-183.

30. Lawson, K., *When Linkage Fails*, in *When Parties Fail. Emerging Alternative Organizations*, K. Lawson and P.H. Merkl, Editors. 1988, Princeton University Press: Princeton.

31. Ferejohn, J.A. and J.H. Kuklinski, *Information and Democratic Processes.* 1990, Urbana and Chicago: University of Illinois Press.

32. Lupia, A. and M.D. McCubbins, *The Democratic Dilemma: Can Citizens Learn What They Need to Know?* 1988, Cambridge: Cambridge University Press.

33. Elberse, A., M.L. Hale, and W.H. Dutton, *Guiding Voters through the Net: The Democracy Network in a California Primary Election*, in *Digital Democracy: Issues of Ttheory and Practice*, K.L. Hacker and J. van Dijk, Editors. 2000, SAGE: London.

34. Boogers, M., G. Voerman, and E. Andersson, *Enquete Politiek & Internet.* 2002, University of Tilburg: Centrum voor Recht, Bestuur en Informatisering.

The Information Ecology of E-Government
V.J.J.M. Bekkers and V.M.F. Homburg (Eds.)
IOS Press, 2005

Responsive E-Government Services:
Towards 'New' Public Management

Hein van DUIVENBODEN
Cap Gemini Ernst & Young, PO Box 2575,
3500 GN Utrecht, The Netherlands

Miriam LIPS
Centre for Law, Public Administration and Informatization,
Tilburg University, PO Box 90153, 5000 LE Tilburg, The Netherlands

Abstract. An important policy goal for many e-government initiatives is to make
government organisations more responsive towards their ecologies. This chapter
describes the heterogeneity of the ecologies of e-government in terms of roles of
citizens and explores possibilities to increase the responsiveness of governments.

1. Introduction

All over the world, policymakers, public managers, politicians, and consultants have
acknowledged e-government as important for bringing about change in government. In
many cases, although the links have not always been made explicit, e-government
initiatives have been designed and implemented based on the range of ideas presented
under the flag of 'New Public Management' (NPM). For instance, an important policy goal
for many e-government initiatives is to make government organisations more responsive
towards society. By means of introducing a customer-oriented approach and to
electronically offer public information and services, the idea in many cases is that
government organisations could function more efficiently and effectively in their
relationships with citizens.

From the position of the 'customer' itself however, i.e. the citizen, the
operationalisation of the concept of responsive government as the provision of electronic
public information and services might be too narrow a perspective on e-government
potentials. So far, for instance, it turns out to be the case that citizens have not had a lot to
say in the reform efforts of government organisations in the field of e-government. Public
management reform in this area has been almost exclusively the business of government,
leading to a situation where the added value of organisational changes in the relationship
between governments and citizens is mainly determined by governments. In many cases,
the outcomes of e-government initiatives have been limited to the implementation of a
website through which citizens are able to get public information and services at one and
the same electronic public service counter (see for instance [1]).

Taking into account the different roles citizens have in their relationships with
government besides their role as a customer, critics indicate the necessity for governments
not to exclusively focus on citizens as customers in their e-government reform efforts, but

also to take the participatory role of citizens into account (see for instance [2, 3]). In addition, in spite of the popularity of the concept of e-government, critics point at the vagueness of its definition. As a reaction, attention nowadays goes to what may be acknowledged as a new form of e-government, namely *responsive* e-government services. Key element of responsive e-government services is the improvement of service quality through the enforcement of citizen orientation instead of customer orientation: that is, meeting the needs of the *citizen* in its different roles instead of exclusively serving the citizen as a *customer* [4].

In this contribution, we discuss the roots and characteristics of responsive e-government services, as we perceive them. To do so, we first place the development of the concept of e-government into perspective of the NPM range of thought. We then further explore the view that the development of e-government has been too narrowly focused on a customer orientation of the citizen. In order to develop an alternative view on e-government services provision, we describe the various roles citizens have in their relationships with government, as well as the unique characteristics of public sector organisations in their relationships with citizens, compared to private sector organisations in their relationships with customers. Next, we present several important characteristics of responsive e-government services that, in our view, will contribute to more effective e-government service solutions from a 'whole citizen' perspective.

2. E-Government and NPM

Until today, in spite of the popularity of the concept of e-government, confusion exists about its interpretation. So far, both the meaning of e-government and its implications are anything but clear. In many cases of e-government, in practice but also in theory, a narrow definition is used that limits the meaning of the concept to the provision of electronic public services (see for instance [5]). But the use of this narrow perspective on e-government is being increasingly criticised, indicating the fact that the potential of e-government initiatives may go beyond electronic public service delivery. For instance, the German Bertelsmann Foundation recently published a study supporting a wider understanding of the concept of e-government. So-called 'balanced e-government' was perceived to be a combination of electronic information-based services for citizens with the reinforcement of participatory elements [6].

The widely used narrow perspective on e-government nowadays can be explained by the fact many governments introduced e-government as a counterpart or part of electronic commerce or e-business and often equated it with the deliverance of governmental services online. Besides, historically, a popular distinction may be observed between the concept of 'e-government' and 'e-democracy', perceiving the provision of electronic public services as something fundamentally different (both in a normative and empirical sense) from organising electronic methods of citizen participation. An additional explanation for the dominance of this narrow perspective on e-government can be found in the observation that most of the effort, money and political attention available for e-government have been devoted to the provision of services online to citizens and businesses (see for instance [7]).

In accordance with their efforts to design and implement e-government from this narrow perspective, many governments perceive citizens as their 'customers'. It is here that we can observe a particular match between e-government developments and the impact of the New Public Management (NPM) range of thought in government organisations. Generally, the customer perspective of the citizen could be found under the flag of the NPM movement in public administration in the 1980's. According to NPM ideologists, government needed to be reshaped in order to function better in modern times: in other words, government had to become more responsive to social developments and therefore had to take a more entrepreneurial position in society. According to Bellamy and Taylor [8], what distinguished the *new* public management from earlier forms of managerialism is a new emphasis on the management and delivery of public services, and how those services are accessed and used. This opinion is empirically supported by the work of Kettl [9], who observes a global reform movement in public management with governments reshaping the role of the state and its relationship with citizens.[1] Kettl perceives the reach of this reform movement both in the number of nations that have taken up the reform agenda, and in the similarity of their basic strategies. In general he distinguishes the following six core characteristics of this reform movement:

- *Service orientation*: how can government better connect with citizens? Government reformers have used market mechanisms to encourage a customer-oriented approach in government services;
- *Productivity*: how can governments produce more services with less tax money? Governments have had to find ways to squeeze more services from the same – or smaller – revenue base;
- *Marketisation*: how can government use market-style incentives to root out the pathologies of government bureaucracy? The strategy of governments has been to replace traditional bureaucratic command-and-control mechanisms with market strategies, and then rely on these strategies to change the behaviour of programme managers;
- *Decentralisation*: how can government be more responsive and effective? In many countries, the reform strategy has decentralised many policy programmes and their service responsibilities to lower levels of government.
- *Policy:* how can government improve its capacity to devise and track policy? Many governments have quite explicitly separated in their organisation the policy function from the service-delivery function, in order to improve the efficiency of service delivery.
- *Accountability for results:* how can governments improve their ability to deliver what they promise? Governments have sought to focus on output and outcomes instead of processes and structures.

Kettl's study clearly shows the reform ambitions of governments around the world, under the flag of new public management, to 'run government like a business'. Also in reshaping their relationship from citizens to customers, the dominance of the economic or 'market' paradigm in the NPM reform efforts of government organisations is evident. To become more entrepreneurial and therefore to meet the needs of the customer rather than the needs of the bureaucracy, government organisations considered user-friendliness, transparency, and holism as important policy goals.

Since the 1990's, especially with the increasing use of the Internet, many governments came to perceive ICT as an important means for implementing NPM's notion of taking the customer as a central focus. In their e-government initiatives, government organisations have been using ICT as an instrument of public management reform (see for instance OECD, 1998), in an attempt to bring about a shift from an internal, bureaucracy-oriented focus towards an external, customer-oriented focus. As a result, in various countries, several models for the organisation of electronic public service delivery are emerging, such as the 'one-stop shop' (or integration model) and the 'no stop shop' (or fragmentation model) [1]

---

[1] Kettl's work is based on a sizeable empirical study towards the transformation of governance in several countries around the world since the 1980's.

One of the most obvious practical examples of the NPM reform movement corresponding with e-government initiatives can be found in the USA, where in September 1993 an important policy document called 'Reengineering through Information Technology' was presented within the framework of the US National Performance Review, a reform effort at the federal level to go 'from red tape to results by creating a government that works better and costs less'. In the accompanying document, the Clinton-Gore administration envisaged the government version of e-commerce, i.e. 'an electronic government that overcomes barriers of time and distance to give people public information and services when and where they would want them'.

3. Toward a More Responsive Government

Clearly, NPM has brought a substantial cultural change to many government organisations around the world. In this change movement, ICTs have been embraced by government organisations as important tools to (further) modernise government. Characteristics of available ICTs have led to policy visions of public managers to enhance efficiency, effectiveness, and accountability by means of e-government initiatives. The unique qualities of the Internet are particularly acknowledged to offer innovative, useful possibilities in the eyes of many policymakers, such as its network character, world-wide coverage, openness, decentralised character, many-to-many communication opportunities, mass-customisation, multi-media support, and availability of distributed knowledge [10]. From this perspective, NPM and ICT seem to be a perfect match for facilitating intended innovations in public administration.

In spite of the NPM policy objective of increasing the responsiveness of public administration and becominging more customer-oriented, it is interesting to note that the 'customer' or the citizen is hardly playing any role in the reform process. Although the change process is often claimed to take the citizens' needs as its starting point, citizens themselves are rarely consulted. This particularly seems to be the case in those change processes aimed at establishing e-government applications [10, 11]. E-government therefore can be acknowledged as a supply-driven concept: the technology offers government organisations new opportunities to reorganise their service provision to their citizens [12].

In one of the very rare citizen consultations on the demands and needs of Dutch citizens towards e-government, citizens indicated to attach particular importance to a short waiting time (71% of the respondents) and specialist help (65% of the respondents) [12]. Expecting that ICT would strongly support these two demands, possibilities were obviously perceived in public service consumption at any time, any place, and in improved access to specialised civil servants (Idem). From this, we may conclude with Lenk and Traunmüller [13] that e-government is clearly transcending NPM in that it may imply innovative, increasingly comprehensive approaches to administrative modernisation, beyond managerialism and economic theory. An important reason for this is that e-government seems to directly act upon the unique production processes in which public services are generated [13]; that is, affecting not only the 'executive', organisational way in which public services are provided, but also the political-administrative, legislative and democratic conditions typical to public activities. Comparably, several authors have stressed the importance for government organisations to not only deal with e-government initiatives in a sense of 'having a website' to serve the customer, but also to deal with the citizens' role as an individual with democratic rights and duties and subject to laws and rules enacted by government [14, 15].

Research in the Netherlands seems to confirm that citizens do perceive different positions or roles for themselves in their relationships with government. While citizens' satisfaction with public service delivery has slowly been increasing over the last decade, at the same time, they are less positive about the quality and performance of policymakers and politicians in force. On the basis of comparing citizen's surveys of 25% of all Dutch local authorities from 1995 to 2001, Hoogwout [16] concludes that the majority (over 80%) of the citizens are positive to very positive on service delivery of local government, but significantly less positive when their opinion is asked on their municipal council. Consequently, we may observe that the citizen approached in his/her role as customer seems to be much more satisfied with public activities than in his/her role as a participant. A popular hypothesis therefore nowadays is that citizens perceive local public service delivery as an activity that has nothing to do with the performance of local managers or politicians (see [16]. It is exactly in this period of time that the practice of e-government has been initiated and further developed in the relationship between government and citizen in many countries around the world.

The NPM range of thought that assumed a connection between increased responsiveness to society and a more entrepreneurial position of government in society may be an explanation for the fact that the concept of responsiveness has been limited in the NPM reform movement to a customer orientation of the citizen. With Kettl, we would argue that the reform effort to enable government to have a more entrepreneurial position in society is not so important in this respect, but the fact that governments are open to a reform process itself and really become responsive is more important. In other words: we argue that to be able to reach out for more responsive e-government services from a citizen's perspective, policymakers should no longer perceive e-government or ICTs in general as a tool to accomplish change in the relationship between government and society, but more as a joint process in which government and citizens together make use of their electronic relationship to arrive at more effective forms of governance in general – not limited to public service delivery that is.

A major question then would be how the emerging structures and relationships resulting from the implementation of ICT developments can promote the interests of citizens *as a citizen instead of a customer* and escape capture by narrow interests [9]? First , we have to take a closer look at the various roles citizens have in their relationships with government. Second, we have to gain more insight in the unique characteristics of public sector organisations in their relationships with citizens -- compared to private sector organisations in their relationships with customers. We do both in the following section in order to gain more insight into the circumstances under which a broader view of the concept of e-government can facilitate serving citizens in a way to meet more adequately meet their needs.

4.   Roles and Characteristics of Relationships Between Citizens and Government

4.1   Roles of the Citizen

One can distinguish many roles of the citizen in its relationship with government: customer, voter, taxpayer, applicant, subject, stakeholder, civil servant (employee) and so on. In this paper we use a four-fold division: the citizen as customer, as 'citoyen', as voter and as subject of the state [2, 17, 18]; see Table 10 .

Table 10: Roles of Citizens and Key Elements

Citizen Role	Key Element
Customer	Transaction
Subject of the State	Law (Enforcement) and Order
Citoyen	Direct Participation
Voter	Indirect Participation

In general, public service delivery concepts tend to focus on the role of citizens as *customers* of government organisations instead of, for example, their position as taxpayers, voters or state inhabitants. However, in most cases the public sector customer role is much different from the private sector customer role.

First, citizens are seldom customers of government agencies on a purely voluntary basis [19]. Most of the times, the relationship between citizen and government concerns specific rights and duties that have been laid down in laws, rules and policy statements that set the standard for service delivery conditions within the government's territory. Citizens can not negotiate the price or quality of services when applying for a new driver's licence, a passport or rental subsidies – because generally the law forbids, hinders or at least does not stimulate government agencies to compete with one another on such matters as price, speed, quality or user friendliness.

Second, citizens cannot 'shop around' in search of say a higher amount of subsidies or benefits. When someone is legally entitled to social security benefits, student grants or – for instance – a building permit, he cannot choose the cheapest or fastest public agency in the region. He will have to apply for this benefit or permit at his local municipal office or at a central state department that is legally authorised for these transactions and is therefore always dependent on a specific organisation's service delivery.

Third, once the right to a certain public service is established, in most cases public sector customers have an absolute right to delivery due to the fact that in that case government agencies have a legal duty to ensure the particular service delivery. Unlike private enterprises, governmental agencies can seldom refuse delivery of the services and goods they have to offer in individual cases. Public services like family allowances, road safety control, fire fighting, education or even prosecution and imprisonment can not be held back from (certain) citizens because the government agency involved has, for instance, too many customers to deal with or is short of personnel or money – let alone the fact that it is virtually impossible for government agencies to file one's petition in bankruptcy.

The apparent incomparability of public sector customers with private sector customers brings some authors to the conclusion that it would be better to not talk about a citizen as a customer of government at all. Hence, some prefer to replace the term 'customer oriented government' with the term 'responsive government' (Derksen et al, in: Hoogwout, 2001). There is, however, some support for retaining the use of the term 'customer' in relation to government activities focused upon citizens.

First, every public sector customer is paying for the services he receives – which is, in a way, similar to private sector circumstances. In general, every citizen is a taxpayer as well and is therefore, though indirectly, paying a certain amount of money every time the government grants him e.g. a licence or a benefit or enforces democratic laws and regulations. This form of indirect payment is most clearly the cases in situations of so-called collective customers – as opposed to individual customers. Government is serving collective customers by building dykes, bridges or roads or by maintaining order or enforcing public safety. Most of the time, the individual customer is also an indirect payer, but not when he applies for a passport or a driver's license and has to pay some legal dues directly.

Second, by using the term 'customer' as a metaphor, government agencies will compensate the fact that they normally don't have an external trigger for improving their service delivery. The bureaucratic culture of most government agencies and the fact that there is no competition with other organisations in order to survive or make a profit generally doesn't make customer friendliness the number one priority – it's just not a characteristic of governments by nature. Over the last few years, the rising popularity of the term 'customer' has brought many public service organisations to implement a quality management system that – among other indicators – forces them to evaluate the citizens satisfaction on a regular base (think e.g. of the popular Balance Score Card method or other remains from the period of Total Quality Management).

Third, there are reasons to treat a public sector customer even better than a private sector customer. This is what Ringeling refers to by the term 'customer oriented plus': precisely because a citizen is not a voluntary customer, he needs to be treated with the utmost respect [2]. As a rule, citizens don't apply for a social benefit or a building permit for pleasure. This is also true for assistance from fire brigades, police or garbage collectors – the incomparability to buying a new wardrobe or going to the movies is obvious. Furthermore, in private sector circumstances both parties normally are satisfied about the transaction that takes place: trading money for something valuable. Public 'services' like taxation or getting a ticket for speeding usually don't translate into happiness of the citizen involved. It is because of this that the national tax agency in the Netherlands uses the slogan 'We can't make it any nicer, but we can make it easier'. The Dutch, along with several other Tax Departments world-wide even lived up to that expectation by being early adopters of the Internet: electronic tax declaration facilities that are in use in e.g. Estonia, Singapore, France and California [4]. In short, in their role as *subjects of the state*, citizens are subject to rules, regulations and decisions made by government authorities. Failure to comply with these rules can lead to penalties varying from (official) reprimands up to imprisonment [18]. This relationship between government and citizen is traditionally vertical, whereby the main role of government is to exercise (democratic) power over the civilian population when necessary. In contrast with this relationship is the increasingly more horizontal one referred to in modern, responsive democratic perspectives, in which deliberation with citizens, checks and balances and the networking society have become popular concepts [20]. However, even in what might considered to be a 'postmodern' information society, the role of the citizen as a subject of the state will not disappear. For example, the absence of criminal law or law enforcement in any democratic state is nearly unthinkable [21].

The perspective of citizens as subjects of the state can easily be related to the classic definition of a bureaucracy: rules must be enforced regardless of the person involved and there is very little room for things like tolerating certain expectations of introducing customer friendliness [2]. Of course, in today's modern welfare states wherein several technological and social developments such as individualisation and horizontalisation might have altered the relationship between government and citizens, citizens and governments are offered many more opportunities to interact in a more informal and flexible manner. In many cases, citizens no longer seem to tolerate strong top-down measures without adequate motivation or a convincing argument. On the other hand, civil servants making decisions in individual cases are no longer the Weberian role model servants without any room for flexibility in interpretation (discretionary powers). From this perspective, placing laws and regulations in force with an adequate motivation on the Internet might help citizens in their role as subject of the state to be aware of what duties and obligations rest upon them and act accordingly.

In the relationship between citizens and the democratic constitutional state, an important role of the citizen is his position as a *citoyen*. This role encompasses his activities as a carrier of democratic rights on a more permanent basis. Referring to the notion of 'citizenship', a citoyen is an individual who participates in policy processes, political parties and social movements. In doing so, he exercises valuable democratic civil rights such as the rights to freedom of opinion and speech, to freedom of peaceful association and assembly, to demonstration and petition and – at least to some extent – the right to access to government information.

For a long time, the role of the citizen as bearer of democratic rights had been narrowed down to his role as a voter (see below). Strong political leadership and loyal grassroots support made direct political participation of citizens less necessary – or so it seemed [2]. As a result, most OECD countries have a strong and dominant system of only a few political parties governing the nation and the citizens are placed in a role of spectators instead of political participants.[2]

Nowadays, the role of the citizen as citoyen seems to be receiving renewed attention as a result of the decreasing importance of political parties and the growing individual involvement or political awareness in society. For example, Van Gunsteren introduces the political ideal of a Neo-Republican Citizen: a citizen who is subject of the state and active participant in political processes at the same time.[3] Depla illustrates the increased importance of the non-electoral role of citizens by pointing to the rise of social movements, demonstrations and the popularity of formal procedures for participation in policy processes of local democracies [22]. The Internet in particular seems to have created many opportunities for supporting the citizen in its role as citoyen. Worldwide access to government and other public information, or electronic debating and meetings are just a few of the new opportunities that may contribute to individual involvement in various democratic processes in society.

As *voters,* citizens can articulate their wishes and needs to government in an indirect manner: by choosing representatives at the local, regional, national or international level. The importance of voters is, of course, clear enough to political parties. However, in today's society, we can question whether the role of the voter sufficiently guarantees the democratic rights of individual citizens. For instance, practices of direct communication and transaction between citizens and civil servants are growing rapidly, leaving the political representative aside. Visiting a local election office every two, three or even four years may no longer be in line with the expectations of modern citizens: a responsive government is not only judged by citizens during election periods, but during each contact with government that citizens have – regardless of their specific roles as voters, customers, subjects or citoyens. Furthermore, apart from the role of voter, individuals are not expected to be aware of playing these different roles in specific circumstances.

Consequently, to serve the citizen as a citizen instead of a customer only, governments may make use of the newly emerging structures and relationships as a result of the implementation of ICT developments for addressing different roles of the citizen at the same time. Responsive e-government services, therefore, can better consider the varying needs of citizens in their different relationships with government – without having to make the citizen actively aware that he or she is playing these different roles.

---

[2] For this, De Beus (2001) has introduced the term spectator democracy.

[3] In Dutch: 'neo-republikeins staatsburger', as stated by Van Gunsteren, cited in Ringeling, 2001.

4.2 Customer Orientation of Public Organisations

If governments or other public organisations intend to become more responsive to the needs of their 'customers', the first thing they ought to do is acquire an adequate picture of who their 'customers' really are, what they really want and what kind of relationships they maintain with the organisation. This so-called 'customer orientation' of public organisations will have direct consequences for designing new forms of more responsive service delivery and relationship management activities towards and with society.

In many ways, the customer orientation in public organisations, and in e-government initiatives more particular, is assessed differently from the customer orientation in the private sector. For instance, while profit is an important criterion for performance measurement in the private sector, the success of government agencies is mostly measured by the effectiveness of policy programmes. One can state that it is all about 'societal profit' in the public sector versus financial profit in the private sector.

Besides, contrary to private organisations, a customer orientation for a government agency can imply delivering services in the most invisible manner possible. After all, true customer orientation in the public sector can be achieved in cases where citizens rarely or never have to physically visit a government counter. While these this so-called 'no-shop perspective' – think of automatic tax filing or continuation of rental subsidies, types of pro-active service delivery – can be the utopia for citizens, it tends to raise wicked paradoxes for government agencies themselves. For instance, being more customer-oriented through no-shop concepts leads to fewer customers in the physical front offices – and the number of citizens that are to be served at these offices are usually the criterion for the government's budget. In addition, many public organisations do not have a very positive image, and becoming more invisible would not help improve that image. In this case, public organisations will lose their identity in terms of a physical place to go.

Another issue in the transformation to a 'customer-oriented', more responsive government is the shift in autonomy in terms of altering the division of accountabilities and competencies. If an (electronic) one-stop shop is set up from the perspective of the needs of the citizen, some other services – from public or private sector origin – are typically added to it. In practice, this would mean collaboration among different parties (joint-up government or public private partnerships) that in turn would mean new divisions of decision making power. Many public organisations tend to have great difficulty redefining accountabilities and authority – especially when losing part of one's own autonomy. Collaboration might in time even threaten one's right to exist as an independent organisation. Besides, government officials and politicians are usually against combining private and public services from an ethical point of view since they don't want to harm their independent position in society.

When designing new forms of more responsive service delivery and relationship management activities towards society, government agencies should not forget that they have a far greater variety of 'customers' than, for instance, private organisations usually have. Citizens, businesses, other government agencies and non- profit organisations are all – and often at the same time – 'customers' of public organisations. In addition, one of the main customers of government organisations is the politician who is ultimately accountable for the public activities undertaken. Often, the most important organisation purpose is to strictly implement the policies formulated by politicians in force – especially now that the importance of public accountability is increasing. This manner of strict politically driven implementation may damage service provision to 'other' customers, such as citizens, businesses and non profit organisations [23]. In fact, *which* party considered to be the 'number one customer' is a strategic organisational choice. As a result, public servants may find themselves in a continuous dilemma: on the one hand, they are expected to strictly implement the policy programmes set up by politicians, while on the other hand they are increasingly confronted with the target group of those programmes that demands a level of service delivery that is better geared to one's individual and constantly changing needs.

4.3   Characteristics of Responsive E-Government Services

From the above we may conclude that the unique characteristics of customer orientation in the public sector require a broad perspective for dealing with citizens in e-government relationships in a 'customer-friendly' way. The characteristics of customer orientation in the public sector make it important for effective e-government solutions to approach the citizen in all of his roles and not only in his role as customer. As a result, a different definition of responsiveness has to be adopted than the one common in NPM thinking. During the 1990's for instance, for many government organisations dealing with NPM-inspired reform efforts, responsiveness meant no longer reasoning 'from inside to outside' but vice versa 'from outside to inside'. The demands and needs of the citizen had to become primary for the products and services provided.

So far, we can observe that while most governments in this reform effort now work on a more customer-oriented basis, they still maintain the attitude of knowing what is best for their citizens: they still determine the demands and needs of citizens by themselves instead of involving citizens in this change process [10]. Government organisations may have become too dependent on anticipating the needs of the citizen when reacting to the citizens might have been more appropriate. Consequently, a necessary policy goal in order to further the ongoing change efforts would be moving from a 'We know what is good for you'-attitude to a 'Let us know what is good for you'- position in developing e-government participation of citizens.

Both theoretical and practical developments seem to confirm this observation of too much anticipation, and along with this, a lack of citizen participation in current NPM-driven e-government efforts. In studying the quality of public service delivery during the 1980's for instance, before the NPM thinking came into use, Snellen defined the criterion of responsiveness as the activities, decisions or projects that are undertaken *in response* to questions, requests and indications of externals in relation to the civil servant. In his view, externals might be for example superiors, legislative bodies, citizens, pressure groups or other government organisations. In current government practice, we can observe a dominant anticipatory attitude in meeting the demands and needs of citizens. From their recent study for instance, the Bertelsmann Foundation concluded that there was little political interest in new forms of citizen participation within the framework of e-government service solutions. Many decision makers in the political and administrative domains would still primarily regard participation as an unnecessary complexity and cost factor: 'such approaches would fall into the "nice to have" category' [6: 10].

In line with Snellen's definition of responsiveness, the meaning of this concept in our view should not need to be inspired so much by a market-oriented, anticipatory attitude of government towards customers, but more by a comprehensive democratic, reacting mode of trying to get to know the desires and needs of citizens "as a whole" and actually doing something with it. Consequently, responsive e-government services would be e-government service solutions in which the regular input of citizens (desires, needs, preferences, complaints, etc.) is embedded and processed in some way.

What, then, would be general characteristics of responsive e-government service solutions in which citizen participation is included in some way so that demands and needs of citizens "as a whole" might be better met? In our view, responsive e-government services would imply flexibility on both the side of the citizen and the administrative organisation to act and react in processes of public service delivery. *Interaction* during the process of public service delivery can be acknowledged as a central element in the design of responsive e-government services. These services can not be determined or standardised beforehand, but in fact may be perceived as outcomes of processes of electronic public service delivery; outcomes that may be different from each other, in accordance with individual circumstances. However, as citizens have a non-voluntary customer relationship with government organisations for a number of public products and services, standardisation in the offering of these products and services can be used to a certain extent. For instance, citizens could be provided with several alternatives as an answer to a particular question, they could actively be informed on issues relevant to all of their citizen roles, or they could have the opportunity to choose to (only) receive information they are specifically interested in.

Another important characteristic of responsive e-government services would be to offer *'whole citizen' access* to existing e-government services. This would imply that citizens would no longer be approached through different service delivery 'silos' of the government organisation in order to be able to make use of various electronic public services or to electronically participate in democratic processes but instead via a one-stop shop beyond the boundaries of individual government departments, public organisations or democratic institutions. By means of this electronic one-stop shop, government organisations could strive for promoting citizen participation in different administrative processes and, with that, for better insight into question patterns of individuals in order to be able to offer products and services accordingly. To be able to better serve the citizen, governments could opt for implementing personalisation options in e-government relationships with their citizens. In this way, governments would not leave each customer with all available service options to choose from, but would provide help with looking for the necessary, applicable government information, services and/or participation possibilities.

As a fourth characteristic of responsive e-government service solutions, we suggest the necessity of not only focussing on the development of (new) electronic front-offices, but of bringing about *necessary changes in both the front-office and the back-office* of government organisations. Only in seriously considering the need to accomplish 'from outside to inside' reasoning in the organisation and also showing this to the citizen by means of delivering what has been promised, will it be possible to simultaneously serve citizens as customers and as participants in political-administrative decisionmaking processes. To possibly further promote effectiveness of responsive e-government service solutions, governments might use the opportunity to provide feedback to the citizen on the way(s) his or her input has been used or processed.

An example of responsive e-government: My Virginia (http://www.vipnet.org/info/)
The US State of Virginia offers a one-stop official government portal through which citizens and businesses can get personalised services. Through the 'My Virginia' home page citizens can access an extensive array of interactive services and information provided by Virginia government entities, such as State agencies, local governments, Colleges and universities, K-12 Schools, Libraries and Museums. 'My Virginia' services include driving licence and vehicle registration renewal, voter registration status check and a polling place finder, legislative and regulatory tracking, professional license renewal, state tax filings, consumer complaint assistance, and Virginia travel planning.

In the State of Virginia, every citizen has the opportunity via the government portal to create his or her personalised Virginia government homepage with only the information and services he or she wants. Through this personal homepage, citizens can select from several information channels (e.g. local government, press releases, local schools, state agency services, local traffic reports, and even lottery results) to automatically receive public meeting notices, legislative tracking updates, voter information, and email announcements. To set up the personalisation page according to the user's choices, a cookie is placed on an individual's PC to store the relevant information. However, no personal information is saved, tracked, or sold. Besides, each citizen can get a personal identification number ("My Virginia PIN"), which he or she can use to access diverse services that go beyond the bounds of individual authorities. Combined with Secure Sockets Layer (SSL) technology, the PIN number allows citizens to safely conduct e-government transactions on the Internet, such as filing tax returns, renewing driver's licenses, viewing and ordering college transcripts, and reviewing unemployment or government assistance benefits. In addition, live online chat assistance is offered to users.

---

5. Responsive E-Government Service Solutions: New Public Management Revisited

Indeed there seems to be a perfect match between NPM and the rise of e-government, but whether this match is an ideal one, particularly from a 'whole' citizen's perspective, is questionable. In introducing an alternative view on the meaning of responsiveness, in contrast to the entrepreneurial approach in accordance with the dominant market paradigm under NPM thinking, the NPM reform efforts in the field of e-government may become more in line with their intentions, namely to better connect with *citizens*. By taking into account the various roles of citizens in e-government initiatives, a satisfied customer of responsive e-government services may well be satisfied with the quality and performance of policymakers and politicians in force.

References

1.   Bekkers, V.J.J.M., *De strategische positionering van e-government*, in *Klantgericht werken bij de overheid*, H.P.M. van Duivenboden and A.M.B. Lips, Editors. 2001, Lemma: Utrecht. p. 49-66.
2.   Ringeling, A.B., *Rare klanten hoor, die klanten van de overheid*, in *Klantgericht werken in de publieke sector. Inrichting van de elektronische overheid*, H.P.M. van Duivenboden and A.M.B. Lips, Editors. 2001, Lemma: Utrecht. p. 33-48.
3.   van Duivenboden, H.P.M. and A.M.B. Lips, *Klantgericht werken in de publieke sector. Inrichting van de elektronische overheid*. 2001, Utrecht: Lemma.

4.   van Duivenboden, H.P.M., et al., *Onderschat debat. Een internationaal vergelijkend onderzoek naar beleidsvisies op informatie- en communicatietechnologie en de democratische rechtsstaat.* 2002, Den Haag: Ministry of the Interior and Kingdom Relations.

5.   Office of the e-Envoy, *Benchmarking Electronic Service Delivery.* 2001, London: Office of the e-Envoy.

6.   Bertelsmann Foundation, *Balanced E-government - Connecting Efficient Administration and Responsive Democracy.* 2002: http://www.begix.de/en/index.html.

7.   6, P., *E-governance. Do Digital Aids Make a Difference in Policy Making?*, in *Designing E-Government: On the Crossroads of Technological Innovation and Institutional Change*, J.E.J. Prins, Editor. 2001, Kluwer: The Hague.

8.   Bellamy, C. and J. Taylor, *Governing in the Information Age.* 1998, Buckingham: Open University Press.

9.   Kettl, D.F., *The Global Public Management Revolution: A Report on the Transformation of Governance.* 2000, Washington DC: The Brookings Institute.

10.   van Duivenboden, H.P.M. and A.M.B. Lips, *Taking Citizens Seriously: Applying Hirschman's Model to Various Practices of Customer-Oriented E-Governance*, in *Governing Networks / EGPA Yearbook*, A. Salminen, Editor. 2003, IOS Press: Amsterdam.

11.   Lips, A.M.B., et al., *Roadmap for Socio-Cultural and Economic Research in Privacy and Identity Management.* European RAPID-project. 2002, Brussels: EU.

12.   Boogers, M., G. Voerman, and E. Andersson, *Enquete Politiek & Internet.* 2002, University of Tilburg: Centrum voor Recht, Bestuur en Informatisering.

13.   Lenk, K. and R. Traunmueller, *The Concept of Electronic Government*, in *Designing E-Government. On the Crossroads of Technological Innovation and Institutional Change*, J.E.J. Prins, Editor. 2001, Kluwer: The Hague.

14.   Bekkers, V.J.J.M. and M. Thaens, *e-Government op een kruispunt van wegen.* Bestuurskunde, 2002. **2002**(8).

15.   Bongers, F.J., C.A. Holland, and B.R. H, *E-government: de vraagkant aan bod.* Openbaar Bestuur, 2002. **3**: p. 25-31.

16.   Hoogwout, M., *Onderschat debat. Een internationaal vergelijkend onderzoek naar beleidsvisies op informatie- en communicatietechnologie en de democratische rechtsstaat*, in *Klantgericht werken in de publieke sector. Inrichting van de elektronische overheid*, H.P.M. van Duivenboden and A.M.B. Lips, Editors. 2002, Lemma: Utrecht. p. 149-166.

17.   van Duivenboden, H.P.M., *Koppeling in uitvoering. Een verkennende studie naar de betekenis van het koppelen van persoonsgegevens door uitvoerende overheidsorganisaties voor de positie van de burger als cliënt van de overheid.* 1999, Delft: Eburon.

18.   Thomassen, J.J.A., *Burgers in twee gedaanten.* 1979, Enschede: Technische Hogeschool Twente.

19.   Lipsky, M., *Street-Level Bureaucracy. Dilemma's of the individual in Public Services.* 1980, New York: Russell Sage Foundation.

20.   Van de Donk, W.B.H.J. and P.W. Tops, *Informatisering en democratie: Orwell of Athene?*, in *Orwell of Athene. Democratie en samenleving*, P.H.A. Frissen, A.W. Koers, and I.T.M. Snellen, Editors. 1992, SDU: Den Haag.

21.   ICT and Government Advisory Committee, *Citizen and Government in the Information Society: The Need for Institutional Change.* 2001, The Hague: Ministry of the Interior and Kingdom Relations.

22.   Depla, P.F.G., *Technologie en de vernieuwing van de lokale democratie. Vervolmaking of vermaatschappelijking.* 1995, Den Haag: VUGA.
23.   Snellen, I.T.M., *Conciliation of Rationalities: The Essence of Public Administration.* Administrative Theory and Praxis, 2002. **24**(2): p. 323-346.

The Information Ecology of E-Government
V.J.J.M. Bekkers and V.M.F. Homburg (Eds.)
IOS Press, 2005

E-Government and NPM: A Perfect Marriage?

Vincent HOMBURG and Victor BEKKERS

Erasmus University Rotterdam, Faculty of Social Sciences,
Public Administration Group, PO Box 1738, 3000 DR Rotterdam, The Netherlands

Abstract. New Public Management (NPM) and e-government are often seen as two sides of the same coin, as they both seem to depart from the classic public administration paradigm. In this chapter, it is argued that it is indeed possible that NPM and e-government reinforce one another, but that this does not necessarily lead to one specific 'new' form of government organisation, or a specific 'new' form of governance. Based on theoretical and empirical reasoning, this chapter presents four trajectories of change and identifies consequences of these trajectories in terms of the information architecture to be used, and the type of accountability that fits each trajectory.

1. Introduction

New Public Management (NPM) techniques as well as electronic government services seem to spread quite rapidly. Until recently, new public management, loosely defined as tactics and strategies that seek to improve the ability of government agencies and their non-profit and for profit collaborators to produce results by means of reinventing government [1, 2], was used exclusively by guru-like consultants and scholars working for governmental organisations. In general, the Weberian, classic public management paradigm remained undisturbed until about the mid 1980s, when it was challenged by techniques and strategies embodied in new public management [3]. Since then, a managerial emphasis on the functional ideas of expediency, efficiency, economy, and calculation of ends seems to have swept through the OECD world [4].

In general, New Public Management focuses on the application of private sector management techniques in the public sector. At first sight, NPM is merely concerned with issues like accruals accounting, the use of performance indicators and techniques for, for example performance-related pay, so it was primarily focused on the internal processes of public sector organisations. However, NPM techniques also include customer orientation, the introduction of market-style relations between governmental organisations and internal and external decentralisation. Therefore, NPM is relevant for the way the context, i.e. the ecology, of government is shaped. As will be demonstrated in this chapter, changes in how information is exchanged or patterns of information relations are connected are far from deterministic. Especially in conjunction with e-government application, NPM refers to very broad patterns of change in the information ecology of e-government.

The aim of this chapter is to assess the impact of both new public management and e-government on the public sector, and to discern one or more trajectories of change based on a critical examination of the theoretical and policy assumptions behind both new public management and e-government. In order to reach this goal, three significant preliminary questions have to be dealt with. These are, first, what are the origins and manifestations of new public management and to what extent does it differ from a 'classic' public administration paradigm? Second, what are the origins and manifestations of e-government? And, finally, where do new public management and e-government meet and what kind of trajectories for reform can be expected at the cornerstones of these reforms? These three preliminaries will be tackled sequentially in the next three sections. In order to answer these questions, the article adopts an analytical approach as opposed to an empirical one.

2.   What is New and Different with New Public Management?

2.1   *The Traditional Public Administration Paradigm*

For more than a century, western bureaucracies have been constructed and constrained by a paradigm known as 'traditional public administration'. Traditional public administration, which is in itself heavily influenced and shaped by Weberian ideas of bureaucracy, is a reaction to, as Wilson noted with respect to the American administration at the end of the 19th century, "(...) the poisonous atmosphere of [city] government, the crooked secrets of state administration, the confusion, sinecurism and corruption ever again discovered in the bureaux at Washington" [5: 206]. In order to prevent the corruption problem, according to the 'classic' public administration paradigm, bureaucracies have to be based on six principles of public service: (1) an apolitical public service, (2) hierarchy and rules, (3) permanence and stability, (4) an institutionalised civil service, (5) internal regulation and (6) equality [6, 7]. These principles are used to curtail the influence and power of the tiny cogs in the wheels of public sector organisations [8] and, in general, to map ways to restrict personal, patrimonial and patriarchal modes of governance. A core concept in the public administration paradigm is the idea of accountability, which is firmly rooted in the writings of Wilson, Taylor, Weber, Goodnow and Gulick [2]: a chain of hierarchical accountability, from citizens to elected officials to appointed officials to government action. In order to make this kind of hierarchical accountability happen, information has to flow directly and exclusively up through superiors, then to ministers, and eventually to parliament. In this conception of accountability, Parliament serves as a filtering institution between community and government. It audits the accounts of public offices and funds used by ministers and officials. In the public administration paradigm, the emphasis is on accountability for finances and fairness [2].

    In the classic public administration paradigm, bureaucratic organisation is a reification of information requirements prompted by a particular accountability mechanism: various functionally differentiated organisational units maintain different sets of files (reflecting functional differentiation of the store of documentary materials) and decomposed general rules, and upper level superiors have access to more condensed forms of information that could be used for (strategic) decision making and accountability.

2.2   *The Emergence of the New Public Management Paradigm*

In general, the classic public administration paradigm has been criticised since the 1970s for resulting in underperformance in the public sector. With the expansion of the scope of markets, citizens increasingly began to think more like customers, even in their experience as users of public services, and in general they also displayed a decline in traditional forms of deference towards civil servants (including public sector professionals such as teachers and doctors). This resentment of citizens with the public service coincided with the development in the academic realm of theories like neo-institutional economics and public choice theory, in which market mechanisms were intensely analysed [9]. In other words, a new rhetoric of choice emerged, which was furthermore fuelled by a kind of managerialisation of organizational life. A number of management gurus became extremely influential, who created a management discourse, in which 'reinvention', 're-engineering', 'entrepreneurial government' played an important role [1, 10, 11]. For example, Osborne stated that "[i]f you want better management, untie the managers' hands and let them manage. Hold them accountable for results – not for following silly rules" [12: 8].

In many subsequent publications, the characteristics of public sector reform have been specified [4, 9]:
- Customer (rather than citizen) orientation [4], or, in other words, a focus on providing high quality services that serve narrower interests of citizens;
- Performance orientation;
- Continuous quality improvement orientation;
- Lean and highly decentralised structures, empowering street-level civil servants;
- Tight cost control mechanisms;
- Emphasis on accountability upwards in relation to performance by decentralised or even privatised units;
- Performance-related systems for recruiting, promoting and paying staff and in general increased flexibility in hiring and firing staff;
- The use of divisional structures in public service resulting in breaking down of former unitary bureaucracies, as well as in interorganisational relations with organisations in private and voluntary sectors ('joined-up government'); and
- More active management and the emancipation of operational management skills (as opposed to policy advice skills which were dominant in the classic public administration paradigm).

Core to new public management seems to be the conviction that democracy can only survive by delivering services efficiently (which is an aim in itself), either by adopting a market orientation or by reengineering the public service itself (which are *means* to the *end* of efficient service delivery). In terms of accountability, there is a shift from accountability for process (finances and fairness) to accountability for performance [2, 13]. According to Behn [13], accountability for process is achieved through record keeping by agencies, which are inspected by (independent or hierarchically superior) auditors for compliance with respect to regulations. If irregularities are observed, individuals are disciplined.

Basically, in new public management, there is an ambition to bypass or complement a hierarchical accountability route which is seen as cumbersome, slow, inefficient and unproductive, by using a system of accountability to 'customers' of government services, using direct mechanisms like user fees, surveys, and user panels much like an enterprise checks whether its goods or services meet customers' requirements. Accordingly, in new public management line of reasoning, accountability information not (only) flows directly 'upwards' to parliament and downwards to citizens, but also directly to the customers involved in using public services. In fact, this may serve two distinct purposes: it may enable consumers to speak up ('voice' their opinions in a direct way; that is, respond politically) or defect (respond economically by choosing an alternative supplier either in the short or long term) [14, 15].

How these underlying ideas and their implementation take shape in various countries, however, fluctuates enormously [16]. This may be due to characteristics of the specific institutional settings new public management ideas and practices are implemented in (in terms of starting points, path dependencies, implementation competencies) [17], but it may also be attributed to the heterogeneous nature of the concept of new public management itself [18]. For example, the notion of customer orientation may collide with the notion of decentralisation when one considers that decentralisation is usually associated with diminished willingness to share information among various agencies [19]. Reasoning from the neo-institutional economic logic that served as a foundation for new public management, it can even be argued that information sharing is not always rational [20, 21], and therefore, service delivery and accountability may be impeded.

One of the implications of heterogeneity and contradictories is that in specific implementations, choices have to be made according to specific circumstances, which, from a global, theoretical point of view, result in variety in new public management practices. Guy Peters has identified four basic, dominant patterns in new public management practices that are more or less internally consistent [6]:

- Market government (emphasising 'pay for performance');
- Participatory government (emphasising empowerment and flatter organisations), which enables citizens to speak up;
- Flexible government (virtual organisations, temporary allocation of staff to tasks); and
- Deregulated government (managerial freedom).

In general, it can be stated that underlying to all patterns of practices is a notion of departure from the classic public administration paradigm - especially the notions of decentralisation (both internal as well as external) conflicts with classic public management paradigm's notion of (strict) hierarchy and rules, and centralisation by integration (or vice-versa). Furthermore, the basic mechanism of the (hierarchical) accountability route is complemented with a product-oriented (as opposed to a process-oriented) accountability route that tries to capture citizens' perception of quality of public services.

The means that are chosen to achieve this, however, vary from direct contact with citizens (both in terms of service appraisal as well as participation), market mechanisms (applied between agencies) and more organic (as opposed to formalised) relationships.

At first glance, the notion of participation and citizenship and new public management may seem an odd couple. Participation draws its substance from community involvement, communitarianism and shared responsibilities, and, by contrast, new public management seems to emphasise the citizens' power of *exit* as opposed to the power of *voice*. Gruening argues that notions of participation are more profoundly anchored in the new public administration reform of the end of the 1960s and beginning of the 1970s than in new public management [9]. Box [22] even claims that new public management takes a very clear and unfavourable approach to participation. New public management writings may indeed fail to elaborate on the advantages of citizenship behaviour within or around the public systems as such, but as Vigoda and Golombiewski [23] have demonstrated, it is quite possible to blend managerialism with active citizenship.

3.   What is New and Different with E-Government?

3.1   ICTs and Public Administration

More and more governments are becoming accustomed to the tools brought about in the new information society [24]. Partly, this is not new. Automated information technologies have been available in many forms for many decades [25, 26]. Until recently, however, specific information technologies, specifically mainframe technologies, tended to be applied in such a way that they replicated the formal structures that already existed in classic bureaucracies. Nohria and Eccles state that "[c]omputer systems and software adopted the 'architecture' of bureaucracy [...]. Not surprisingly the language of information systems became the language of bureaucracy" [27: 120]. In as early as 1960, Bendix used the metaphor of a teller machine to explain that bureaucracy "(...) is like a modern judge who is a vending machine into which the pleadings are inserted together with the fee and which then disgorges the judgment together with its reasons mechanically derived from the code" [28: 421].

Later on, especially since the late 1970s, new generations of technologies became available that began to eliminate the architecture of bureaucracy. Personal computers (PCs) and especially Internet technologies are supposed to have distinct transformative powers that, in specific societal and organisational dynamics, can be used to accelerate changes inside and around governments [29]. Often, the term 'e-government' is used to refer to the application of specific Internet-related technologies inside and around governments. However, in a broader sense, the type of technologies used could also include wide area networks in general (including but not limited to the Internet), mobile telephones, personal digital assistants used by street-level bureaucrats, and so forth. The aims to which these technologies are put to use differs enormously: better delivery of government services to citizens, improved interactions with business and industry, citizen empowerment through access to information [30], or more efficient government management in general. The resulting benefits can be less corruption, increased transparency, greater convenience, revenue growth, and/or cost reductions.

In a narrow definition, e-government is mostly defined as the production and delivery of government services through ICT applications [31]. In this chapter, we more broadly describe e-government as the use of information and communication technologies, especially internet and web technology, by a public organisation to support or redefine the existing and/or future relations with 'stakeholders' in the internal and external environment in order to create added value.

Before analysing what e-government has to do with new public management, there is at least one issue that can be commented on beforehand: the concept itself seems to be based more on pragmatic experiences and visions [32-36] and management consultancy (inspired by e-commerce experiences) than on a solid theoretical view. In terms of academic knowledge, there is an abundance of empirical research which is focused on the effects of ICT on the functioning of public administration [37, 38], but a solid theoretical base seems to be lacking: Gruening thoroughly analysed the origins of 24 characteristics of new public management in 14 schools of thought on public administration, and concluded that "the *use of information technology* seems to be a characteristic of NPM that has no specific theoretical roots. It is strictly a pragmatic idea, used where it is useful" [9: 17]. In general, the conclusion that the use of ICTs in organisations has no theoretical roots can be contested [see for example 20, 29, 39] but how ICT is dealt with in new public management writings particularly, certainly lacks theoretical rigour.

3.2   Variety in E-Government Initiatives and Relationships

On the shop floor of many government organisations, e-government initiatives originate in rethinking the interaction between government and citizens. Traditionally, the interaction between stakeholder groups like citizens or businesses and government agencies occurred in a government office. With emerging information and communication technologies it is possible to locate service centers closer to stakeholders. Such centers may consist of an unattended kiosk in the government agency, a service kiosk located close to the citizen or company, or the use of a website.

The interaction between citizens and governments, however, is a multifaceted phenomenon. It is possible to distinguish many roles citizens (as primary stakeholders) can play in relationship to governments: customer of public services and goods, voter, taxpayer, subject of regulation, contender, employee (civil servant), private person who wants his privacy to be respected, or even entrepreneur who wishes to sell goods and services to government agencies. Accordingly, many types of interactions can be distinguished, like government-to-citizens relationships (G2C), government-to-business enterprises (G2B) and intergovernmental relationships (G2G). In each and every type of interaction, information and communication technologies can be applied, accounting for various types of e-government.

In the international practice of e-government, various types of e-government services can be discerned [40].

A dominant type of e-government is G2C with a focus on service delivery [31, 40]. This type predominantly addresses citizens and businesses in their roles of customers. In practice, this type often takes the form of citizens receiving information, contacting civil servants and/or performing transactions using a web site as a one-shop-no-stop delivery channel. Fountain provides the example of an International Trade Data system that provides businesses with licenses and permits that are required under international and federal legislation [41]. In practice, such a form of service delivery brings along a need for G2G interaction because tens of agencies are involved in the execution of policies regarding international trade, safety, health inspection, and so forth.

Another form is G2C interaction aimed at voters. This type of interaction is often referred to as online voting. At this moment, online voting takes place in, among other places, Australia (Australian Capital Territory), Brazil, Canada, Germany (Niedersachsen), New Zealand, and the United States (California) [42]. In many cases, e-voting occurs alongside postal voting and regular voting.

A third form is G2C interaction with 'citoyens' [31]. This type of interaction often takes place in discussion forums, and is aimed at participation of citizens, interest groups and other stakeholders in the policy process and decision making about, for instance, urban and rural planning projects like the reconstruction of a neighbourhood, a shopping mall or the planning of a rail road. Grönland mentions examples of local electronic forums in the Swedish city of Bollnäs, where citizens engage in electronic discussions with the local politicians [43].

Apart from these forms, which are all targeted at pro-active, responsible and demanding citizens, there are some services that target the less benevolent aspects of citizens. E-government services can also be used for criminal prosecution or enforcement of legislation. Sometimes, this occurs in concurrence with or under the heading of, service delivery. For example, in many countries, internal revenue services are frontrunners in the application of e-government. One of the more important motives for tax agencies to use e-government services is to promote compliance of taxpayers by supplying them with accurate and more compelling information.

In general, the added value of e-government initiatives can be traced back in terms of increased quality of services, increased transparency, improved efficiency for citizens, improved participation, and increased accountability. In some situations, e-government initiatives are identified as direct or indirect enablers of joined-up government (JUG). For example, in the British policy document 'Modernising Government', ICTs are mentioned as leverages of joined-up government, albeit ICT are merely viewed as front-office delivery channels rather than as back-office coordination mechanisms; so, ICTs are viewed as indirect enablers of joined-up government (as opposed to direct mechanisms like pooled budgets across Departments, cross cutting performance measures and appraisal systems which reward team-working across traditional boundaries) [44]. On the other hand, in the Danish national E-Government Strategy, it is explicitly recognised that the public sector should work and communicate electronically using an electronic infrastructure so that it can take full advantage of the potentials of keeping information in an electronic format throughout the work process.

In sum, it can be stated that there are reasons to assume that e-government services in practice mark a deviation from the classic public administration paradigm. E-government's main characteristic 'redesign of relationships with internal and external stakeholders' potentially results in all kinds of lateral communication flows and semiformal coordination mechanisms, which are incompatible with classic public administration's principle of integration and centralisation of bureaucracy. Furthermore, classic public administration's accountability route is challenged by consultation mechanisms that are often present in e-government initiatives.

4. Synthesis: Trajectories of Change and Configurations of Public Service Organisations

4.1   ICT and Direction of Reform: Divergence

The theoretical rationale for assuming a 'marriage' between new public management and e-government seems to be that e-government affects information costs within and between organisations, and reduced information costs are expected to change the comparative advantage of governance mechanisms and institutional arrangements [45]. In other words, the assumption is that because of reduced information costs produced by e-government services, the public service organisation embodied in new public management writings has a comparative advantage over the unitary bureaucracy of the classic public administration paradigm. As Hammer puts it, it may be that the use of information and communication technologies provide many, if not all, of the benefits once made administrative centralisation and specialisation of administrative functions such as reporting, accounting, personnel, purchasing or quality assurance attractive, without sacrificing any of the benefits of decentralisation [10]. Reschenthaler and Thompson predict four major shifts that arise because of changes in information costs that are quite compatible with the shifts inherent in new public management:
-   The efficacy of the market has increased relative to government precision and control, which could result in more outsourcing and privatisation;
-   The efficacy of the market and other self-organising system has increased relative to hierarchically coordinated systems, which could result in decentralisation;
-   The efficacy of decentralised allocation of resources and after-the-fact control has increased relative to centralised allocation and before-the-fact control, which could result in the use of performance indicators instead of the classic budget mechanism;
-   The efficacy of process-oriented structures has increased relative to functional structures [45].

From this line of reasoning and the authors they are quoting, it is clear that authors such as Reschenthaler and Thompson explicitly use neo-institutional economics as a starting point in order to identify trends like the use of market-style forms of coordination, and internal and external forms of decentralisation, which are by themselves enabled because of the availability of alternatives to bureaucratic allocation mechanisms like performance indicators. The degree to which these effects can be attributed in practice to ICTs embodied in e-government initiatives, however, is not a clear-cut factual statement. The original claim is more or less directly transplanted from business-to-business networks into public service organisations, and even within the original business domain, the empirical validity of the hypothesised trajectories is doubtful. Reschenthaler and Thompson's expectations were discussed previously with respect to internal decentralisation [7, 46]. In the relation between ICTs and (de)centralisation, there seems to be a centralisation thesis [47, 48], a decentralisation thesis [49, 50], a contingency explanation [51] and a social choice explanation [52]. In this context, Groth states that the debate on the relation between ICT and centralisation seem to function like a Rorschach test: "those who think central control is a good thing eagerly eye what they see as the opportunity to use automation [...] to strengthen management's grip on the organisation, whereas those who would like to wrestle power away from bosses finally see their chance to decentralise operations, devolve responsibility, and empower employees" [7: 325].

Analogously, in other strands of the literature, there are various theses about the relationship between ICTs and hierarchical dissemination. In a classic article, Malone, Yates and Benjamin argue that in general, ICT lowers information and coordination costs, and claim that by using ICT, market-like mechanisms ('electronic brokerage') are favoured over hierarchical coordination mechanisms ('electronic integration') [53]. In a similar vein, Davenport, Eccles and Prusak state that "(...) as organisations make widespread use of information technology, information will flow freely and quickly eliminate hierarchy" [54: 54] Various studies support this claim [53, 55]. On the other hand, various authors conclude that electronic hierarchies are more commonly observed than electronic markets [56-58]. Furthermore, Clemons, Reddi and Row have formulated the 'move-to-the-middle' hypothesis [59], and Holland and Lockett remark that ICTs "(...) do not affect directly the evolution of governance structure such as markets or hierarchies [...]. However, [ICTs] can affect all of them in some way enabling a much greater flexibility of outcome both in the short and longer terms. (...) In essence, [ICTs] enable organisations to do what they want much more efficiently and flexible" [60: 409].

We can state that the theoretical and empirical backing of the successfulness of the marriage between new public management-like reforms and e-government, and projecting a single trajectory on the basis of an assumed marriage may be highly speculative. On logical grounds, there is no one best way of merging new public management and e-government, at least not without having to accept a number of internal inconsistencies. For example, the required investments in e-government may contradict the focus on cutting costs emphasised in new public management, and the notion of (public) accountability may be diametrically opposed to effects accruing from contracting out. An alternative line of reasoning, which is presented here, is to envisage *various* trajectories, each based on combinations of attributes of new public management and e-government strategies. In general, two sets of trajectories emerge from the marriage between e-government and new public management. The first one is concerned with an external perspective, that is, with a perspective on the relationship between government and citizens. The second one is concerned with an (government) internal perspective, referring to the changes that could occur within and between bureaucratic organisations.

4.2 The Interface with the Outside World

The external trajectory builds upon e-government's notion of the relational competencies of ICT: the capabilities of ICT to (re)consider relationships with other actors (citizens, societal organisations, and firms) [24]. In general the reengineering aspect of this reform trajectory is concerned with the redesign of the 'interface' between government as a whole on the one hand, and citizens, firms and societal groups on the other hand.

A first trajectory within this set is especially concerned with service delivery. We refer to it as a '*service orientation*'. Other authors refer to this trajectory as digital new public management [61] and a 'managerial model' [40]. In general, this trajectory emphasises service delivery to firms and citizens in their role of consumer of services, purely within the executive realm. In order to do this, executive organisations may use proactive delivery of services through profiling their clients. Accountability is sought in reporting on performance of the service delivery, preferably directly to the users of services (for example by querying user panels). In a way, the consumers' preferences penetrate executive organisations [39] by 'magnetising' the orientation of the executive organisation in terms of both service delivery and accountability. Underlying information processes focus on generating performance indicators in terms of costs and quality of services for accountability purposes. "A key claim is that ICTs will allow for more accurately targeted communication of citizen requests and faster responses. Long-established state objectives [...] can be furthered through support and facilitation of the information economy and the enhancement of agencies such as the police, the armed forces, the prison service and the courts" [40: 6].

A second trajectory is concerned with mediating the interaction between citizen and government. It is referred to as '*consultation*' [see also 40] and it slightly borrows the notion of participatory government from new public management and especially leans on specific participation services as exemplified in the e-government literature. Typical examples that fit within this trajectory are advisory referendums, e-voting, and electronic town meetings. The focus of accountability is communicating information on process to general or even specific societal groups. This trajectory treats the citizen primarily as voter. Related to this, there is also a trajectory that focuses on electronic, bi-directional mediation between government on the one hand and societal groups on the other hand using electronic forums. This model builds on the assumption that the knowledge that is required for policy formulation, -formation and –execution is discursive and malleable and emerges from interaction between societal groups – including but not primarily government. In this trajectory, electronic discussion environments are the basis for transforming social capital into policies. This trajectory borrows slightly from new public management the notion of participation and breaking down governments, but especially from e-government's focus on participatory services. Accountability focuses on process and is targeted directly at citizens in their role of 'citoyen'.

These two trajectories indicate how interaction between citizens and governments change as a result of new public management and e-government reforms. These trajectories, however, do not indicate how government organisations themselves (or: relationships between various government organisations) could be affected by the combined reforms of new public management and e-government.

4.3 Internal Structuring of Government

With internal trajectories, reference is made to "changes in internal government operations that come about as IT is used for automation, cooperation and integration among government agencies and as a tool assisting in decisionmaking processes" [43: 55]. In this context, internal trajectories refer to the changes in the executive realm that stem from reforms of new public management and e-government combined.

A first 'internal' trajectory affecting relationships within and among governments is a type of reform that builds upon new public management's emphasis on joined-up government and tight cost control, and e-government's characteristics of a more efficient and cooperative interaction in and among governmental agencies using (standardised) interorganisational information services. Such a trajectory is referred to as a 'digital NPM' scenario [7, see also 41, 61]. We refer to this trajectory as *'bureaucratisation'*. It is a trajectory that indeed supersedes specific implementations of new public management reforms in the sense that "NPM methods placed a premium on single organisations handling discrete service tasks in a financially independent way, with minimal policy integration with partner agencies, the logic of Web development is much more integrative. Internet and Web changes are now one of the strongest forces for 'joined-up government', for a 'holistic' approach to data acquisition and utilisation instead of the previously highly compartmentalised and non-communicating data 'silos' of NPM's fragmented departments and agencies" [61: 2]. In order to realise any of the external trajectories mentioned above, relationships between governmental organisations are coordinated more tightly by means of centralising by informating [7, 62]. By developing an government-wide information architecture, it is possible to increase control through automatic collection, aggregation and presentation of vital policy information, and thus to enable cross organisational performance measures [44]. In fact, what is happening in this trajectory is that Weberian control is optimised by means of conscious direction of processes to great depth and/or great breadth. Weber's iron cage is optimised not through visible direction, but through the standardisation of primarily data, but secondarily operations, enforced through a government-wide information architecture.

A trajectory that is more or less opposite to the above trajectory is a trajectory that is based on blurred boundaries between agencies and departments [39] and ubiquitous e-government technologies [27]. It is based on new public management's notion of lean and highly decentralised structures, empowering street-level civil servants, and breaking down unitary bureaucracies in a web of relations with organisations in semi-public, private and voluntary sectors, and e-government's focus on external relationships and transactions. The trajectory that emerges is also referred to as leading to virtual organisations, "an admittedly voguish term" [27: 110]. Nonetheless, various forms of virtual organisations have been observed in and around public bureaucracies [63].

We call this trajectory *'virtualisation'*. The main difference with the classic public administration paradigm is that the store of documentary material is no longer controlled by means of functional differentiation and vertical integration. Rather, this trajectory indicates that ICTs in themselves are an alternative form of control that have made it possible to manage the store of documentary material in ways less crude and labour intensive than in the bureaucracy of the public administration paradigm. Whereas in the 'bureaucratisation' trajectory, control through structure is strengthened by informating bureaucratic control in an information architecture, here, the necessity of hierarchical structure is discussed: with current database and web technology, it is possible to maintain a store of documentary material that seems to have no 'real' structure but can be assembled and disassembled according to organisational and personal requirements.

4.4 Synthesis: Four Trajectories and their Consequences for Accountability and Information Requirements

By combining both the external and internal trajectories, four trajectories of marriages between new public management and e-government can be discerned (Table 11). As is the case with the archetype of bureaucracy, these configurations may be understood as ideal types: heuristic tools for identifying and classifying empirical phenomena in a way that aids further research. While one of the models is likely to be the dominant one in any specific empirical case, there may be some degree of overlap and intersection.

Table 11: Four Trajectories of Reform

		Internal Structuring	
		Virtualisation	*Bureaucratisation*
Interface with outside the world	*Service orientation*	"Electronic mediation for service delivery"	"Electronic hierarchy for service delivery"
	Consultation	"Electronic consultation enabling choice"	"Electronic consultation enabling voice options"

In practice, it is clear that it is hard to identify pure forms of the identified configurations. For example, inasmuch as electronic hierarchies truly exist, they are passive, supply oriented information services providers that rarely engage in contact and transaction services. Furthermore, in practice, there seems to be an emphasis on the development of electronic hierarchies to a lesser degree, forms of electronic mediation at the expense of services embodying democratic innovation [40].

These remarks notwithstanding, it is possible to explore these trajectories and to identify how they differ from the classic public administration paradigm. This analysis is focused on how each trajectory deals with the core idea of accountability, and how mechanisms of accountability are reinforced and enabled by the way ICTs are envisaged, or, in other words, how each trajectory is supported by an information architecture.

The first trajectory, 'electronic mediation for service delivery' idealtypically results in a service network: a loosely coupled network of public, non-governmental and private organisations that produces public goods. Inclusion in the network is based on temporary hierarchical fiat or on a fixed-term agreement, where renewal of the agreement (and thus renewed inclusion in the network) is at least partially dependent on perceived quality of service. As an illustration, the Amsterdam Public Traffic Authority's budget is partially dependent upon the results of a survey among users of the public transportation.

In this trajectory, political principals determine how the service network is configured based on the performance of the network in terms of perceived quality. Thus, accountability is not focused on 'fairness' or 'process', but on 'product', and accountability information with respect to product quality is reported to political principals. If the quality is substandard, politicians may reconfigure the network by not renewing agreements, and, in general, tender for alternative sourcing of public service delivery. An example of such a mechanism is the use of quality indicators by schools and semi-autonomised public health institutions in the Netherlands and in the United Kingdom.

In general, the information architecture that serves as the backbone of the organisational network has to facilitate a minimal degree of lock-in in the service network in order to make entry and exit of public, non-governmental and private organisations in the network possible. Therefore, the architecture does not necessarily aim for integration of programmes and services. Fountain refers to this situation as virtual integration, a coordination mechanism that functions "without changing their structure, jurisdiction, or budgetary autonomy" [41: 26-27]. A typical information architecture in this trajectory has characteristics of a clearinghouse or reference index, instead of an integrated 'data silo'. For example, in the Netherlands and in Belgium, social security schemes are executed in a network of semi-autonomous organisations. In the Netherlands, a dedicated information service called RINIS, connects, among others, municipal welfare services, the national social insurances institute (UWV), the Student's Loan Institute (IB Group), and the tax agency, by enabling them to query each other's databases using a dedicated message service. The information service, which is hosted by a small foundation and is funded by he participating members, does not enforce data standards among the participating organisations (other than the use of the Dutch social security number, SoFi, to identify citizens), nor does it strive for integration and harmonisation of procedures. Each of the participating organisations in this social security network retains its informational autonomy and therefore, the (informational) lock-in is minimal [20, 21]. The Belgian 'Kruispuntbank' is a comparable initiative, albeit it is anchored more firmly in legislation, and a bit more missionary in character in the sense that in the beginning of the 1990s, civil servants of the Kruispuntbank were stationed at other organisations participating in the social security network in order to streamline procedures and set up ICT facilities. Furthermore, de Kruispuntbank actively promotes harmonisation of legislation. But as an information service, it merely refers to decentralised databases rather than embodies an integrated information service.

The second trajectory, 'electronic hierarchy for service', marks a different perspective on both accountability and the information architecture. Here, data standardisation through the use of centralised databases is seen as a forerunner of (expanded) structural change in government bureaucracy in the sense that it creates a platform for integration efforts. Thus, the information architecture of this trajectory is based on integral, centralised databases that enforce bureaucratic control. In a sense, here, informatisation and especially integration *optimises* bureaucratic control. In other words, informational control is a device used for the sake of discipline in and between organisations because informational control is explicitly used to standardise underlying (inter)organisational procedures. A typical example of this trajectory is the Dutch network of agencies and organisations dealing with immigrants, asylum seekers and political refugees. Here, standardisation of information by dedicated standardisation committees has resulted in, among other things, harmonisation of data and procedures.

The accountability mechanism at work is basically accountability for fairness and finances, and it is emphasised and enforced in an information architecture that ties organisations together in a bureaucratic structure: the information architecture consists of one or more relatively centralised databases that more or less enforce common procedures to be used. Here, informatisation is the precursor for further standardisation, formalisation and (implicit) centralisation.

In the third trajectory, 'electronic consultation for choice', the focus is on enabling citizens (some) degree of freedom with respect to how public services are produced and/or delivered. Again, the example of public health institutions can be used: in the Netherlands, the Dutch Association of Hospitals gathers and publishes information on waiting lists for therapies offered by specific hospitals. In contrast to electronic mediation, accountability mechanisms are not directed at political principals, but at the citizens directly (public accountability): competing service providers provide performance indicators to the general public in order to generate legitimacy. Perceptions of quality of services help organisations to pass the evolutionary filter of legitimacy.

The information architecture that supports this trajectory is essentially a data warehouse application, ideally managed by a separate governmental or non-governmental organisation that monitors the performance of various competing service channels and/or providers. This application may be supplemented by procedures guaranteeing access and safeguards for the validity of the information provided. Note that the information architecture of this trajectory may resemble the information architecture of the electronic mediation trajectory, but the accountability mechanism differs, especially in its direction (public accountability versus political accountability).

The final trajectory, 'electronic consultation for voice', is based on the assumption that a relatively unitary, public service producing bureaucracy proactively generates accountability information and targets and distributes it among citizens, allowing them to cast their opinions. The manner in which this takes place, however, does not address the bureaucracy directly but their political principals. Accountability refers to finances and fairness primarily. The information architecture that supports this trajectory basically resembles the architecture of the electronic hierarchy, notwithstanding that accountability and therefore, information, is targeted at citizens, for example using websites as channels. An example is the commitment of five Dutch agencies to report periodically to the general public on their functioning.

5. Conclusion and Discussion

Bureaucracy became a bad word in the last decades of the 20th century and in the beginning of the 21st century. The new rhetoric (and possibly also the reality) of reforms stemming from new public management and e-government are stirring, analysed as separate types of reform but even more stirring when analysed in conjunction. At first sight, there seems to be a successful marriage between the reforms implied by new public management and e-government, but the variety of concepts embodied in these reforms as well as results from empirical research on the interrelation between 'technological' and 'organisational' variables suggest that various types of redesign of interorganisational relationships and, in particular information relationships can be envisaged. A single marriage between new public management as a managerial innovation and e-government as a technological innovation is a fallacy: ICT and e-government strategies can affect new public management strategies (and vice-versa) in such a way that they enable various trajectories. The views of Symonds, Dunleavy and Margetts, that indicate that seem to indicate that there is one best way of merging new public management and e-government, are therefore contested.

On the other hand, an 'anything goes scenario' can also be disputed. As has been demonstrated and illustrated, every trajectory brings about different requirements (1) with respect to the accountability and (2) with respect to the architecture of the information provision, and various manifestations of accountability mechanisms and routes, and information architectures that support these mechanisms and routes. In general, if one tries to analyse the information requirements that emerge in the different trajectories, various accountability mechanisms and information architectures emerge. Reforms adopting a new public management or an e-government flavour therefore urge their initiators to reconsider basic concepts of accountability and information architectures. Inversely, a specific architecture for e-government applications may have profound effects on how accountability mechanisms are shaped and how government and citizens interact, and therefore it requires careful consideration.

[handwritten note: No research / no data or evidence / poor use of the lit...]

References

1.   Osborne, D. and T. Gaebler, *Reinventing Government: How the Entrepreneurial Spirit is Transforming the Public Sector*. 1992, Reading, MA: Addison-Wesley.
2.   Behn, R.D., *Rethinking Democratic Accountability*. 2001, Washington D.C.: The Brookings Institute.
3.   Hood, C., *A Public Management For All Seasons?* Public Administration, 1991. **69**(1): p. 3-19.
4.   Pollitt, C.P., *Is the Emperor in his Underwear? An Analysis of the Impacts of Public Management Reform*. Public Management, 2000. **2**(2): p. 181-199.
5.   Wilson, W., *The Study of Administration*. Political Science Quarterly, 1887. **2**(2): p. 206.
6.   Guy Peters, B., *The Future of Governing: Four Emerging Models*. 1996, Kansas: Kansas University Press.
7.   Groth, L., *Future Organizational Design*, in *Future Organizational Design*, L. Groth, Editor. 1999, John Wiley & Sons: Chicester. p. 325-344.
8.   Bovens, M. and S. Zouridis, *From Street-Level Bureaucracy to System-Level Bureaucracy: How Information and Communication Technology is Transforming Administrative Discretion and Constitutional Control*. Public Administration Review, 2002. **62**(2): p. 174-184.
9.   Gruening, G., *Origin and Theoretical Basis of New Public Management*. International Public Management Journal, 2001. **4**(1): p. 1-25.
10.   Hammer, M., *Don't Automate, Obliterate!* Harvard Business Review, 1990. **68**(4): p. 104-113.
11.   Peters, T.J. and R.H. Waterman, *In Search of Excellence*. 1982, New York: Harper and Row.
12.   Osborne, D., *Bureaucracy Unbound*, in *Washington Post Magazine*. 1996: Washington. p. 8.
13.   Behn, R.D., *The New Public Management Paradigm and the Search for Government Accountability*. International Public Management Journal, 1998. **1**(2): p. 131-164.
14.   Hirschman, A., *Exit, Voice and Loyalty. Responses to Decline in Firms, Organisations and States*. 1970, Cambridge: Harvard University Press.
15.   Duivenboden, H.P.M.v. and A.M.B. Lips. *Taking Citizens Seriously*. in *EGPA*. 2001. Vaasa.
16.   Pollitt, C.P. and G. Bouckaert, *Public Management Reform: A Comparative Analysis*. 2000, Oxford: Oxford University Press.
17.   Hood, C., *Paradoxes of Public-Sector Managerialism, Old Public Management and Public Service Bargains*. International Public Management Journal, 2000. **3**(1): p. 1-22.
18.   Lynn, L.E., *A Critical Analysis of The New Public Management*. International Public Management Journal, 1998. **1**(1): p. 107-123.
19.   Landsbergen, D. and G. Walken, *Realizing the Promise: Government Information Systems and the Fourth Generation of Information Technology*. Public Administration Review, 2001. **61**(2): p. 206-219.
20.   Homburg, V.M.F., *The Political Economy of Information Management*. 1999, Groningen: SOM.
21.   Homburg, V.M.F., *The Politics and Property Rights of Information Exchange*. Knowledge, Technology and Policy, 2001. **13**(3): p. 49-66.
22.   Box, R.C., *Citizen Governance: Leading American Communities into the 21st Century*. 1998, Thousand Oaks: SAGE.

23. Vigoda, E. and R.T. Golembiewski, *Citizenship Behavior and the Spirit of New Managerialism: A Theoretical Framework and Challenge for Governance.* American Review of Public Administration, 2001. **31**(3): p. 273-295.

24. Gascó, M., *New Technologies and Institutional Change in Public Administration.* Social Science Computer Review, 2003. **21**(1): p. 6-14.

25. Fletcher, P.T., et al., *Managing Information Technology: Transforming County Governments in the 1990s.* 1992, Syracuse: School of Information Studies.

26. Kraemer, K.L. and J.L. King, *Computers and Local Government.* 1977, New York: Praeger.

27. Nohria, N. and J.D. Berkley, *The Virtual Organization (Bureaucracy, Technology and the Implosion of Control),* in *The Post-Bureaucratic Organization.*, A. Dennelon, Editor. 1994, Sage: Thousand Oaks. p. 108-128.

28. Bendix, R., *Max Weber: An Intellectual Portrait.* 1960, CA: University of California Press.

29. Gazendam, H.W.M., *Variety Controls Variety. On the Use of Organization Theories in Information Management.* 1993, Groningen: Wolters-Noordhoff.

30. Edmiston, K.D., *State and Local E-Government.* American Review of Public Administration, 2003. **33**(1): p. 20-45.

31. Moon, M.J., *The Evolution of E-Government among Municipalities: Rhetoric or Reality?* Public Administration Review, 2002. **62**(4): p. 424-433.

32. National Audit Office, *Better Public Services through E-Government.* 2002, National Audit Office: London.

33. National Performance Review, *Conversations with America.* 2000, National Performance Review. p. http://npr.gov/converse/converse.htm.

34. European Commission, *Living and Working in the Information Society.* 1996, European Commisson. p. http://europe.eu.int/comm/off/green/index_en.htm.

35. European Commission, *Building the European Information Society for all of us.* 1997, European Commission. p. http://www.cvut.cz/cc/icsc/nii/forum/building.html.

36. European Commission, *Government Online.* 2000, European Commission. p. http://europe.eu.int/comm/information_society/eeurope/actionplan/index_en.htm.

37. Snellen, I.T.M. and W.B.H.J. van der Donk, *Public Administration in an Information Age. A handbook.* 1998, Amsterdam: IOS Press.

38. Danziger, J.N. and K. Viborg Andersen, *Impacts of Information Technology on Public Administration: An Analysis of Empirical Research from the Golden Age of Transformation.* International Journal of Public Administration, 2002. **25**(5): p. 591-627.

39. Bekkers, V.J.J.M., *Grenzeloze overheid. Over informatisering en grensveranderingen in het openbaar bestuur.* 1998, Alphen aan den Rijn: Samsom.

40. Chadwick, A. and C. May. *Interaction Between States and Citizens in the Age of the Internet: 'E-Government' in the United States, Britain and the European Union.* in *APSA.* 2001. San Francisco.

41. Fountain, J., *Building the Virtual State.* 2001, Washington DC: The Brookings Institute.

42. Aarts, C.W.A.M., R.E. Leenes, and J.S. Svensson, *Kiezen op afstand Monitor.* 2001, Ministerie van Binnenlandse Zaken: Den Haag.

43. Grönlund, A., *Emerging Electronic Infrastructures (Exploring Democratic Components).* Social Science Computer Review, 2003. **21**(1): p. 55-72.

44. Minister for the Cabinet Office, *Modernising Government.* 1999, Minister for the Cabinet Office: London.

45.   Reschenthaler, G.B. and F. Thompson, *The Information Revolution and the New Public Management.* Journal of Public Administration Research and Theory, 1996. **6**(1): p. 125-143.
46.   George, J.F. and J.L. King, *Examining the Computing and Centralisation Debate.* Communications of the ACM, 1991. **27**(7): p. 650-665.
47.   Lee, H.C., *The Impact of EDP upon the Pattern of Business Organizations and Administration.* 1965, Albany: State University of New York.
48.   Whisler, T., *The Impact of Information Technology on Organizational Control,* in *The Impact of Computers on Management,* C.A. Meyers, Editor. 1967, MIT Press: Cambridge.
49.   Blau, P.M., et al., *Technology and Organization in Manufacturing.* Administrative Science Quarterly, 1976. **20-40**.
50.   Meyer, M.W., *Automation and Bureaucratic Structure.* American Journal of Sociology., 1968: p. 256-264.
51.   Breukel, A.W.V., *Strategic IT, but not by ITself.* 1996, Groningen: SOM.
52.   Schrama, G., *Keuzevrijheid in organisatievormen: Strategische keuzen rond organisatiestructuur en informatietechnologie bij het invoeren van personeelsinformatiesystemen bij grote gemeenten (Freedom of choice in organizational forms: strategic choices regarding organizational structure and information technology surrounding implementation of personnel information systems in large municipalities).* 1991, Enschede: UT Press.
53.   Malone, T.J., J. Yates, and R.I. Benjamin, *Electronic Markets and Electronic Hierarchies.* Communications of the ACM, 1987. **30**(6): p. 484-497.
54.   Davenport, T.H., R.G. Eccles, and L. Prusak, *Information Politics.* Sloan Management Review, 1992. **34**(1): p. 53-65.
55.   Brynjolfsson, E., et al., *Does Information Technology Lead to Smaller Firms?* Management Science, 1993. **40**(12): p. 1628-1644.
56.   Hart, P. and D. Estrin, *Inter-Organisational Networks, Computer Integration, and Shifts in Interdependence: The Case of the Semiconductor Industry.* ACM Transactions on Information Systems, 1991. **9**(4): p. 370-398.
57.   Steinfield, C., R. Kraut, and A. Plummer, *The Impact of Interorganizational Networks on Buyer-Seller Relationships.* Journal of Computer Mediated Communication, 1996: p. Http://jcmc.huji.ac.il.
58.   Johnston, K.D. and P.W. Lawrence, *Integrating Information Technology in a Bank Merger. Fit, Compatibility and Models of Change.* Journal of Strategic Information Systems, 1996. **5**(5): p. 189-211.
59.   Clemons, E.K., S.P. Reddi, and M.C. Row, *The Impact of Information Technology on the Organization of Economic Activity: The "Move to the Middle" Hypothesis.* Journal of Management Information Systems, 1993. **10**(2): p. 9-35.
60.   Holland, C.P. and G. Lockett. *Strategic Choice and Interorganisational Information Systems.* in *HICSS.* 1994. Hawaii: IEEE Press.
61.   Dunleavy, P. and H. Margetts. *The Advent of Digital Government: Public Bureaucracies and the State in The Information Age.* in *Annual Conference of the American Political Science Association.* 2000. Washington.
62.   Zuboff, S., *In the Age of the Smart Machine: The Future of Work and Power.* 1988, New York: Basic Books.
63.   Bekkers, V.J.J.M., *Voorbij de virtuele organisatie? Over de bestuurskundige betekenis van virtuele variëteit, contingentie en parallel organiseren.* 2001, Den Haag: Elsevier Bedrijfsinformatie.

Public Accountability in the Information Age[1]

Albert Jacob MEIJER and Mark BOVENS
Utrecht University, Utrecht School of Governance,
Bijlhouwerstraat 6, 3511 ZC Utrecht, The Netherlands

Abstract. This chapter summarizes empirical findings on the influence of information and communication technologies (ICTs) on organisational, professional, political, legal, and administrative accountability. ICTs enforce and challenge these traditional accountability arrangements and call for new forms of accountability. Both local accountability practices and linkages between government practices and the (accountability) environment are affected. We conclude that we need to understand the linkages between information ecologies and their environment to grasp the nature of public accountability in the information age.

1. Introduction

Public accountability is a key concept in public administration and embodies the central value of accounting for delegated authority. In the context of government, public accountability is a key element of information ecologies since the exchange of information is a prerequisite for accountability. Governments use a variety of information and communication technologies (ICTs) to improve service to citizens and to enhance their input in policy processes. These ICTs can also, sometimes quite inadvertently, play a role in processes of public account giving.

An early example of the role of ICTs in public accountability is the 1999 Dutch parliamentary investigation of an airplane that crashed into Amsterdam in 1992. One of the politically sensitive issues was the fact that the airplane had contained some sort of uranium and thus how the Dutch National Aviation Agency had dealt with the uranium became part of the parliamentary investigation. At the time of the crash, the Dutch National Aviation Agency, as a very early adopter, had already introduced a system for internal and external e-mail. Individual officials preserved the e-mail messages they considered to be important for their work or personal dealings. This preservation of information proved important for external accountability. An inspector at the agency gave copies of internal e-mail messages to the committee. Eventually it turned out that the use of e-mail instead of telephone calls had increased the transparency of communication within the agency and thus facilitated external accountability [1].

ICTs can thus be used to support traditional forms of public accountability, such as parliamentary inquiries, but they may also facilitate new forms of accountability. In this chapter we explore how governments can be held accountable in the information age. We argue that the focus on public accountability highlights a crucial element of information ecologies: the linkages between these ecologies and their environment. To understand the nature of these linkages, we begin with brief discussion of public accountability.

---

1 Previous versions of this chapter were presented at EGPA 2003 Conference in Oeiras and the E-government Workshop of JURIX 2003 in Amsterdam.

2. Public Accountability: A Key Concept in Democratic Governance

Public accountability is increasingly considered to be the hallmark of democratic governance. Democracy remains a paper procedure if those in power cannot be held accountable in public for their acts and omissions, for their decisions, their policies, and their expenditures. Public accountability, as a set of practices of account giving, therefore, is one of the important elements of information ecologies.

As a concept, however, 'public accountability' is rather elusive. It serves as a synonym for many loosely defined political desiderata, such as transparency, equity, democracy, efficiency and integrity [2-4]. As we see it, 'public accountability' refers to institutionalised practices of account giving. For the purpose of this chapter, we define accountability as a social relationship in which an actor feels an obligation to explain and to justify his conduct to some significant other [5, 6]

This relatively simply defined relationship contains a number of variables. The actor, or *accountor*, can be either an individual or an agency. The significant other, which we call the *accountability forum* or the *accountee*, can be a specific person or agency, but can also be a more virtual entity, such as the general public.

The relationship between the actor and the forum, the account giving, usually consists of at least three elements or stages. First of all, the actor must feel obliged to inform the forum about his conduct by providing various sorts of data about the performance of tasks, about outcomes, or about procedures. Often, particularly in the case of failures or incidents, this also involves the provision of justifications. This then, can prompt the forum to interrogate the actor and to question the adequacy of the information or the legitimacy of the conduct. This is the debating phase; hence, the close semantic connection between 'accountability' and 'answerability'. Third, the forum usually passes judgment on the conduct of the actor. It may approve of an annual account, denounce a policy, or publicly condemn the behaviour of a manager or an agency.

In passing a negative judgment, the forum frequently imposes some sort of sanctions on the accountor. These sanctions can be highly formalised, such as fines, disciplinary measures or even penal sanctions, but often the punishment will only be implicit or informal, such as the very fact of giving an account in front of television cameras, or of having your public image or career damaged by the negative publicity that results from the process.

The obligation felt by the accountor can also be both formal and informal. Public managers will often be under a formal obligation to give accounts on a regular basis to specific forums, such as their superiors, supervisory agencies, or auditors. In case of unpleasant incidents or administrative deviance, public managers can be forced to appear in court or to testify before parliamentary committees. But the obligation can also be informal, or even self-imposed, as in the case of press conferences, informal briefings, or public confessions.

Finally, the conduct that is to be explained and justified can vary enormously, from budgetary scrutiny in case of financial accountability, to administrative fairness in case of legal accountability, or even sexual propriety when it comes to the political accountability of Anglo-American public officials.

In the daily life of modern public managers operating in a democratic system, there are at least five different sorts of forums that they may have to face up to, and therefore also five different types of potential accountability relationships, and five different sets of norms and expectations:[2]
-   Organisational accountability

---

[2] These forms are adapted from [5], [6] and [7].

- Professional accountability
- Political accountability
- Legal accountability
- Administrative accountability

Organisational accountability primarily takes place *within local practices*. This type of accountability shapes relations and information exchanges between managers and civil servants within government organisations. Professional, political, legal, and administrative accountability form a *linkage* between practices within government organisations and the relevant environment of these organisations.

Public managers have to deal with all of these types of accountability. The introduction of ICTs in government organisations, however, has led to changes in the functioning of government. ICTs have influenced these five accountability relationships in different ways. In this chapter, we look at each of these five accountability relationships and describe the influence of ICTs for understanding both the changes within local practices and the changes in linkages between local practices and the environment.

3. Information and Communication Technologies

It does not seem to be an exaggeration to state that nowadays most government organisations could not function without ICTs. Information and communication technologies are used to support the key functions of government. ICTs are both used *within* government organisations and in the contacts between the organisation and the '*outside world*' (citizens, companies, other organisations). Database systems, workflow management systems, e-mail systems and web technology systems are all used to support government operations, engage citizens, and provide government services. These various information and communication technologies are integrated in complex information systems. Databases, for example, are connected to websites, workflow management systems use the facilities of office systems, and expert systems may be connected to e-mail applications.

In an analytical way, however, different qualities of separate technologies can be identified. Zuboff distinguishes between 'intrinsic' and 'emergent' qualities [7]. Orlikowski indicates that these 'intrinsic qualities' are not neutral: they facilitate certain actions whereas they might hinder others [8] Workflow management systems, for example, facilitate standardised processing of documents but may make it more difficult to deal adequately with exceptional cases. According to their 'intrinsic qualities', three types of information and communication technologies can be distinguished:

Societal ICTs facilitate openness and may hinder the formation of boundaries between organisations and countries. Examples are the World Wide Web and Usenet.
Organisational ICTs facilitate central steering and may hinder the handling of non-standard cases. Examples are enterprise resource planning systems, such as the SAP systems used for financial administration and workflow management systems.

Personal ICTs can be used to support the work of individual employees, but may hinder central oversight. Examples are e-mail applications, text editors, and mobile telephones.

The characteristics of these technologies are not deterministic [7, 8]. Societal technologies, such as web technology, can be used within organisations; and organisational technologies, such as database systems, can be used by individuals. Nevertheless, these technologies have acquired different characteristics through processes of technological and social construction. Technologies tend to have different effects on public accountability because of their differences.

We can better understand the differences between these groups of technologies if we put them in the perspective of information ecologies. An information ecology is a system of people, practices, values, and technologies in a particular local environment. [9] The three groups of ICTs influence these local environments differently. Societal ICTs open the local environment up to the wider environment and even to people on the other side of the world. Organisational ICTs change power relations *within* local environments since they facilitate steering of local practices. Personal ICTs support individuals in shaping local environments according to their preferences.

The use of ICTs in government can influence local practices of civil servants. Accountability relations are elements of these local practices, but they also connect local practices to relevant actors in the environment of government organisations. ICTs can thus influence the variety of accountability relations within these local practices and the accountability relations between these practices and the environment. To understand the impact of ICTs on accountability, we summarize major empirical findings on the influence of these various types of ICTs on each of the accountability relations that we have distinguished. *NO summaries here*

4. Organisational Accountability in the Information Age

4.1 Accountability to superiors

The first, and most important accountability relation for public managers is organisational. Their administrative and political superiors will regularly, sometimes on a formal basis such as with annual performance reviews but more often in daily informal meetings, ask them to account for their assignments. This usually involves a strong hierarchical relationship and the accounting may be based on strict directives and standard operating procedures, but this is not a constitutive element. Senior policy advisors and project managers will often have a considerable amount of autonomy in performing their tasks, and yet may strongly feel the pressures of organisational accountability. Strictly speaking, this is not yet 'public' accountability because these account givings are usually not accessible to the public at large. Nevertheless, this organisational accountability is the *sine qua non* for the other, external forms of public accountability.

4.2 ICTs and organisational accountability

Various researchers have investigated the impact of the use of organisational ICTs on organisational accountability. Zuurmond indicates that bureaucracy is transformed into 'infocracy' [10]. In an infocracy, control is not exerted through bureaucratic structures but through the information structure. This information structure controls the behaviour of civil servants and also renders their behaviour transparent to their superiors. The organisational accountability of civil servants is increased since superiors have more means to monitor their behaviour and ask them to account for their behaviour. At the same time, one can argue that there is less need for ex-post accountability since ex-ante control is increased because civil servants can no longer escape from organisational procedures (see also [11]). The account giving has become less explicit and overt because in the infocracy, the behaviour of civil servants is increasingly controlled ex-ante through the information structure, instead of ex post through answerability to their superiors.

Student grants in the Netherlands: Civil servants used to have a fair degree of autonomy in deciding who received a student grant or loan. They used their discretionary powers to evaluate whether a student was in need of a grant and looked into the personal situation of the student. This was a source of professional pride but also of personal biases. Nowadays, the provision of public grants to students is fully automated. This expert system is based on the law concerning student grants, and legal procedures have been encoded in computer programmes. Civil servants only have to enter data in the system and the system then decides who will receive a grant. Organisational accountability concerning the use of discretionary powers is no longer relevant [12].

Research by Meijer [1] indicates that the use of personal information and communication technologies (such as e-mail and text editors) may have the opposite effect on organisational accountability.[3] He states that these ICTs hamper organisational accountability because these ICTs render the behaviour of civil servants less transparent to their superiors. Superiors do not know who civil servants are communicating with and lack control over information storage. Meijer argues that these changes require a shift from organisational to professional accountability.

The Dutch Ministry of Foreign Affairs: At the Dutch Ministry of Foreign Affairs, e-mail facilities are used for both business and personal communication. Business communication at the ministry follows official, functional lines and e-mail addresses are connected to functional mailboxes of embassies, consulates or directorates. In practice, however, little use is made of this form of communication. Civil servants prefer to use either the protected network, fax or snail mail. Apart from the functional e-mail addresses, civil servants also have a personal e-mail address. This personal address is used for both private and work related communication. Civil servants use personal e-mail according to their own standards and decide whether they need to preserve e-mail messages and in what form. Central management has no control over this use of e-mail. [1]

The findings of Zuurmond and Meijer seem to be contradictory. A closer look at their research, however, indicates that the findings apply to different administrative processes. The findings of Zuurmond and Zouridis concern the use of organisational ICTs (large database systems) in large-scale policy execution. Meijer's findings concern the use of personal ICTs in policy development. This seems to indicate that organisational accountability is strengthened in certain parts of government and hampered in other parts of government through the use of ICT.

4.3   New forms of organisational accountability

The transition from bureaucracies to infocracies (or even information refineries [12]) may demand new forms of organisational accountability. The object of accountability has shifted from the execution of business processes to the design and implementation of information infrastructures. In terms of Mintzberg [13]: accountability in the technostructure becomes more important than accountability in the operating core. A question that remains unanswered is whether accountability relations in the technostructure will be of an organisational or rather of a professional nature. Will organisations set up

---

[3] The changes Meijer describes fit well within Hekscher's ideas about post-bureaucratic organisations. Hekscher indicates that in these organisations, individuals in network relations structure their actions according to the mission of the organisation [13].

information structures in the technostructure to control the design and implementation of information structures in the operating core? Or will organisations rely on profession accountability to assure the quality of information structures in the operating core?

5. Professional Accountability in the Information Age

5.1 Accountability to professional peers

Many public managers are, apart from being civil servants, professionals in a more technical sense. They have been trained as engineers, doctors, veterinarians, teachers or police officers. This may imply accountability relationships with professional associations and disciplinary tribunals. Professional bodies establish codes with standards for acceptable practice that are binding for all members. These standards are monitored and enforced by professional bodies of oversight on the basis of peer review. This type of accountability will be particularly relevant for public managers who work in professional organisations, such as hospitals, schools, psychiatric clinics, police departments or fire brigades.

5.2 ICTs and professional accountability

In line with their findings on organisational accountability, Zuurmond, and Bovens and Zouridis stress that professional autonomy is limited through the use of organisational information and communication technologies [11, 14]. Operating procedures are embedded in software and professionals cannot evade these procedures. This not only applies to administrative professionals but also increasingly to doctors and police officers. Use of ICTs leads to a process of 'deprofessionalisation' in government and thus to less professional accountability.

Other developments, however, point to an increasing professionalisation in government and thus to a shift in professional accountability. The use of ICTs may lead to accountability relations for occupational groups that were not previously recognised as professions – e.g. 'information professionals'. Electronic data processing auditors in the Netherlands, for example, have formed professional associations and standards for acceptable practice. This indicates that civil servants in the local environment of a public organisation are trying to improve their position by strengthening linkages with their – professional – environment.

5.3 New forms of professional accountability

Traditional professions such as doctors and lawyers have well described procedures for entrance to their professional community. One may wonder whether these new communities of information professionals will be at the same distance from the general public as classic professionals. It seems likely that in the near future (information) professionals in government will not only be held accountable by professional peers but – through societal ICTs – also by 'amateurs'. LINUX and the open source movement may provide interesting models for public forms of professional accountability in the information age.

6. Political Accountability in the Information Age

6.1   Accountability to elected representatives

For managers in the public sector, accountability to political forums, such as elected representatives or political parties, can be very important facts of life. In parliamentary systems with ministerial responsibility and a general civil service, such as Britain and The Netherlands, this political accountability is usually exercised indirectly, through the minister. Increasingly, however, public managers also have to appear before parliamentary committees, for example in the case of parliamentary inquiries. In the American presidential system, senior public managers, heads of agencies for example, are often directly accountable to Congress. In administrative systems that work with political cabinets and appointees, as for example in the US, France, or Belgium, public managers will also find they have an informal and discrete, but not to be disregarded, accountability relationship with party bosses. Public managers, especially those with a professional or legal background, often find political accountability difficult to handle, if not threatening, because of the fluid, contingent and ambiguous character of political agendas.

6.2   ICTs and political accountability

Meijer indicates that the use of organisational ICTs in government increases the informational and the analytical transparency of government organisations [1]. Local practices are opened up to the environment of government organisations. Political fora can profit from these changes in government because they are often interested in policy evaluations. However, Meijer also points at the danger of an information overload. Government agencies generate enormous amounts of information and it seems unlikely that elected representatives will be able to deal with all of this information adequately.

> The Dutch Central Information Agency: An example of the inability to use all relevant (digital) information is a Dutch parliamentary inquiry into the use of various methods of investigation by the police. The Central Information Agency of the Dutch police is the central actor in exchanges of information concerning police suspects. To perform this task, this agency uses an elaborate database system to manage data about suspects. This database system can be considered a rich source of information for evaluating the functioning of the Dutch police organisation. However, the parliamentary enquiry committee did not directly use these digital data. The committee limited itself to a paper report that showed numbers that were generated with the database system. In this case, ICT created many opportunities for fact-finding, but these opportunities were left unused for lack of expertise and resources to analyse it [1].

6.3   New forms of accountability

In the context of government and ICTs, direct accountability to citizens is the most debated form of political accountability [1, 15]. Direct accountability could be an addition to – rather than a substitute for – indirect accountability. New technologies can facilitate a 'digital agora' so that modern rulers can then be held accountable in the same way as Greek rulers. Societal ICTs are important here: citizens can have direct access to information about the functioning of government agencies and use communication technologies for a public debate. Local practices in government organisations are thus not only opened up to the political environment but also to (individual) citizens. Northrup and Thorson give the interesting example of the Korean government that enabled citizens to monitor the process of permit applications [16]. They claim that this form of transparency enables accountability and reduces corruption.

7. Legal Accountability in the Information Age

7.1   Accountability to courts

Public managers can be summoned by courts to account for their own acts, or on behalf of the agency as a whole. Usually this will be a specialised administrative court, but, depending on the legal system and the issue at stake, it can also be a civil or penal court. In most western countries, legal accountability is taking on increasing importance to public managers as a result of the growing formalisation of social relations [17]. Legal accountability is the most unambiguous type of accountability since legal scrutiny will be based on detailed legal standards, prescribed by civil, penal, or administrative statutes or precedent.

7.2   ICTs and legal accountability

Legal accountability of digital governments used to be a matter of debate for legal scholars. Can electronic information be admitted as evidence? What is the legal value of a digital signature? These questions, however, seem no longer relevant as countries all around the world are granting digital information the same status as paper information. This does not mean, however, that the digitisation of government does not have an impact on legal accountability. Meijer has indicated that e-management and the use of organisational ICTs increases both the informational and the analytical transparency of government organisations and that, therefore, fact-finding by legal fora is facilitated [1].

   However, legal forums so far have made little use of these additional opportunities and keep on using the same information that they used in the 'paper situation'. Opportunities for linking local practices to the legal environment are rarely used. One may ask whether this is a problem: legal accountability is not hampered. One may even wonder whether there is still so much need for legal accountability. Empirical research seems to indicate that the legal quality of routine decisionmaking has increased because of the use of organisational ICTs [12, 18]. Humans are likely to make more mistakes than computers. In this respect, the use of ICTs seems to lead to a change from ex-post to ex-ante legal accountability. On the other hand, one may argue that legal checks and balances may no longer be adequate since the power of government organisations over citizens has been increased by their use of information and communication technologies. The net result of these developments may be that citizens have less legal protection against the abuse of power by government organisations.

7.3   New forms of legal accountability

De Mulder indicates that the use of ICTs has led to 'fourth generation law': law that is interactive (like spoken law) and can be distributed on a large scale (like printed law) [19]. In research on commercial applications of ICTs this is often labelled 'mass customisation'. ICTs can be used to pre-programme decisionmaking in highly individual cases. Traditional forms of legal accountability are incapable of dealing with use of power since they were designed to evaluate individual cases. De Mulder therefore called for a new form of legal accountability that can check on 'mass customisation' in government.

8. Administrative Accountability in the Information Age

8.1 Accountability to auditors and controllers

In addition to courts, a whole series of quasi-legal forums that exercise independent and external administrative oversight and control has been established in the past decades. These forums vary from Ombudsmen and national or local audit offices to independent supervisory authorities. They exercise regular financial and administrative control, often on the basis of specific statutes and prescribed norms. This type of accountability can be very important for public managers that work in quango's and other executive public agencies.

8.2 ICTs and administrative accountability

The increase in the informational and analytical transparency of government organisations because of the use of organisational ICTs also facilitates fact-finding by administrative fora [1]. ICTs can increase the quantity and the quality of the information which they need for evaluating government policies and government decisions.

> The Dutch Ministry of Finance: The Ministry of Finance is responsible for collection of national taxes. A wide variety of information systems is used to execute this task. Additionally, the ministry advises the minister in developing tax policies. Data about income taxes in the Netherlands are gathered in a database system for policy analysis. As it turned out, this system was not only helpful for policy analysis but also for administrative accountability. The National Audit Office was able to use data from this database system to calculate the effects of certain legal arrangements. Without the digital application, this type of fact-finding would have been practically impossible. In this case ICTs created many opportunities to analyse data and can therefore facilitated fact-finding [1].

8.3 New forms of accountability

The development of more direct forms of accountability through societal ICTs may also be impacted by administrative accountability. Auditors and controllers may no longer function as separate accountability forums, but may function as support mechanisms for direct accountability. Auditors and controllers can monitor the quality of the information which government agencies present to citizens and indicate whether this information is reliable and complete. This evaluation could take the form of a (required) hyperlink on government web pages. Auditors would then monitor the linkage between the local practices of government organisations and the wider environment.

9. ICTs and Public Accountability: General Trends

So far we have focused on effects of the use of ICTs on specific types of accountability. On the basis of empirical research we can also identify several general trends. These trends refer to changes in government that influence various types of accountability.

The first general trend is the blurring of boundaries between public organisations: "When informational domains entangle, it is quite difficult to find out where something has gone wrong. And, if information is shared and refined, where lies the right of ownership? Who is responsible for the use of new, virtual databases that are based on the combination and refinement of data which is stored in database management systems in different organisations with different jurisdictions?" [20: 74]. The blurring of organisational boundaries may have serious implications for the organisational jurisdiction which can be described as the exclusive authority of an actor as a unified entity to determine right and obligations of citizens in a task domain with (a certain degree of) discretion for which the actor is legally and politically accountable [20]. This means that blurring of boundaries influences political, legal, and administrative accountability. It may also aggravate the problem of many hands [21, 22]. Who is to be held accountable? And who can provide the required information?

The second general trend is an increase in transparency. More data are recorded and there are more ways to retrieve these data. The use of ICTs leads to a more 'transparent state'. Meijer indicates that the increased transparency may be the result of deliberate actions, but often results unintentionally from efforts to improve the execution and management of work processes [1]. We have seen that this transparency facilitates fact-finding by all accountability forums.

The third general trend is an increase in the diversity of mechanisms for accountability. New mechanisms do not replace old forms of accountability but supplement the traditional mechanisms. From the point of view of information ecologies, we observe that the diversity of information ecologies increases: local practices consist of a wider variety of information exchanges. One can argue that this strengthens the robustness of local practices since they are less dependent on traditional mechanisms.

The blurring of boundaries and the increase in transparency effectively result in stronger linkages between local practices within government organisations and the (professional, political, legal, and administrative) environment. ICTs create additional opportunities for monitoring whether government practices conform to external standards. One may wonder, however, whether this opening up of local practices has only positive effects. Nardi and O'Day describe that the opening up of local practices in the operation room of a hospital negatively affected the work of anaesthesiologists and nurses [9]. The same might happen in government: the protection of a local practice may be needed for creating trust and self-confidence of civil servants. The lack of protection might result in risk avoidance, goal displacement, and stressful working conditions [23].

10. Public Accountability in a Network Society

We think that the changes in the accountability relations of government require a new conceptualisation of public accountability. The public consists of all kinds of other societal actors (journalists, societal groups, intermediaries, etc.). These societal actors increasingly add dynamic, informal and non-hierarchical accountability relations to the existing accountability relations through formal institutions. The only way that we can get a grip on the accountability of government is by placing government in a network society. Northrup and Thorson suggest that we move the focus from e-government (the institutions of government) to e-governance (the larger web of formal and informal institutions) [16]. This transition means that public accountability does not relate to accountability relations between government agencies and society but concerns a wide range of horizontal accountability relationships between societal actors. Public accountability concerns accountability for public affairs, and government is not the only entity that deals with these affairs..

This transition will affect all phases of accountability processes. In the information phase, there will not be one single source of information. Information will increasingly be provided and contested by various actors. The debate phase will change with regard to participants and the structure of the debate: the debate will be open for many participants and will not always be structured according to formal procedures. Most actors will not dispose of formal sanctions. It seems probable that publicity and public exposure will develop into dominant sanctions.

The impact of ICTs on informational aspects of accountability has received a lot of attention in empirical research. The role of ICTs – especially the Internet – in the debating and sanction phases of accountability processes has scarcely been investigated. A further conceptualisation of public accountability in the information age requires more research into the role of ICTs in the debating and sanctions phases of public accountability processes.

References

1. Meijer, A., *De doorzichtige overheid. Parlementaire en juridische controle in het informatietijdperk.* 2002, Delft: Eburon.
2. Mulgan, R., *Accountability: An Ever Expanding Concept?* Public Administration, 2000. **78**(3): p. 555-575.
3. Behn, R.D., *Rethinking Democratic Accountability.* 2001, Washington D.C.: The Brookings Institute.
4. Dubnick, M.J., *Seeking Salvation for Accountability.* 2002, Annual Meeting of the American Political Science Association: Boston.
5. Romzek, B.S. and M.J. Dubnick, *Accountability,* in *International Encyclopedia of Public Policy and Administration. Volume 1,* Shafritz, Editor. 1998.
6. Pollitt, C.P., *The Essential Public Manager.* 2003: Open University Press.
7. Zuboff, S., *In the age of the smart machine: the future of work and power.* 1988, New York: Basic Books.
8. Orlikowski, W.J., *The Duality of Technology: Rethinking the Concept of Technology in Organizations.* Organization Science, 1992. **3**(3): p. 398-427.
9. Nardi, B.A. and V.L. O'Day, *Information Ecologies: Using Technology with Heart.* 1999, Cambridge (MA): The MIT Press.
10. Zuurmond, A., *From Bureaucracy to Infocracy: Are Democratic Institutions Lagging Behind?*, in *Administration in an Information Age. A Handbook,* I.T.M. Snellen and W.B.J.H. van de Donk, Editors. 1998, IOS Press: Amsterdam.
11. Bovens, M. and S. Zouridis, *From street-level bureaucracy to system-level bureaucracy: How information and communication technology is transforming administrative discretion and constitutional control.* Public Administration Review, 2002. **62**(2): p. 174-184.
12. Zouridis, S., *Digitale disciplinering.* 2000, Tilburg: University of Tilburg.
13. Mintzberg, H., *Structure in Fives: Designing Effective Organizations.* 1983, Englewood Cliffs: Prentice Hall.
14. Zouridis, S., *Information Technology and the Organization Chart of Public Administration,* in *Public Administration in an Information Age. A Handbook,* I.T.M. Snellen and W.B.J.H. van de Donk, Editors. 1998, IOS Press: Amsterdam. p. 245-258.
15. Raab, C.D., *Electronic Confidence: Trust, Information and Public Administration,* in *Public Administration in an Information Age,* I.T.M. Snellen and W.B.H.J. Van de Donk, Editors. 1997, IOS Press: Amsterdam.

16.   Northrup, T.A. and S.J. Thorson, *The Web of Governance and Democratic Accountability.*, in *Proceedings of the 36th Hawaii International Conference on System Sciences*, R. Sprague, Editor. 2003, IEEE Press: Big Island.

17.   Friedman, L.M., *Total Justice*. 1985, New York: Russell SAGE.

18.   Groothuis, M.M. and J.S. Svensson, *Expert System Support and Juridical Quality*, in *Legal Knowledge and Information Systems JURIX 2000: The Thirteenth Annual Conference*, J. Beuker, R.E. Leenes, and R. Winkels, Editors. 2000, Koninklijke Vermande: Lelystad.

19.   De Mulder, R.V., *The Digital Revolution: From trias to tetras politica*. Public Administration in an Information Age, ed. I.T.M. Snellen and W.B.H.J. van de Donk. 1998, Amsterdam: IOS Press.

20.   Bekkers, V.J.J.M., *Wiring Public Organizations and Changing Organizational Juridisctions.*, in *Public Administration in an Information Age*, I.T.M. Snellen and W.B.H.J.v.d. Donk, Editors. 1998, IOS Press: Amsterdam. p. 57-77.

21.   Thompson, D.F., *Moral Responsibility of Public Officials: The Problem of Many Hands.* American Political Science Review, 1980. **74**: p. 905-916.

22.   Bovens, M., *The Quest for Responsibility: Accountability and Citizenship in Complex Organisations*. 1998, Cambridge: Cambridge University Press.

23.   Halachmi, A., *Performance Measurement: A Look at Some Possible Dysfunctions.* Work Study, 2002. **51**(5): p. 230-239.

The Information Ecology of E-Government
V.J.J.M. Bekkers and V.M.F. Homburg (Eds.)
IOS Press, 2005

The Information Ecology
of E-Government Revisited

Victor BEKKERS and Vincent HOMBURG
Erasmus University Rotterdam, Faculty of Social Sciences,
Public Administration Group, PO Box 1738, 3000 DR Rotterdam, The Netherlands

Abstract. In this chapter the authors discuss the added value, relevance, advantages and disadvantages of information ecology as a perspective on e-government. Throughout the book, the concept has been refined in a step-by-step manner, resulting in a view of e-government as the local co-evolution of developments in technological, socio-organisational, economic, cultural and economic organisational environments.

1. Introduction

Our odyssey through the worlds of e-government has come to an end. We have looked at several manifestations of e-government, in the front office as well as the back office. The local flavour of e-government could be understood by visiting several countries. Different kinds of e-government services have been described. Often, these descriptions went beyond sheer public service delivery; possibilities of using ICT to enhance the political participation of citizens and to improve the public accountability have been discussed and analysed as well. New intermediaries and new, virtual organisation patterns have been identified in the slipstream of e-government. Although the rhetoric of many policy programmes regarding e-government proclaims the same benefits, the variety of e-government is an intriguing phenomenon. How can we explain this variety? In this book we have used the notion of the information ecology to grasp the outcomes of a number of e-government initiatives in several countries. What are the lessons to be learned? There are lessons regarding the outcomes of e-government as well as lessons about the strengths and weaknesses of using notion of the information ecology to understand the outcomes of e-government. This final chapter of this volume will deal with these and other questions.

In section two, we return to the notion of the information ecology as it was introduced in the first chapter. In section three, we discuss the findings of the several contributions. In section four, we discuss the strength and weakness of the notion of the information-ecology. An outlook is presented in section five.

2. The Information Ecology of E-Government

In many policy documents regarding e-government, a combination of determinism and voluntarism of the role of technology is evident. In the deterministic view of ICT, it is seen as an autonomous, undeniable and exogenous force. The notion of the *information society*, in which government operates, also reflects this idea: the omnipresence of ICT will open up new horizons to enhance the legitimacy of public administration.

In the voluntaristic view of ICT, technology is seen as an enabling technology which, provided the 'right' people use it, will create desirable outcomes. In this view, ICT is a neutral set of tools that can be used to reinvent government in a more customer-oriented, responsive and efficient way. In many policy documents, e-government is indeed seen as a set of tools and a strategy to redesign the machinery of government.

However, as we have argued in the first chapter of this book, research into the effects of ICT in public (and private) organisations has shown us that very few general effects of ICT can ever be discerned; the outcomes are greatly influenced by the specific setting in which ICT has been developed, introduced and implemented. In many e-government policy documents, the existing political, socio-organisational, economic and institutional setting has been rather neglected. Since an ecological approach of ICT use in organisations focuses on the co-evolution of different kinds of environments that produces a selection process of the technological variants, which will ultimately be used and implemented, we have introduced the notion of the information ecology for understanding the contextuality of e-government. Inspired by Davenports [1] and Nardi and O'Day's [2] work on the information ecology, we have distinguished the following features of an information ecological approach of e-government.

- E-government can be seen as a system, which is marked by strong interrelationships and dependencies between different parts. E-government is not only about the use of ICT, it is also concerned with other aspects of the organisational environment in which ICT is used, such as the strategy of the organisation, the qualities of the staff, the dominant culture and structure of the organisation and the distribution of power and power resources within the organisation.
- In an information-ecology of e-government, there are different kinds of actors and different kinds of tools. Hence, actors see different kinds of opportunities for e-government. This is why it is the local context that determines what kinds of technologies and opportunities will be envisioned. This is the main reason that e-government in Amsterdam has different features than e-government in Paris, London or Barcelona. But even within the municipality of Amsterdam, we see a striking variety of e-government applications.
- It is not only technological considerations that play an important role in the selection process. We should also consider the interaction between the technological environment of e-government and other environments, like developments in the political, socio-organisational, cultural and economic environment. The relationship between these different environments can be understood in terms of co-evolution.
- The co-evolution of these different environments of e-government generates variety of possibilities, threats, applications and all kinds of possible changes that require selection. However, this selection process does not take place on the basis of a powerless and open dialogue. Within these specific environments, various kinds of different actors can be distinguished, with different positions, interests and with all kinds of powerful resources at their disposal. This is why we should pay attention to the interactions between the stakeholders who are involved, the strategies they employ to safeguard their positions and interests, and the choices they make. It is important to look what values these actors attach to the role and meaning of e-government in relation to the goals they possess. Moreover, it is important to bear in mind that in the technology itself, specific values, i.e. like the potential to control, are embedded; values that can also be linked to the values that these actors attach to possibilities and threats of e-government. The result is that the introduction of technology in organisations can

hardly be understood in terms of a rational and linear process. Rather, it is the outcome of a complex and unpredictable process of interactions, in which power, exchange, and communication play an important role. If we want to understand this complex interplay, it is important to recognise the fact that these interactions are local and that e-government has a local flavour.

- At the same time the co-evolution of these specific (and local) environments and the interaction between the stakeholders who are dominant in those environments are institutionally embedded. The behaviour of these actors is influenced by 'rules', by historically developed practices. For instance, Scandinavian countries traditionally, have a more open attitude about the protection of privacy while the Netherlands and Germany consider it a more serious issue; this will obviously influence the nature of e-government design in these countries.

3. The Flavours of E-Government as an Information Ecology

In this section we present the major findings of the contributions. We show how e-government has been shaped at several levels: the policy formulation level and the implementation level. Moreover, we show how the formulation of e-government policy programmes and the implementation of these policies have been shaped by the co-evolution of technological, socio-organisational, political an economic environments as well as by the complex interplay of stakeholders.

3.1   *The Locus and Focus of E-Government: Revealing the Information Ecology*

Zouridis and Thaens explored e-government as a phenomenon by looking at the locus and focus of e-government. This enabled them to investigate the anatomy of e-government. They described some examples of different e-government services, situated in a broad variety of policy sectors (e.g. education, public safety, social security). They conclude that the manifestation of e-government primarily takes place on the operational level of public administration. This can partly be explained by the fact that the emphasis lies on public service delivery, in which citizens are primarily seen as consumers. E-government can be seen as the final electronic piece of the implementation of public policy programmes. There is hardly any relation between e-government and the agenda setting and political decision-making phases of the policy cycle. In the realms of politics, e-government is primarily used to support democratic supervision and representation, in which citizens are mostly seen as voters.

Not only is the locus of e-government limited, but the focus of e-government is also limited. How does e-government approach public administration? Public administration is seen as the production of public services and the reinvention of public administration through ICT, and because of this, it is primarily viewed as an information management challenge. The rationale the colours the bias of many e-government programmes is an economic and professional one. ICT is primarily used as a tool to improve the efficiency of government in terms of cost reduction and as a tool to enhance the legal professionalism in the application of rules and regulations in such a way that a citizens acquires the specific rights (like a subsidy or a permit) and obligations (like a tax assessment) in a consistent and legally defendable way. The dominant image of government in many e-government projects is that of government as an 'information processor' [3].

3.2   Trends and Consolidations in E-Government Information Ecology

Janssen and Rotthier showed that there is an interesting convergence between the central ideas that have been put forward in the policy programmes on e-government of a number of OECD-countries at the policy level, even though these countries themselves rarely conclude that there is convergence between them. They conclude that a process of e-government policy transfer has taken place that has produced a number of striking similarities. The goals of these strategic e-government programmes, the instruments they have used and a number of operational e-government policy programmes (focusing on identification, authenticity, security, privacy and architecture) resemble each other to a large extent. Looking at the work of Janssen and Rotthier, we can speak of an e-government ideology that countries and organisations share and that has a rather limited locus and focus. However, the interesting question is whether the sharing of this common frame of reference concerning the goals and instruments of e-government will also produce the same outcomes, because the real challenge lies in the implementation of these programmes. Understanding the outcomes of the implementation process could be understood in terms of an information ecology.

Zouridis and Thaens' contribution and Janssen and Rotthier's contribution show us that an ecological approach to e-government should pay attention to the ideological environment that influences the shaping of e-government. To some extent, e-government can be seen as a public management ideology that legitimises the reform of public administration in a more efficient and client-friendly way. Actors within a public organisation appeal to these values in order to legitimise the changes to be made.

Moreover, in Janssen and Rotthier's contribution, the notion of an information ecology has been used to understand the introduction of a variety of ICT applications as specific front office applications or even as front office organisational models. The realisation of these front office applications is not seen as a technological issue, but as the result of a complex interplay between people, values, working processes etc. Such an approach can also be found in the work of Davenport [1].

3.3   The Political Economy of the Information Ecology

In Bekkers and Homburg's chapter on the back office of e-government, the policy level has been set aside in order to address the question of how organisations that are involved in e-government operations overcome a number of barriers which are typical for e-government. Several reasons are provided. The major challenge is to organise a process of co-operation between these back-offices. In their contribution, Bekkers and Homburg studied the emergence of five basic registration systems. These registers store authentic information that has been gathered at the source and is used by several back offices that use the same information for different operations and functions.

The notion of the information ecology returns to the forefront here in at least three ways. First, the lessons that have been drawn from the case studies show that other environments, besides the technological one, also influence in the shaping of the interorganisational information systems. For instance, the cases of the Residential Information Register and the Vehicle License Register show that the introduction of these registers have had serious consequences for the working process, the culture and the qualifications of the staff of the organisations involved. Second, not only the organisational environment, but also characteristics of the legal environment and the institutional environment have played an important role in the shaping of these registers. Since both registers were based on a special law, the legal environment and the parallel drafting of the law and design of the functional design of the registers was a major challenge because layers and system designers have different frames of reference. The institutional environment played an important role because the relationship between actors has been based on legally and historically developed and accepted 'rules'. In the case of the Residential Register, the distribution of power between the Dutch municipalities and the Ministry of Internal affairs challenged the established 'rules' between them. Third, this contribution showed us that the shaping of both registers has taken place in closely and loosely linked arenas in which stakeholders (which are sometimes the same, sometimes they are different) try to influence the nature and organisation of the register. This chapter demonstrates the added value of an information-ecology approach, but at the same time it underlines the importance of viewing the information ecology as a set of political economies (or arenas) in which power, the exchange of resources, negotiation and communication play an important role.

3.4   *Boundary Management in the Information Ecology*

In the chapter on 'E-government, Changing Jurisdictions and Boundary Management', Bekkers demonstrated that the introduction of e-government has important implications for the management of the boundaries of public organisations. The introduction of e-government challenges the nature of public organisations in several ways that go beyond the introduction of the Internet. It affects the structure, the culture, the power relations and the working processes in the organisations-- a point that has also been made in Davenport's work on the information ecology. Moreover, it has been made clear that e-government also challenges the nature of existing information domains between organisations and new information domains sometimes be created. However, this interorganisational dimension is not present in Davenport's approach on the information ecology. In this chapter, it interesting to see how e-government can be understood in terms of the co-evolution of the technological, specific intra-organisational environments and the interorganisational environment of e-government projects, which become manifest in the interplay between relevant actors or stakeholders in these environments or domains.

In public administration, organisational boundaries also have an important normative function. They refer to the jurisdiction of a public organisations that can be challenged if the boundaries of this jurisdiction begin to blur or perhaps even enlarged through the use of ICT. Hence, in this chapter attention has also been paid to the institutional environment that also influences the shaping and nature of e-government.

3.5   *Virtual Organisations as Outcomes of the Information Ecology*

E-government has been an important incentive for the massive use of ICT in public administration. This process had started years before the e-government hype of the late 1990s. In the slipstream of e-government, we see that a variety of new types of organisations in the public sector emerge; organisations which, according to Bekkers, can be described as virtual organisations. E-government focuses on the establishment of new information, transaction and communication relations between a government organisation and important stakeholders in its environment, like citizens, companies, other government agencies and civil servants. Through ICT, an informational space has been created that enables actors to share information and to communicate with each other across internal and external organisational boundaries.

In this chapter, we have seen that the creation of virtual organisations as informational space can be understood from the interplay between characteristics of the ICT network (focusing on the nature of the infrastructure and the characteristics of the information architecture), the socio-organisational network of actors (like the degree of interdependency between them, the degree to which collective and coordinated action develops between them), and the characteristics of the virtual organisation itself (like the degree of formalisation and the degree of inclusion and exclusion). A typology has been developed which shows a number of different virtual organisations in the public sector. E-government contributes to the emergence of a set of contingent patterns of virtual organisation. The notion of the information ecology helps us to understand that these virtual organisations - which are at the same time, the outcomes of e-government and a necessary condition for many e-government services - cannot be understood from a functional and instrumental perspective on the use of ICT alone. To some extent, they can be understood in terms of the co-evolution of technological and socio-organisational networks.

3.6   New Intermediaries in the Information Ecology

Sometimes the emergence of virtual organisations can be perceived in terms of the rise of new intermediaries, as described by Edwards. In his contribution, we see that e-government not only deals with public service delivery, but that ICT could also stimulate the participation of citizens in public debate and in political decision making.

In this chapter the notion of the information ecology has been used to understand the emergence of new 'species' and new 'niches'. New intermediaries are viewed as 'species' that may succeed in joining the 'community' of existing species of intermediaries within various democratic regimes in the Netherlands. The interesting question will be which of these new intermediaries as emerging species will survive and what the implications for the position of the existing intermediaries will be. In other words: what does this selection process look like?

3.7   Politicians in the Information Ecology

Not only is it interesting to look at the influence of the political environment on the shaping of e-government, but we can go one step further by looking at the role of one actor or group of actors. In this case it is the role and position of politicians in the design of e-government. In a municipal case study, Jæger has conducted an empirical investigation of the role of politicians and their political views. She concludes that in the shaping of e-government, politicians do not play a major role. This is rather surprising because e-government also intrinsically influences the role and position of citizens, politicians and administrators in the political system as well as the communication and information exchange between them. She suggests three reasons for the importance of looking at politicians' assumptions regarding e-government. First, politicians define technology as apolitical. Second, they define the division of roles between politicians and administrators as fundamental for the separation between politics and technology. Third, politicians do not relate to the development and implementation of technology.

Because of the intrinsic political nature of e-government, Jæger argues that politicians should review their role in and vision of e-government. The absence of politicians in the definition of e-government could explain, for instance, why e-government has a limited focus and locus in terms of public service delivery.

3.8   Love and Marriage in the Information Ecology

In the chapters of Homburg and Bekkers, and Van Duivenboden and Lips, we see that two separate developments in the political environment of public administration have been brought together: e-government and new public management. A new reform agenda seems to be emerging. In Homburg and Bekkers' chapter, four strategies have been described that express the marriage between the ideas of e-government and NPM. First, there is the possibility of electronic mediation for electronic service delivery. A second strategy is using ICT to facilitate electronic consultation in order to determine whether the delivered services meet certain quality and accountability standards. As a third related option, e-government could provide forms of electronic consultation that enable voice options. E-government provides citizens with the possibility of casting their opinions about the quality of the services to be delivered. Fourth, electronic service delivery can be improved by the introduction of 'hierarchy', in terms of more control and coordination, in public administration that improves the exchange of information. The notion of the information ecology can help us to understand why a specific issue of this reform agenda has been put into practice. Moreover, it shows us that the political values in public administration are changing and that new values emerge that can inspire technological driven changes with profound non-technological implications.

In Van Duivenboden and Lips' contribution, the possibility of marriage between e-government and NPM has been explored further. The result of this marriage is a more responsive government, which could be put in practice by the four options that have been described by Homburg. Van Duivenboden and Lips suggest that the responsiveness of government could increase if governments address citizens not only as passive consumers, but also as engaged citizens. An engaged citizen in a responsive government implies two things. First, citizens should have the possibility of giving his opinions in order to be dealt with as a 'whole person'. Second, government should provide feedback information in response to the requests of citizens and in relation to the choices he or she has made. From an ecological point of view, it is interesting to see why e-government, up until now, has not been defined as responsive e-government. What kind of strategies do relevant stakeholders, who are involved in designing and implementing e-government, use to promote or to prevent more responsive e-government projects?

We have just been thinking about a marriage between NPM and e-government, which could lead to the emergence of new species in the information ecology of e-government. However, if we take into account the attention that has been given to the notion of accountability in public administration, it is possible to think about a 'ménage à trois' between e-government, NPM and accountability. In their chapter, Meijer and Bovens consider the idea of several kinds of legal, professional, political and administrative accountability in the information age. The wiring of public and private organisations by the network technology creates threats as well as opportunities for public accountability. Meijer and Bovens show how ICT can open new horizons in order to design and/or redesign public accountability. After all, accountability no longer has to be restricted to a hierarchical (vertical) form of monitoring and control. Especially network technology makes it possible to design more horizontally accountability arrangements which recognises the network character of today's society.

4.   E-Government as an Information Ecology Revisited

In this volume, we have explored the potential of an information ecological approach to e-government. First we have amended the notions of the information ecology, as described by Davenport and Nardi and O'Day, in order to create a richer perspective on information ecology. In a richer perspective, the introduction of ICT in organisations is not only seen as the local co-evolution of developments in technological, socio-organisational, economic, cultural and economic (intra and extra) organisational environments; attention should also be paid to the interaction between stakeholders, developments and values which are present in these environments. If we look at the results of the exploration, the next question is: What do the findings imply for the use of the 'information ecology'-concept?

4.1   Uniformity versus Locality

An interesting point of discussion is the claim that the outcomes of technological interventions can only be studied by considering the specificity and locality of outcomes. This claim is not always fully supported (the contributions of Zouridis and Thaens, Janssen and Rotthier, and Van Duivenboden and Lips). For example, the issue has been raised that the locus and focus of e-government is rather limited. E-government is primarily seen as electronic service delivery while the citizen is primarily seen as a consumer. What does this convergence regarding the goals and nature of e-government imply for the claim that it is important to take the local context of ICT interventions into account?

First, it is important to make a distinction between the level on which the drafting of e-government programmes takes place and the implementation level. The claim of contextuality should primarily be understood on the implementation level, within and between organisations. In the chapters on the back office of e-government (Bekkers and Homburg), the boundary management of e-government (Bekkers) and the emergence of virtual organisations (Bekkers), this has become rather evident.

Second, it is interesting to see that a convergence of ideas regarding e-government can be understood in terms of management reform ideology. The notion that 'common beliefs' (which relate to specific values of relevant stakeholders) in the environment of organisations can play an important role in the way ICT interventions take place is not an explicit point of attention in the information ecology approach. According to Meyer and Rowan [4] these 'common beliefs' refer to the institutional environment as a reservoir of 'rules' (like developed practices, common beliefs, routines, ideologies etc.) in which an organisation operates and to which an organisation refers. Meyer and Rowan show us the importance of 'myths' and 'ceremonies' that legitimise the transformation of organisations to meet changing environmental conditions in order secure success, survival and resources. New public sector management techniques, but also reforms like e-government can be seen as myths and ceremonies, which, if adopted and performed well, add to legitimacy of an organisation. Implementing e-government can be viewed as a ceremony that an organisation has to go through in order to meet the myths of 'efficiency' or the myth of 'client friendliness'. Conformity implies success; non-conformity implies failure. Hence, the existence of specific management or reform myths within the environment of an organisation can explain the uniformity in the promises of technological change.

4.2   The Institutional Environment

In another way, the institutional environment also plays an interesting role. The 'rules', of which this environment consists, not only reflect emerged and established management practices, but they also refer to other practices, taken-for-granted assumptions, techniques routines and procedures. In the chapter on boundary management and the chapter on back office integration, we have seen that the institutional environment could be seen as a separate environment. But, at the same time, it could also be seen as an overarching environment in which the specific co-evolution of the technological, socio-organisational, political and economic environments took place. Especially for public administration, the recognition of the importance of an institutional environment is important because public administration is in essence a rule-oriented conglomerate of organisations.

4.3   The Interorganisational Dimension

Within the information ecology literature we have studied, the emphasis lies primarily on the organisational level [1, 2] or on the user group level like the use of ICT by librarians or gardeners [2]. Our work on e-government shows the importance on the interorganisational level in order to understand the outcomes of e-government. This is not surprising, because the nature of e-government implies that ICT interventions are focused on the (re)design of (existing) information exchange, transaction and communication relations between a government organisation and several target groups in its environment (like citizens, companies, societal organisations and other public organisations). This implies that in an information ecological approach the interorganisational level should be taken into consideration in order to assess the outcome of a technological intervention like e-government.

4.4   Species and Niches

Edwards makes an interesting observation in relation to e-government from an ecological perspective. He perceives the emergence of new intermediaries as new species that are looking for a niche in an existing and institutionalised environment. Not only new intermediaries but also new e-government services that have been described in terms of front office arrangements (Janssen and Rotthier), responsive e-government arrangements (Van Duivenboden and Lips) and e-government-NMP-accountability combinations (Homburg and Bekkers, Meijer and Bovens) can be described as species that compete with the dominant e-government species. The interesting question will be how the selection takes place in a population of many e-government species.

4.5   Stability and Change in the Information Ecology

Another interesting issue is stability and change in an information ecology. When we look at the dominant practice of e-government, we can observe that the emphasis is on electronic service delivery. The potential of ICT innovation is primarily related to process innovation. ICT is used to redesign the quality, efficiency and efficacy of the existing information exchange, transaction and communication relations and processes. From an information ecology perspective, it is interesting to see why up until now e-government did not contribute to the establishment of institutional renewal and institutional innovations, even though we have seen that new species of technologically-driven innovation have emerged. In the public administration literature on the effects of ICT on public organisation, this observation is known as the reinforcement hypothesis [5]. This hypothesis, based on empirical research, states that ICT tends to extend and reinforce the prevailing biases of governmental structures and processes. It would be interesting to see if notions can be generated from an information ecology perspective that help us to understand why outcomes of e-government can also be understood in terms of reinforcement.

It would also be interesting to see if the ideas that have been formulated by scholars of the 'punctuated equilibrium approach' of stability and change in policy sectors could be combined with the information ecology approach of e-government – both approaches are inspired by an biological and evolutionary perspective. In the theory of the 'punctuated equilibrium', a distinction is made between long periods of stability in a policy sector, which are then disrupted by punctuated changes in which a new paradigm emerges because the internal and external pressure on the existing paradigm simply becomes too much [6]. The narrow locus and focus of e-government can be understood in terms of a policy monopoly. As a result, it would be interesting to follow the development of e-government over a period of several years in order to understand stability and change in the nature of e-government from an information ecology perspective.

5. Outlook

In this book we have explored the significance of e-government in terms of an information ecology approach. We have used this approach, after reformulating it to some extent, in order to understand the complex interaction of actors and environments that are related to technological innovations in and between organisations. The next step might be to develop a comparative case study of similar organisations or a longitudinal case study of a large, highly compartmentalised organisation in which the shaping of e-government can be studied intensively. We can only hope that this bookcan contribute in some way to further research activities.

References

1.   Davenport, T.H., *Information Ecology: Mastering the information and knowledge environment.* 1997, Oxford: Oxford University Press.

2.   Nardi, B.A. and V.L. O'Day, *Information Ecologies: Using Technology with Heart.* 1999, Cambridge (MA): The MIT Press.

3.   Zinke, R.C., *Administration: the image of the administrator as an information processor*, in *Images and Identities of Public Administration*, H.O. Kass and B.L. Cantron, Editors. 1990, SAGE: Newbury Park. p. 183-201.

4.   Meyer, J.W. and B. Rowan, *Institutionalized organizations: Formal structure as myth and ceremony.* American Journal of Sociology., 1977. **83**(2): p. 340-363.

5.   Kraemer, K.L. and J.L. King, *Computing and Public Organizations.* Public Administration Review, 1986: p. 488-496.

6.   Baumgartner, F.R. and B.D. Jones, *Agendas and Instability in American Politics.* 1993, Chicago: Chicago University Press.

Author Index